Anonymous

The Red Letter

Anonymous

The Red Letter

ISBN/EAN: 9783744659055

Printed in Europe, USA, Canada, Australia, Japan

Cover: Foto ©Thomas Meinert / pixelio.de

More available books at **www.hansebooks.com**

The Red Letter

August

TEN CENTS

LITERATURE

1.

ART

To Poster Collectors

A copy of the first *Red Letter* poster, "In the Library," by E. B. Bird, will be sent, postpaid, to those remitting the amount of subscription, $1.00. ✦ Single copies of the poster, 25 cts. ✦ Copies of *The Poster's* Poster, "Miss Art and Miss Litho," by E. B. Bird, may be obtained of the publishers for 15 cents. ✦ The Red Letter, 903 Exchange Building, Boston.

Are You Interested in Black and White Art?

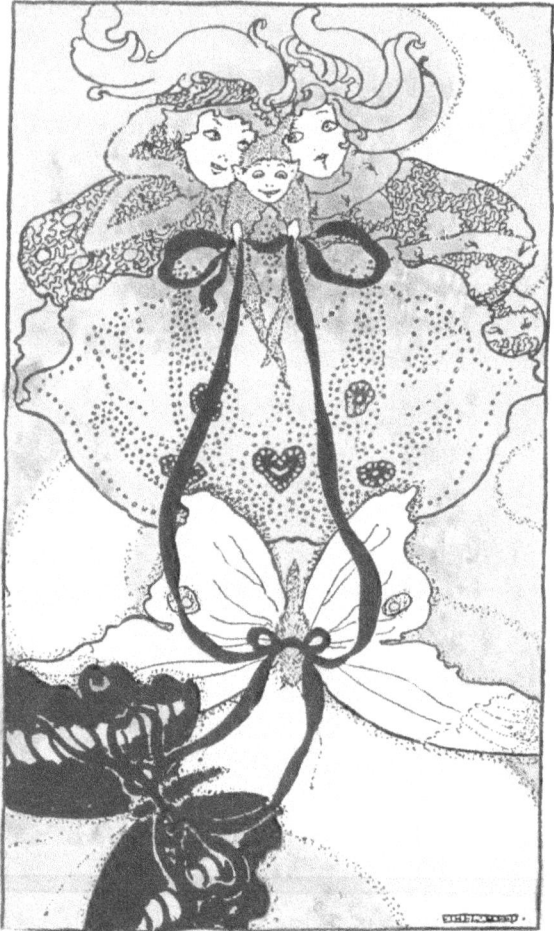

The Goblin's Chariot
By Ethel Reed

AUGUST, 1896. VOLUME I., NUMBER I.

The Red Letter

An Illustrated Monthly

" 'T will while away an hour or so with picturings and print."—MARLOWE

To a Fair Lady

A Rondel

FAIR Lady, you were clad in white
 When first your gentle eyes I met,
 And never shall my heart forget
The vision of that August night.

With the pale moon's transcendent light
 You shone, in your clear heaven set;
Fair Lady, you were clad in white
 When first your gentle eyes I met.

Bend, Moon of Women, from your height,
 Soothe with your smile Earth's care and fret,
 Let us be happy in your debt,
Since you Love's varied charms unite;
Your soul and you were clad in white
 When first your gentle eyes I met.

Louise Chandler Moulton

Goin' to the Fourth

POTTSVILLE was going to have a grand Fourth of July celebration. The town was one hundred years old, and had never
had a genuine patriotic observance of the day. Neither had it
celebrated the one-hundredth anniversary of the arrival of the
first settler from Massachusetts, the spring before. Now it had
been decided by the town fathers to celebrate these two important
events in one, and have a Fourth of July that would attract not
only the denizens of Pottsville, but those from all the neighboring towns of Heath,
and Edenville and Perkinsville. For weeks the inhabitants of these towns had

forgotten to accost each other with the usual remark about the weather, because the all-absorbing question had been, " Goin' to the Fourth ? "

Farmer Wilkinson lived 'way up in the northeast corner of Pottsville, on the farm which his father had settled as a pioneer, and had wrested from the wilderness with his stout axe and many years of hard labor.

When he had brought his young wife home forty-five years ago, they had not lived apart from the world; they had gone regularly to meeting and to mill, and had attended whatever was going on in the way of social festivities, like quiltings, raisings, sewing-bees and corn-huskings; but it was now many years since they had been off the farm for more than half a day at a time, and then only when it became absolutely necessary to go to the village store for such supplies as they could not raise on their stony acres.

In their early married life one little daughter had come to them, who had lived to grow up a rosy-cheeked, fun-loving maiden. They had made an effort in those days to let Elvira get out among young companions, and had sent her away to school one or two seasons, to get advantages which had not been possible to her mother and father when they were young. As a consequence, Elvira had fallen in love with the handsome dancing-master; and when her father sternly refused to let him come to the little brown farmhouse to see her, she had slipped away unobserved one night and never came back. From that time, for years, Elvira's name had not been mentioned.

It was a week before the Fourth that Farmer Wilkinson had been obliged to go to Pottsville Corners to buy his semi-annual barrel of flour. In the one store, which served as post-office, general merchandise emporium and men's and women's club-room for the town, the talk had all been of the coming celebration, and half a dozen different men had asked him the inevitable question, " Goin' t' the Fourth ? "

As usual after his visit to the village, Farmer Wilkinson had gone home and detailed every item of gossip to the patient wife, who seldom saw the few friends who remained of her youth.

The day before the Fourth she had surprised him by saying : —

" Azariah, what's the reason we can't go t' the Fourth? Kind o' seems 's if I sh'ld like to get out once more. We ain't be'n off the place sence last October."

Azariah whistled under his breath and looked out of the window. Then he laid down his knife, poured out half a cup of tea into his saucer and drank it. Then he leaned back in his chair.

" Wal, Sary, I be'n kind o' thinkin' of it myself, though I kind o' mistrusted p'r'aps you wouldn't want to go. It's considerable of an undertakin' fer old folks like us, you know."

Then he resumed his knife and finished his pie.

" Well, I do want ter go, if it's a pleasant day, that is. You know I ain't no great fer gaddin' round, but I sh'd like ter git out once more an' see somethin', an' termorrer'll prob'ly be the biggest time Pottsville's ever seen."

" Wal, all right," said the old man. " We sh'll hev to be up bright an' airly to git the chores done if we're goin'."

And so the next morning, before the sun had cleared the eastern horizon, the old farmer was rattling the milk-pails down toward the barnyard, where stood the mild-eyed cows waiting to be let out into the green pastures. He felt unusually young that morning. He remembered a certain Fourth of July just forty years ago, when he and Sarah and little Elvira, a toddling thing not two years old, had started off for a Sunday-school picnic in the south part of the town. He remembered just how fresh and pretty Sarah used to be, and even recalled the sprigged calico gown which she wore. And little Elvira, how pretty she had looked in the white sun-bonnet and the fine pink chintz gown, with the little flaxen curls waving about her face, and the happy, gleeful laugh when he had tossed her into her mother's lap in the wagon as they started off.

" Poor gal," he said to himself with a sigh. " I'd give a hunderd dollars to know where she is an' what's become of her. It's a turrible thing to have yer own children grow up, an' lose track of 'em like that : an' mother, no wonder she's grown old an' lost her good looks. Mebby I was to blame." The old man was standing still and gazing toward the east. There was a tear in his eye. " The gal knew what she wanted, an' there's no use in goin' ag'in natur, an' I'll never git over it, I know. Whoa there, Daisy : so there, Daisy. You want ter be milked, don't ye ? " for the pet cow had rubbed up against him impatient to be off after her breakfast of clover.

Meanwhile, in the house " mother " was preparing a good breakfast of codfish and cream and warm biscuits, and skimming the milk, and feeding the hens, and getting all in readiness for her unwonted outing. She, too, was thinking of the day forty years ago when she had gone to the picnic with little Elvira and Azariah. How handsome he had looked to her that morning ! young and strong, and able to take such good care of her and the little baby that nestled in her arms. And the baby — but old Sarah could not think of her. She turned resolutely from the thought of the child and stooped to give a saucer of rich, creamy milk to the cat who rubbed up against her foot. And then " father " had come in with the milk, and it must be strained, and the pigs must be fed, and so many things must be done.

And then breakfast was over, and the unwonted task of dressing up in their best must be gone through with. For it was a task. The best bombazine had been carefully brushed the night before, and the brown silk shirred bonnet had been carefully gone over with the whisk broom ; but it was a matter of good deal of moment whether a deep embroidered collar should be worn, or the white ruffles which she had bought two years before in an extravagant mood, only to lay away in the top bureau drawer and never wear. She tried them both and finally decided to wear the ruffles, although she knew they would never be fit to be seen again.

And as for " father," there were so many details of his costume to be looked after. His boots must be greased ; his hair must be cut ; and then he was determined

The Red Letter

An Illustrated Monthly

Published by H. Walter Stephenson
Edited by Harry Draper Hunt
Under the art direction of E. B. Bird

¶ The subscription rate is one dollar
a year. Entered at the Boston Post
Office as second-class mail matter.
The trade supplied by the American
News Company and its branches. Ad-
vertising rates on application.

The Red Letter Magazine,

Boston.

296 Boylston Street.

not to change his shirt, while she argued that the one he had put on clean Sunday was not the proper garment to wear to the celebration on Wednesday. After a wordy tussle she had succeeded in getting a clean shirt on to him; but she had had to take hold and dress him as though he had been a baby, or he would not have worn a collar, nor the black silk stock which was a remnant of the extravagances of his youth. Neither would he have carried a white pockethandkerchief, a red bandana being deemed good enough for all occasions by him. But finally they were ready, and settled in their old buggy, with a big bundle of hay tucked in behind for Rosinante.

"There," said Sarah at the last minute, " I've forgotten to put up any lunch. Hadn't I better do it now ? "

" No," said her lord and master. " It's be'n many a year sence we've had a Fourth. We'll go to the tavern an' git our dinner to-day, jest like rich folks."

At nine o'clock they started. All along the way people were just driving away from their doors; whole families packed into wagons, buckboards and carryalls; children sitting in front on salt-boxes, and children sitting behind with their feet dangling off. Farmer Wilkinson remembered when Elvira used to sit on the little cricket in front of them, when they used to go to church every Sunday. He wondered if mother remembered it too. But they had not talked of Elvira for many a long year.

The little green which marked the center of Pottsville was indeed gay when they drove up to it shortly before ten o'clock. Never before had that quiet spot been so crowded with people, and there was a temporary band-stand and a speaker's platform draped with the national colors. From the flagstaff in the center, too, floated the stars and stripes; and there was a lemonade and peanut stand at its foot, to further emphasize the national holiday and prove that Pottsville was master of all the necessary adjuncts of the day.

Farmer Wilkinson helped his wife to alight near the speaker's stand and went and " put up " his horse under the " meetin'-house " shed; then he returned and saw her comfortably seated on one of the benches where she could see and hear all that was to transpire. And then he joined a group of grey-haired boys on the meeting-house steps who were actively discussing the day's festivities. They were not so far away but that they could hear (except the deafest of them) every word spoken on the platform a few feet across the green; and the band (composed of a cornet and drum from Heath, an alto horn from Edenville and a flute and snare-drum from Pottsville) made music that, whatever it lacked, certainly was fairly audible throughout the entire village.

They played " Hail Columbia " and " Gem of the Ocean " while the people gathered; and then the two ministers escorted Squire Penniman to the platform, and a trio of girls in white sang America, and the exercises were fairly begun.

It seemed to old Sarah Wilkinson that she had never listened to sweeter music or more eloquent speeches in her life; and probably she had not; while her consort over on the meeting-house steps applauded heartily at times and shook his head dissentingly at others. For Farmer Wilkinson was a shrewd old fellow and had views of his own on most matters, — views that could not be overthrown by a brief outburst of Fourth-of-July eloquence.

Noon came all too soon, and with it the " spread-eagle " torrent of eloquence ceased to flow. Dinner was always ready in Pottsville at prompt twelve, and patriotism could wait. In the general break-up of the audience Sarah Wilkinson, all unused to crowds and bustle, felt quite lost and forlorn ; for among these younger generation of people there were but few she remembered. But as soon as possible " father " came to take her to the tavern. As they started, a voice called him by name.

" Why Uncle Azari'," it said. " You here ? And Aunt Sar'y ? Why, ain't you renewin' your youth ? "

" Wal, yis, we be, kind o'," was the farmer's reply. " Thought we might as well git out once more afore we die. How's your folks ? "

" Come over'n see," was the hearty response. " Where ye goin' for dinner ? "

" We was goin' to the tavern," said the farmer.

" Wal, you ain't," said the younger man, Abner Swett. " You ain't goin' to no taverns 'slong's we've got a house an' a dinner. You come along with me."

" I guess we better go to the tavern," put in Mrs. Wilkinson, seeing her better half waver. " We'd cal'lated to. We don't owe you no visits."

" Come now," responded the hospitable Abner. " You don't want to talk that to me. I owe you many a good turn, Uncle Azari', an' I don't forget it. The idee of your goin' to a tavern an' payin' for a dinner."

Farmer Wilkinson had not begrudged the prospective dollar for their two dinners ; but he had become fairly grounded in the belief that a dollar saved is as good as a dollar earned ; and to refuse Abner's offer would be distinctly flying in the face of Providence ; and so they went to Abner's. And nobody ever knew that it was a keen disappointment to one of them that she could not just for once in her lifetime experience the luxury of dining at a hotel. And there was no one to tell her that Mrs. Swett's dinner was vastly preferable.

But the fun of a whole year, with the honest, hard-working people of Pottsville, was concentrated into the afternoon. Patriotism had had its fling in the more formal exercises of the morning. From two to four joy was unconfined and mirth reigned supreme around the little village green. For there were bag-races and hurdle-races and a potato-race. There was a game of base-ball to absorb the men's attention, and plenty of gossip to make the day memorable for the women. Sarah Wilkinson thought she had never seen anything so funny as the bag-races — until the potato-race ; then she laughed until she cried, and her poor old sides ached. And when, at half-past four, her lord and master signified that it was time to be going home, she felt younger than she had for years.

They had a pleasant ride home in spite of the fact that the thermometer indicated eighty-five and the dust rose in clouds around them. There were so many interesting bits of news, so many personal experiences to be interchanged between these two old people so dependent on each other, that they did not notice the minor discomforts of the day in the pleasure of talking it all over. They had gone more than half way home before Sarah noticed how tired she really was; and even then "father" talked unceasingly for another dusty mile; and then they fell into silence. Suddenly Farmer Wilkinson saw as in a vision, himself and Sarah and two-year old Elvira coming over the same dusty road forty years before. It was just along here, by that clump of birches, that the baby, overcome by a sudden access of love, had put her arms around his neck and kissed him with her soft rosy lips. He had remembered it many times, although he had never spoken of it, not even to Sarah.

They passed the clump of bushes, and a carriage drove by them. It went on a few rods and turned into the next farmhouse gate. A group of little children ran laughing and calling out a glad welcome.

Farmer Wilkinson turned and looked at Sarah. On her face was the hungry look he had seen so often of late.

"Mother, I'd give a thousand dollars to see Elviry's children run out to meet us like that," he said. It was the first time he had mentioned the girl's name in years.

Sarah lifted the corner of her old-fashioned shawl and cried into it. The farmer looked the other way and swallowed hard.

"Ef there was any way to find her," he began. But he said no more, and they rode the rest of the way in silence, — a sad reaction from their brief holiday.

It was not long, however, before their old brown house was in sight. Sarah had stopped crying, and was conscious of a sense of sheltering love and care the moment she caught sight of its brown roof. She had lived there nearly fifty years.

The farmer, too, was conscious of a similar relief at the sight of the old house, though in a lesser degree, as befits the masculine mind. As they drew nearer, he noticed with some alarm that the side-door was open, but he said nothing to "mother." And then they were at the gate.

And then dawned the real happiness of old age for these two people.

Two little children ran around the corner of the house, one a boy of six, and one a toddling girl of two, with flaxen curls and eyes like Elviry's.

"I guess you're my grandpa," said the boy, "aren't you? An' my gran'ma?"

Just then a middle-aged woman appeared at the door. She was in widow's weeds. "Father, Mother!" she cried. "I've come home. Forgive me."

The two old folks were on the door-step now. Grandma sat down and drew the two children close to her, kissing them over and over again, and clasping them to her hungry heart. But Farmer Wilkinson reached out both arms and took the black-robed woman to his breast. "Elviry."

The word was a sob; but it breathed infinite peace and content.

Helen M. Winslow

At Night   By John Sloan

In Love's Name

A Tableau in Three Parts

The Child

HEAVEN'S gift — a child!

A wee, bonny thing, with merry eyes, and mouth waiting to be kissed. Little dimpled arms that at a word close unforgettably around one's neck. Soft little trembling hands that creep confidently into larger ones for protection. Daring, runaway little feet that lead others a dizzy but willing dance. A brown, closely cropped little head that nestles on broad shoulders for comfort, or peeps mischievously from behind curtains at unexpected moments. A bewitching voice that echoes through the house from morning until night. A gay little tongue that startles with its questions. A precious morsel of flesh and blood that fills hearts to bursting from love of her.

The darling child!

The Debutante

A starry night, with a jingle of sleigh-bells in the crisp air. A light from her windows shines on the sleigh below.

Clad all in pale yellow she stands before the mirror. The dainty, creamy throat lifts proudly like the round stem of a flower.

She's aglow with delicious expectancy; in a quiver of excitement, like a bird about to try its wings for the first time.

Tho' a dreamy smile hovers around the wonderful eyes and half-parted lips, not a detail of her gown escapes her; this shoulder-knot a little lower, that wave of hair down, so.

The whole household is at its idol's feet.

Bouquets and boxes of flowers are handed lavishly in to her, for this, her first ball. "Which will she wear?" She reads the cards. Not the violets, nor the marguerites, nor the orchids — there's a shadow over her face — nor the La France roses, — ah, it passes — but these, the American Beauties, his favorites. Tenderly she separates the long stems — no maid's touch here — selecting one with crumpled petals — she and somebody else know how it happened — for her hair.

Fur boots are drawn over the pretty feet that will so soon skim a polished floor — with him.

Around the exquisite, lithe young body loving hands wrap the warm velvet cloak, and over the beautiful head the filmy lace hood.

There, now she is ready. With fond, admiring eyes they stand back, like an artist, to gaze at the ravishing apparition.

Gathering her flowers lightly together she gives a last, swift, serious glance of inquiry at herself in the mirror.

Is she beautiful enough — for him?

Oh, hurry, hurry, hurry, she will be late—and the beloved image is beyond their reach.

After the Ball

Ah, ha! "My Lady Nicotine"; and only a year since that ball.

The mocking eyes are maddening in their mysterious depths; in spite of the satirical curves the luscious lips are very tempting; they're no longer parted in a dreamy smile, nor does she study any more with inquiry her own face in the mirror. She knows now that "things are not always what they seem"; she "has loved not wisely but too well."

The heart that has throbbed with all the wealth of a woman's love now beats evenly, coldly.

The hand that once welcomed with a bewildering caress now hangs passionless at her side.

There's a fascination about the defiant, almost reckless poise of the head.

He told her to "go to the devil"; there she stands, in the magnificence of her ripe, young beauty, the devil's own.

In unguarded moments do those lips never quiver pitifully?

Never a ring of bitterness in the light laughter? Is there nowhere a tinge of sadness lurking, a faint halo of remembered sweetness?

Back of the mockery and the satire is there just a glimpse of the once beautiful but now blighted soul?

No, no; she's "My Lady Nicotine"; perhaps it did not hurt much after all; there's no "heart upon her sleeve."

But the debutante's sweet mouth has been kissed; she was too beautiful—for him.

Frances A. Hoadley

His Grace

"His Grace"

TO the servants in the palatial Darracut mansion he was known by no other name than "His Grace." At first there was considerable curiosity as to his identity, and many questions were asked concerning him; but he was loth to say much about himself even to so good a friend as Mrs. Darracut, for to her he had only confided such facts as served to excuse his frequent visits.

"His Grace" appeared to be about sixty. His beard was slightly gray and his deep-set eyes had not altogether lost their lustre, though his pale, emaciated features told of much suffering. Always sad and thoughtful, he would have excited sympathy from even the most casual observer.

It was in the spring of the previous year that he had first called on Mrs. Darracut. Briefly he told his errand. He had heard she possessed a picture — the portrait of a young girl. He had known the artist, also the girl herself, whose name, he said, was Grace. Would she allow him to see the picture?

Consenting to the simple request, Mrs. Darracut led the way to the rear apartment and drew aside the curtains, revealing the features of a wonderfully handsome girl, scarcely out of her teens. Many had admired before now the life-like portrait; but no one had ever been moved to tears as was "His Grace"; and not wishing to intrude upon his sorrow, Mrs. Darracut retired that he might hold silent communion with this counterfeit of one who had doubtless been close and dear to him.

Weeks rolled by and he came frequently to feast his eyes upon this mute witness of a past; but a day came when Mrs. Darracut was no longer able to greet him. An incurable malady confined her to her room.

One cold, bleak morning "His Grace" found the curtains drawn, the emblem of death on the bell handle. He paused a moment on the sidewalk, and the tears which fell were but the natural outlet of a sorrowing soul. The only person who had shown the least interest in these later years of his life had gone. She had possessed the one thing which made his life worth living. Would he ever again be able to look upon those heavenly, soft blue eyes, that flaxen hair? Over and over again asking himself this question, he slowly and sadly retraced his steps. A few days later came the funeral, and then the house was closed.

* *
*

The following month the newspapers announced that the sale of "the entire contents of a fashionable Back Bay house" would take place at one of the leading auction rooms. The exhibition of the goods during the few days prior to the sale attracted many people, among them a frail, unkempt individual, whose forlorn appearance made him the subject of frequent inquiry.

Totally oblivious to his surroundings, one article enlisted his entire attention — the portrait of a fair-haired, blue-eyed girl.

The day of the sale arrived. The gentlemanly auctioneer mounted his little stand, remarking that the paintings would be disposed of first. The old man slid noiselessly into a front seat, his eyes riveted on a half-dozen canvasses leaning against the wall. One by one they were knocked down, until finally the auctioneer announced the "Portrait of a Girl, by the famous artist, V."

The picture was brought forward and placed on the easel. Every one marveled as the strong light, focussed upon it, seemed to endow the features with the very breath of life. Nervously the old man bent forward, every line of his face depicting eagerness and anxiety.

As he listened to the auctioneer's description of the picture, its marvelous drawing, its superb coloring, the fine texture of the work and the extreme beauty of the face itself, which gazed so radiantly at the assembled crowd, the old man's features took on an intensely interested expression, and an occasional nod and a low murmur showed him to be in entire accord with the auctioneer's praises.

A bid was asked for. A benevolent looking gentleman offered a hundred and fifty dollars. Fifty was added to it by another. As three hundred was reached a frail voice down front murmured twenty-five. Another raised it twenty-five. A few moments' lull, and the old man, one hand clutching the back of his chair, his face of ashen hue, nodded the auctioneer a similar raise.

At this point the latter importuned one of his aristocratic patrons to take the picture. Such a chance would never occur again. Would he not offer another twenty-five; if not the gentleman on the front seat would get it. But the aristocratic patron was obdurate. He had reached his limit.

"Going once — going twice — going three times," slowly called out the auctioneer, "and sold to Mr. ———."

The old man staggered out of his chair, and with a stifled cry, "My Grace, my Grace, at last," fell heavily to the floor. Willing hands removed the prostrate form. A physician who happened to be present gravely shook his head and remarked that it was a case of heart failure due to excessive excitement.

John H. Wilson

N "The Love Affairs of a Bibliomaniac" Eugene Field has undoubtedly added to that list of bedside books he loved so well to read; and the company is rather a good one.

¶ I MUST confess that "Platonic Affections" is a very wearisome book. However, it is strictly proper, and is therefore a somewhat notable volume in the Keynotes Series, in which it is published.

¶ THERE is a very fancy gilt snake coiled up in a wreath of pretty pink roses on the cover of "Effie Hetherington." This is undoubtedly symbolical of something. Perhaps they both represent Effie—the rose Douglas thought her, the snake she really was. This is a very good interpretation, anyway. To those who like to revel with the hero in a mass of unrequited affection, I suggest the book. None will keep the tearfully sympathetic reader in a state of greater dampness.

¶ I DIDN'T like to begin "Casa Braccio" at first, for it was a two-volume affair, which are things I generally leave to the last, after the manner of putting off misery as long as possible. However, I finally made up my mind and, setting my teeth hard, plunged; and as soon as I had commenced, my dislike was all over and I was glad I'd come. For the book holds one with a grip that I have not felt for a long time. The narrative goes along rapidly but easily, with no disturbing fits and starts. The characters are not animated puppets with all the wires visible, while the plot and incidents are both well conceived and carried out. Whenever such a book as this is published, which unfortunately is seldom, and the work of an American, those folks who look to England as the home of the best and only in Anglo-Saxon literature have to stop and think a moment.

¶ "AND this time he held out his hand to her, but just as she reached to grasp it the train started."
That is the way with the majority now. The train starts and—that's all. No one, of course, ever has the faintest idea where the train is going. No one, equally of course, can possibly surmise what the author intended to convey. Probably this is the

acme of art. There is no doubt but that it is very puzzling, likewise extremely unsatisfactory. It is, however, rather the fad to close with one of these endless endings; to die with a sort of female tiger gasp that will admit of any interpretation. But is this exactly fair to the gentle reader? To inveigle him along page by page and then to drop him in the midst of nowhere. To smile sarcastically as he, groping for something tangible, becomes more involved with every step. "Oh, but," says my realistic friend with a sneer, "we really can't bother about our readers and endings, you know. *We* depict life."

But even admitting this very doubtful hypothesis, shouldn't some conclusion be indicated? Shouldn't at least a hint convey some idea of the end of it all?

Being a bit old-fashioned myself, I prefer one of those so-called good old-fashioned endings.

"'Oh, Penelope,' he whispered, 'that song of thine was a true prophecy. Love *has* found out the way.'"

This, you see, conveys the necessary information. We instinctively know they are married and live happily ever after; and knowing that, we toss down the book with a feeling of satisfaction. We feel, for the time being, happy ourselves. For have we not lived for a time in a little world peopled by Penelope and Bryan Fairfax and the others? Have we not gone through all their trials, and should we not now, at the end, rejoice with them?

"Which," sneers our realistic friend, "is all very childish."

Of course it is childish, the whole thing is childish. But isn't childhood the golden age? And our realistic friend must admit that those who have stooped to humor this childish whim of having it all come out right, have a faculty of both exceeding in sales and outliving in popularity those who cater to that very exclusive, pessimistic cult which deals in "sordid realism."

For love, you know, makes the world go round, and is then not a factor to be ignored or treated patronizingly.

We will admit, however, that there are exceptions to this rule. Well, then, let them all be irrevocably damned, but let there be no doubt about it.

"A little sigh followed; the limbs fell slowly back, and the eyes, with their dreadful terror, stared vacantly into Farrell's ghastly face.

"The coverlet went on rustling as the bed-clothes settled down."

PREPARATIONS

By E. B. BIRD

"Motionless, she stared fearfully at the two bodies."

These, you see, all do the business very completely.

Personally, I do not care for them as a steady diet, though I cannot but admire their definitiveness, their brutal disregard for feelings. The author has at least the courage of his convictions and does not nervelessly beg the question with a vapid interrogation.

¶ THE reason that a rich man is rarely thankful for his dinner is because a rich man's dinner is usually a matter of course.

¶ THOSE South Sea Islands must be a very cozy place in which to pass a winter or so if Mr. Louis Becke's "Ebbing of the Tide" be true. And the tales seem as if they were, for they have an air about them that is very convincing, and mightily interesting withal.

¶ Now that Mr. Robert Barr has achieved a fame as magnitudinous as that of Mr. Richard Harding Davis, and has risen to the Narcissus-like dignity of having his portrait used in an illustration in "A Woman Intervenes," he ought to be at least comparatively happy.

¶ THE Keynotes Series, inasmuch as it is the outcome of what may be called "*The Yellow Book*" phase of the present ideas as to the construction of English fiction, is worthy of more than passing attention, more, however, as a class of productions than as separate volumes. The various units of this series run on approximately the same plane, and between the same lines.

Their mission is the solution of the problematical, the striving with the unnaturally realistic, the using of the allegorical for the promulgation of divine truths.

All have been written in a delightfully frank and free and easy mode of expression; but none, with the prominent exception of "The Woman Who Did," have ever sufficiently outstepped the bounds of that which should be spoken and that which should be only thought, to have both merited and received especial attention.

The majority, too, plainly show that they have been written by those who possessed the deluding and devastating gift of cleverness.

THE
LAWN PARTY
By E. B. BIRD

They have, as a rule, I believe, enjoyed but a limited circulation, which is unfortunate, since no collection of books shows so concisely and ingeniously the manner in which our younger English friends look on life.

Although as a class they are not such food as we should care to have the mental digestion of the young and innocent thrive upon, to those who, when they meet a spade, are able to recognize it as such, they will undoubtedly prove soothing and often quite interesting reading.

¶ WHENEVER the idea strikes me, I cannot for the life of me help smiling very broadly. Just imagine for yourself the horrified indignation of Mr. Cedric Errol, My Little Lord Fauntleroy, at the tempestuous advent of his youngest sister, Mistress Clorinda, Her Grace of Osmonde.

Just imagine, I say, his carefully smoothed golden hair rise, and his little velvet suit fairly bristle, as he looks into Miss Vivian's violet eyes and recounts in indignant accents how naughty Clorinda had been swearing at the stable boys, or galloping off on Rake, or strutting about in some of his own little clothes; or mayhap poking a very stiff man under a sofa after having played with him for a time with the loaded end of a riding whip.

A pretty sister for his correct little lordship, indeed!

¶ IF some kind friend will point out to me the peculiar æsthetic or other value possessed by Scotch dialect, I will probably nearer approach adequately appreciating Mr. Crockett's "Lilac Sunbonnet."

As it is, I have had to skip paragraphs, pages, chapters. However, there is the consolation that the various square feet of dialect so overlooked did not at all bother the story; which is quite a pretty, orthodox, old-fashioned love episode, such as is really refreshing in this realistically problematical, erotically *fin-de-siecle* age.

In "Cleg Kelly," however, Mr. Crockett has been less lavish with his dialect, and I read it all. Cleg is a delightfully interesting little rascal, and his adventures as the champion stone-thrower of the Sooth-Back were well worth the chronicling. But the end of the book I do not like so well. It is all so rabidly improbable.

Major-General Theophilus Ruff with his " False Friend "

PATRIOTISM
BY E. B. BIRD

and " False Love," and his automatic doors and canned dollars, seems a true wanderer from our old but ever present friend, " the penny dreadful."

¶ THIS is an age of relativity. Nothing can be known except in the only ways that it can be known. That makes us all phenomenalists; in these insipid days who would not be a phenomenalist?

The outspired poet has trilled, " Things are seldom what they seem," and we all know they are not, know it to our heart sickness. Few things will stand the test of proximate inspection. Those that do we find to be insufferable, vapid and inconsequential; not worth the while. In verity, the most satisfying and complacential things are those that we know the least about. Ignorance is a bliss, knowledge, a blister.

We are always disillusioned when we get close to things and men. Stand under the dome of St. Peter's and gaze aloft on Michael Angelo's creations; they are adjectiveless. In propinquity, they are, to the beholder, handfuls of pigments, incoherent, inconcinnous. Distance alone makes and enhances value. No man is a hero to his valet, nor to his wife; each knows him to be an ass with a lion's head on, removable as his shirt.

Blessed St. Nature was beneficent to us mortals; our eyes are non-microscopic. Were it otherwise and life would be keyed to the utmost of neurotic intensity in our endeavor to escape the mountains that were in reality but sand-grains. We would choke on microbes that were visioned as whales; gnats would be in sooth camels.

He is indeed a philosopher who takes things as he finds them and does not seek to penetrate into the arcana of nature and men and women. For my part I am content to take things as they appear to me. Curiosity is a vulgar propensity of the mind; it never pays to exercise it; the returns are always small and disgusting. I never examine a Corot with a reading glass, never scalpel my friends for dissective purposes, never botanize a Jacqueminot rose to discover the source of its perfume. It is enough for me to have them as they are; their appearance to me is satisfying, and when I have harmony and satisfaction I have that which makes life complete.

IN THE GARDEN
By E. B. BIRD

JDCCCXCVI

To Peter Bell, "A primrose by the river's brim a yellow primrose was, ... and nothing more," and that is all it could be expected to be to him. And it is all it could be to anyone, be he poet, painter, priest, or pedagogue. What would you have it be? a narcissus? a pansy? a skunk cabbage? Or would the primrose be more to one if it were known as *primula vulgaris?* Would it be more of a flower? Peter Bell had all there was in the primrose when he knew its name and took it for what it was. Peter was a philosopher and was much more of a man than Wordsworth intended he should be.

Men, things, and women should be viewed in perspective, and all depends on the point of view of the beholder. Everything should be estimated relatively, not absolutely. Things are absolute only when we get close to them, and then their purpose and use is not understood. When we take things as they are and do not seek to know why they are, take them collectively, not individually, take them freely, not questioningly, then are we making this stage in our existence quite worth while stopping in.

¶ I TRUST that Mr. Harte will find "*The Lotus*" easier steering than was "*The Philistine*," and that he will not again find himself on the lee shore of incompatability.

¶ MR. FREDERICK THOREAU SINGLETON of "*Poster Lore*" and Kansas City will soon bring both himself and his very artistic little periodical to the more aesthetically congenia. atmosphere of Boston.

¶ THIS endeavoring to sell a five-cent periodical for ten cents is hard enough under any circumstances; but one may as well kill his baby at home privately as to try to make it live at the latter price, when previously it has gone at the former.

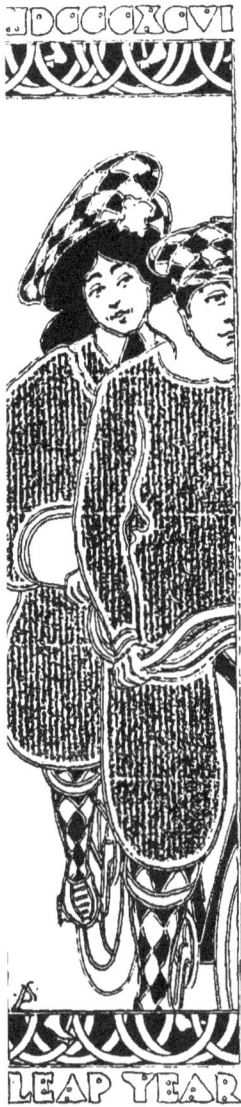

THE BICYCLERS
BY FRANK BIRD MASTERS

LEAP YEAR

The Poster and Decorative Work

¶ WE shall endeavor to present in this department a continuation of the good work started by " *The Poster*," and we trust that the readers of that very bright little periodical will be at least satisfied with the change.

¶ THROUGH the kind permission of Messrs. Chas. Scribner's Sons, we are able to present a small reproduction of their August poster by Will H. Low.   It is a most magnificent affair, being reproduced in twelve colors, but has unfortunately, in its composition, far more of the pictorial than the poster spirit.

The coloring is beautiful, the drawing excellent, but the details are too evident, its carrying power inferior, and it reminds one, sad to say, of those exquisite picture cards that Prang gives us at Christmas.

¶ WE think that we could start this department with nothing more fitting than a short eulogistic résumé of the style and work of that very remarkable young man, Aubrey Beardsley. Not that Beardsley has been spared warm praise, for he has been lauded to such an extent that there is no doubt but that he must unfortunately suffer oblivion — the fate of all who are so unlucky as to become a fad or start a cult — and that twenty years hence his name will be as little known as it was twenty years ago. If his is not genius, it is talent of a sufficient merit to be easily mistaken for its more divine relative.

Springing into prominence some two years ago, he has in that short time so changed the art of decoration, and so demonstrated its possibilities in the heretofore-thought limited field of black and white, as to open vistas of almost unlimited expansion.

Falling under the spell of the Japanese, he has modified their exquisite work and given it the strong stamp of his own irresistible individuality to such an extent as

to have exerted an influence greater than that of any other man of the last fifty years: an influence traces of which will never be obliterated. No one ever better understood the value of a line than did Beardsley. No one ever better expressed that value than did he.

There is a facility and range to his work that many apparently choose to ignore. Seeking as he does, for the most part, the repulsive and the hideous, he will now and then turn out some conceit of exquisitely dainty conception and execution. But the strength and virility of his work itself will speak far more ably for him than any written words, and through the kind permission of Messrs. Roberts Bros. and Copeland & Day, we can present some little-known specimens, also a portrait that should be strikingly natural in that it is as eccentric as himself.

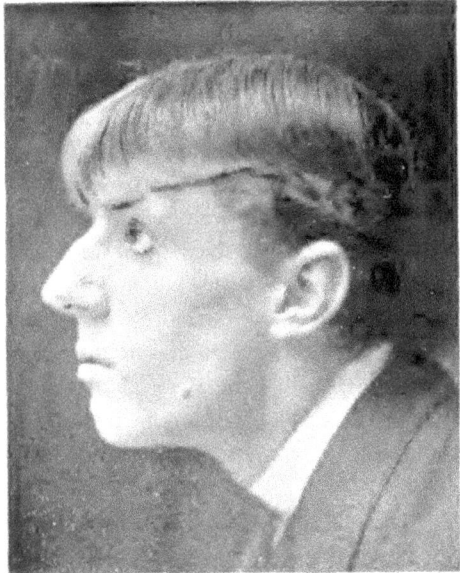

PERMISSION COPELAND AND DAY

AUBREY BEARDSLEY

¶ THE wisdom displayed in these special articles, which every now and then our enterprising press bestows upon us, may be truly said to be appalling. A short time since, the Boston *Herald* essayed one on the poster, from which I cull the following : " Grasset, who inspired W. H. Bradley, and Aubrey Beardsley into the bargain." This will perhaps be news to other collectors than myself. Perhaps also the square inspired the circle.

There is a saying, or, if there isn't, there should be, to the following effect : It is right to call a spade a spade ; but before doing so, find out whether it is not some other agricultural implement.

PERMISSION ROBERTS BROS.

THE MIRROR OF MUSIC
BY AUBREY BEARDSLEY

¶ COMING as it does from Mr. Wilbur C. White-head, one of the leading collectors of this country, the following cannot help being worthy of note: —

" I was talking with the superintendent of our Art School here the other day, and she asked me what I thought the future was in regard to poster art. I said 'that the poster would have to improve to live; that the grotesque would not survive much longer in my opinion. It was very well for a time, as long as it was a novelty, for it attracted attention. It is becoming common now, and in time will no longer attract; people are beginning to look for more true art and less of the absurd, grotesque caricatures that have been labeled "Beardsleyisms." I am not an admirer of the Beardsley-Bradley etc. style. It is effective, or I should say, *was* effective in attracting attention, but it does not satisfy.' "

While differing somewhat from Mr. Whitehead's evident estimate of the work of Beardsley and Bradley, we readily admit that their various inferior imitators are beneath notice. These daubing copyists also do much to deceive the unthinking public as to the real worth of these master decorators, since everything that is odd and ill drawn must be at once dubbed Beardsley-Bradleyism.

¶ To one observant of the small things, the increase of lithography over printing in the manufacture of posters cannot be otherwise than noticeable and interesting. The reasons for this — it can hardly be called encroachment, since it is but the survival of the fittest — are neither strange nor difficult of explanation. The price, being practically the same, is thrown out of consideration. Perhaps the greatest advantage is the liberty given the artist of making his sketch in the colors in which it will be reproduced,

THE DANCING FAUN
By AUBREY BEARDSLEY

which, as can be easily seen, is no small one. More delicate tones are also obtainable, and all doubts about the serious question of register are completely dissipated. Altogether the change is for the better.

Editorial

I is not with the intention of filling a long-felt want, of giving the most for the least money, or of conferring an inestimable favor upon the reading population of the world, that this first number of THE RED LETTER is given out.

We realize that the market is apparently overcrowded with what purport to be magazines. We know that new ones are born to-day to die to-morrow. We understand perfectly that every shade and variety of thought and expression is apparently more than adequately represented. We meet every day periodicals who feed their readers upon great names alone; others who serve only such matter as the publisher himself makes and passes out under fictitious appellations. We see those that consist solely of pictures, those that offer only solid letterpress; those again who affect the antique, others who strive after twentieth century effects.

Yet notwithstanding this we still have sufficient courage to become a unit in the multitude. We believe that a magazine of merit will be supported, that there is always room for something better than there is, that quality will, to a certain extent, hold its own against quantity. We believe that a magazine exploiting the newest and best in decorative and illustrative art, side by side with letterpress as good, will gain and hold a certain circulation; somewhat limited it is true, but still worthy the best efforts of someone to secure. This then will be our field, and one we believe that is not already too overcrowded.

Whether we succeed or fail, we know, is dependent largely upon ourselves. We do not think that only the unworthy obtain the golden pinnacle of success; but that merit is the largest and surest stepping-stone to the coveted goal of enormous circulations. We realize that a magazine, such as we hope to make, must look to its first support from the younger men, from those who, like ourselves, have yet their own peculiar niche to carve and fill. To them, then, we appeal. However, we do not believe in fostering the productions of these should youth be their only recommendation. Again, we do not believe that a reputation will make all that one produces wholly good or equally bad. We believe that a mixture of the old and the new will benefit both. That it will instill vitality into the former, and help to disabuse the latter of its yet unproved idiosyncrasies.

In a word, then, we shall endeavor to present the newest, brightest and best in literature and art, without descending to the sensational or becoming faddy. We make no boasts of what the future will bring forth: the time for this will be most fitting when it has already appeared. We ask only to be judged on what we may present.

The Red Letter

An Illustrated Monthly

Edited by Richard Gorham Badger
Under the art direction of E. B. Bird

The subscription rate is one dollar per year. To Foreign countries one dollar and twenty-five cents. The trade supplied by the publishers direct. Advertising rates on application.

The Red Letter

Boston

¶ *The Editors would be pleased to examine contributions to both the literature and art of* THE RED LETTER. *All that is found to be unavailable will be returned as soon as possible provided proper stamps are enclosed.*

¶ *The next number of* THE RED LETTER *will contain original contributions by Clinton Scollard, Miss Helen Leo Reed, Charles Knowles Bolton, Theo. B. Hapgood, Frank Bird Masters, and others.*

¶ *Houses that have issued meritorious posters and desire to have them reproduced are requested to correspond with the publishers.*

¶ *Copies of the first volume of "The Poster," appropriately bound, may be secured from the publishers at one dollar.*

The Heintzemann Press Boston

Fine Plate Makers & Blanchard and Watts Engraving Co 36 Colum—bus Au Boston

Sunday Globe ✦ouer✦ 250,000

THE LARGEST CIRCULATION IN NEW ENGLAND

Daily Globe ✦ouer✦ 180,000

The Boston Daily & Sunday Globe

The Melody
by
Florence P. England

SEPTEMBER–OCTOBER, 1896. VOLUME I., NUMBER 2

The Red Letter

An Illustrated Monthly

" 'T will while away an hour or so with picturings and print." — MARLOWE

The House of Time

THIS is the House of Time,
   Shaped wondrous fair,
Set by a hand sublime
   In spacious air.

The broad blue rafter-bars
   One sun doth fret ;
There are the pale gold stars
   For carcanet.

All this above ; below,
   Wide wastes of foam,
The rock, the shriven snow,
   The leafy loam.

The House is full of forms
   That, restless, range ;
These ever-varying swarms,
   How swift they change !

Clay charged a little space
   With ardent breath ;
A shadow on the face,
   And life is death.

Strange ! — and no reason writ
   In prose or rhyme ;
Ah ! who shall fathom it, —
   The House of Time ?

Clinton Scollard

Separation

A SMALL island is in a certain harbor near a famous watering-place. By day it is a pretty spot, with its narrow, pebbly beach and slightly indented shore. The most of the island is occupied by an old fort with gray walls and grass-grown ramparts.

The fort has not been garrisoned for twenty years. An Ordnance Sergeant, in charge of the government property, and his family are the only inhabitants. Once the fort was thought a good defense for the great city, distant only a few miles. But the improved guns of modern warfare have made a mockery of the old fortifications. It is twenty years since the troops went away. Weeds now cover the ramparts, and blades of grass are pushing themselves between the gray blocks of masonry.

Pleasure parties sometimes row over from the summer resorts in their little pleasure boats. They ramble over the parade-ground, walk under the dark arches, and wonder that people ever could have lived in the curious casemates.

At night the island is more beautiful than by day, less on its own account than because of its surroundings. As the sun goes down, lights on the neighboring shores twinkle like stars. Hundreds of electric lamps dazzle the eyes, and here and there a more brilliant gleam comes from hotel or lighthouse.

One July evening toward sunset a little boat rowed across the channel from the hotel. The Ordnance Sergeant strolled to the end of the pier, and a lady who stepped from the boat showed him her pass.

She left her boatman at the water's edge, and, attended only by her maid, walked toward the fort. Several times she looked around her as if only half knowing her way. Passing through the sally-port, she climbed the stone steps to the ramparts, and walking slowly along, paused at a corner where an old-fashioned gun was mounted.

" The very spot," she said aloud, " and yet how changed."

When she last had stood there, bugle tones summoning to retreat had fallen on her ear. Now the silence was broken by the harsher whistle of a passing excursion boat. Yet, except that the once trim ramparts were now ill-kept, the general surroundings were little changed. The alteration was in the lady, now so little like her former self, that slim girl of twenty, who had then said to the young officer beside her, " We shall never forget this place."

" Never," he had replied, kissing her.

They were newly betrothed, and they were taking a last look at a favorite rendez-vous. Her month's visit at the fort was at an end. The next day she would return home.

"Forget this place, never," he continued: "this cannon, this bird's nest," and then they had laughed.

How often they had sentimentalized over the nest which a daring bird had built in the very cannon's mouth.

As the middle-aged woman now half absent-mindedly ran her hand into the cannon, she pulled out a little bundle of straw shaped into a nest.

"But it isn't the same," and she brushed a tear from her eyes. Sadly enough now she recalled that last moment when she had clung to her lover's neck.

"In twenty-five years," she had said, "we shall come back to this very spot — twenty-five years from to-day — to talk over this happy summer, even if we have been separated —"

"Separated," and a look of pain had crossed his face. "Nothing shall ever separate us —."

"Except death," she had added.

"Nonsense," he had replied, "when one dies the other shall go, too."

"A double suicide," she had laughed; then, more seriously, "We feel sure of each other now, but men are so fickle —"

"They haven't much reputation in that direction compared with women; but you, my dearest, I do not doubt you, so why do we waste these last hours talking of separation?"

How earnest they both had been — then. Yet now, on the appointed day, she alone had remembered that promise through those long twenty-five years.

"To think that I should return here alone," she said to herself. "It did not seem then as if anything could come between us. But men do not know themselves, and young men least of all. Why should I expect him to be different from the rest? Ah, how I loved him, and how he seemed to love me! Ah, well —"

Here she broke down, and if Marie, her maid, had stood nearer, she would have been surprised to hear her mistress, the so-called impassive leader of society, actually weeping.

At this moment a step approaching startled the lady, and but for the tears in her eyes she would have reproached Marie for coming so near.

Before she could say a word, an arm was thrown around her waist.

"What, Eleanor, *you* here, too?" cried a man's voice.

"Yes," she said weakly; "I — I —"

"Come, now, don't pretend. You remembered. You're just as bad as I."

"Am I? Well, I never thought that you would —"

"Ah!" he interrupted. "It all came back to me yesterday. How strange it was that we should be staying near the fort which neither of us has seen certainly for twenty years. Then I began to count how long it was since *that* summer — you remember, Eleanor. Heavens, it doesn't seem like twenty-five years. You look as young as you did, Eleanor. Well, then I remembered all our heroics about coming here again. But I didn't think I'd find you here. Really, I'm afraid people will gossip."

"Yes," she answered bitterly. "I believe they say we are on the verge of a divorce."

The man colored a little.

"Well, I believe that Sunday paper paragraph was good enough to add it would merely be for incompatibility of temper or something of that kind. Well, Eleanor, sometimes I wish my uncle hadn't left me that fortune. If I'd stayed in the army I wouldn't have been troubled with any superfluous wealth — even after thirty years' service. We couldn't have gone such separate gaits — "

He still held her hand.

" I didn't know you cared," she said almost timidly.

" Cared," and he looked at her until her heart almost stood still.

" But I have cared, too," she apologized. " I have been jealous, people say — "

" No," he interrupted, "people said — "

" The future people shall say only what you wish them to say. Come, come, don't cry. Neither of us has anything awful to confess, we are both forgiven. It was really fate that brought us to this neighborhood this summer. But for this opportunity for sentiment, we might have made that newspaper paragraph truth instead of libelous gossip."

" Well, we won't prosecute the publisher," she laughed.

" No, we'll try to live it down. There, Eleanor, see the moon just behind the lighthouse. One walk around the ramparts. Upon my word, we haven't had a tête-à-tête for ten years."

It seemed a long time to Marie before her mistress and her mistress' husband returned to the pier. She almost wondered if it wasn't a dream even when they all rowed back together in the same boat, with her master's canoe in tow behind.

As husband and wife walked arm in arm up the broad plank walk toward the hotel, the electric lamps overhead seemed to glare at them with curiosity. The old fort across the channel was invisible, yet, wizard-like, it stood more plainly before the eyes of the two than the great hotel itself.

Helen Leah Reed

When Hearts Are Twain

WHEN hearts are twain that would be one,
 And but a word may show it;
When faith is broken, scarce begun,
 Life's gone before you know it.
Though bare existence be retained,
 The joy of living's done.
The charm of life and love departs
When by misfortune kindred hearts
 Are twain that would be one.

Geo. Allan England

BUNGLY AND WINKLE
WINE MERCHANTS 🍇
1273 WASHINGTON STREET
SKOWHEGAN MAINE

Suggestion for an
Announcement
by Frank Bird Masters

A Village Operator

PHRAIM HOLT, the Skimby postmaster, brushed the flies from his forehead and gave a groan.

"Good land o' Nod, how these plaguey things do stick!" he ejaculated, as he walked across the little store to gaze intently, but with unseeing eyes, on a row of chocolate mice which stared back at him from under the glass case with unblinking orbs of white sugar.

"If I'd had any notion 'twas goin' to be so hot, I wouldn't have offered to stay here and look after Jed's stock this afternoon, ye can jest rely on *that*," continued Mr. Holt, morosely, removing his gaze from the mice, and addressing some elderly cocoanut cakes a little farther along in the case. "I must say I supposed there'd be some passin', even if nobody come in, but I haven't laid eyes on a livin' creatur' sence Jed started. Sakes alive! I shall be clean eat up with these pesky flies!"

As he wandered aimlessly about the store, he suddenly heard a brisk step on the flagstones, and hurrying to the door he encountered a stout, middle-aged man, who held a large umbrella over his head and carried a bag. The newcomer mounted the steps, entered the store, set his bag on the counter, and, last of all, closed his umbrella.

"Good afternoon," he said briskly. "Where is Hawkins? I've walked over here from Bumsted. Hot, ain't it?"

"Jed," replied Mr. Holt, disdaining useless formality, "is to a baseball game over to the Center, and will be for some hours, if not days, judgin' as usual. Is there anythin' I can do for ye?"

"Not unless you're going into the calico line," responded the other. "Seems to me I remember your face; name's Holt, ain't it? Help Gregg sort mail, don't you? How is Gregg? My name's Perkins. I've been off the route for three years, so I've lost track of some people."

"I can't inform ye as to Josiah Gregg's health," said Mr. Holt dryly. "He left town more'n ten months back; he wa'n't feelin' over and above chipper when he went, but most likely he's picked up some sence. *I'm* postmaster now."

"Is that so?" said Mr. Perkins, with a show of interest. "What started Gregg off? Is there any place I can sit down here awhile?"

"I can accommodate us both with seats, sech as they be," said Mr. Holt, producing two wooden chairs on whose worn backs and seats the faint traces of a once gay pattern still lingered. "We'll get 'em out in the middle o' the floor, where we'll ketch what little air there is stirrin', and tilt 'em back against the stove. Lawzee! I wisht I had a fan!"

" Here's one you can use," said Mr. Perkins, opening his bag and drawing out a paper fan ; " I generally think it makes me warmer to keep a fan going."

" Maybe it does when you let up on it," responded the postmaster, vigorously plying the article in question, " but I cal'late t' keep this up for one spell. Whew ! ain't it refreshin' ! "

" Well, now, how about Gregg leaving town ? " asked the dry-goods drummer, when he had succeeded in balancing his chair against the stove, a feat which Ephraim Holt, with an ease born of long practise, had accomplished some moments before.

" Well," said the postmaster, with evident relish for the task before him, " I shall have to begin clear'n back when Will Acres set out to marry Statiry Phillips. Old man Phillips favored Will in his courtin', but *Mis'* Phillips would fly right out at anybody that said the indications seemed to p'int to a match 'twixt the young folks. Howsever, after fussin' for upwards o' three years, she give in, and Will got his bride.

" Statiry wasn't a pooty gal — she favored her father, and had a kind of a pudgy figger and look — but she was easy-goin', and jest suited Will. He was well meanin' but high tempered, from a boy ; he used to have words with his mother sometimes, and Mis' Phillips said once that *she* presumed he hastened her death, but it wasn't so. Mis' Acres was consumptive, took it from her family on both sides, and Will was a good son to her, even if he did speak up quick once in awhile.

" Will an' Statiry set up housekeepin' on the Stedman place. He wasn't drawn towards farmin', but he did the best he knew. He wrote a beautiful hand, and he'd had offers of an excellent opportun'ty to book-keep in Nashuy, but I don't know's he'd ever have felt to go there if old Mr. Phillips hadn't died when they'd been married about five years.

" He left three hundred a year to Statiry, and two thousand down ; all the rest to the old lady, knowin' 'twould come round to Statiry, of course, when *she* died. There wa'n't any outlyin' relations.

" Mis' Phillips proposed to Statiry and Will to go and live with her, and see her through. Will didn't covet the plan, but Statiry told him *if* they went *he* could go to Nashuy and only come home for Sundays. Jeems, their baby, was goin' on two.

" Well, they moved over. Will aimed to please Mis' Phillips when Sundays come, but some way he missed it. They used t' have reg'lar set-to's about Jeems's fetchin' up ; to be sure, Jeems had undertook to fetch *himself* up, and his relations' ideas didn't trouble him much, I reckon.

" They hitched along for about four years. The old lady never went off for a day, and she grew dreadful snappy and aggravatin.' Will was doin' first rate in Nashuy, and Statiry went down there off and on, leavin' Jeems to keep his grandma company. There wa'n't any trouble between Will and his wife, but he didn't get in the old lady's way any more'n need be, those years.

" Well, one day, two years back, Statiry came home from Nashuy and found the old lady real sick. I presume likely Jeems had tuckered her out ; she nor his ma hadn't a mite o' *purchase* on that child's will — neither one on 'em. The old lady'd been failin' for some time, though she wouldn't own to it.

" She took to her bed and never left it again. She kep' Statiry and Mary Jennin's (the hired gal) on the keen jump waitin' on her, and she *aimed* to have Jeems fetched up by her bedside, but he broke loose now and agin.

" She'd made her will and done well by Statiry — she told her so one day — and we were lookin' to hear of her death 'most any time, when one afternoon as Josiah Gregg, Jed, an' I set here, Jeems come runnin' in. He cruised round the stove, and sent the cat spittin' off with her tail as big as three, and says he : 'Mr. Gregg, please set right down to the telegraph machine and send pa word 't grandma's dyin'; the doctor says she won't live through the night.'

" Then, before the words was off his tongue, he was careerin' up the road agin ! We hollered after him till we was all hoarsed up, but he never looked round.

" 'Well,' says Josiah, 'I expect I shall have a piece o' work to *send* this message, for I can't hardly ever tick 'em up from the Junction after four o'clock; I guess the young lady 't operates this branch goes vis'tin' afternoons.'

" Sure enough, there wa'n't a sign o' life at the Junction from that time till the office shet up for the night. We counselled together and decided all Josiah could do was to send that message off fust thing in the mornin', soon as he got a return tick from the Junction.

" When I got here next mornin' Josiah was walkin' round kind of uneasy, and, says he, ' Ephraim, I s'posed that Acres child had orders to say his grandma couldn't last through the night, so I sent the message that she *died* last night, and *now* I'm kind o' scairt ! '

" Well, it appears 't on his way to his store that mornin', Will stepped into the telegraph office to send a message to Statiry, and the man says, ' There's a telegram jest come for you, Mr. Acres.'

" Will, he took it, an' read, ' Mis' Phillips died last night.'

" He got leave o' absence from his employer, and then he bought a handsome funeral piece — Mary Jennin's told me 'twas a wreath of everlastin's, picked out with glossy leaves — and started for Skimby.

" The depot wagon don't go down for that noon train in hot weather, so Will walked up the back road. He's been heard to say that the walk seemed real short and pleasant that day.

" When he come near the house, he see Statiry drawin' down one o' the livin'-room shades. When she spied him, she let go her holt, and the shade flew clear'n up to the top. She opened the door, and Will says, ' Wasn't you expectin' me ? '

" ' Why, not *to-day*,' says she. ' We'd better go right up and see mother.'

" They begun to mount the stairs, and when they got 'most to the top a voice come out o' the old lady's room. ' Statiry, why don't you answer me ? What was that noise jest now ? '

" Will come nigh fallin', it give him sech a start, but Statiry shoved him up an' into the room. There was Mis' Phillips bolstered up in bed, with Mary Jennin's fannin' her ! Statiry marched Will up to the bed, and said, ' 'Twas seein' Will comin' that made me let go the window-shade, mother ; the noise you heard was when it flew out o' my hand.'

"'What's in that box you're heftin', William?' says the old lady.

"Will has allowed sence that his wits clean left him. He jest stammered out, '"T —'twas for you!' not knowin' what he said, seemin'ly.

"'Hand it here, then,' says she, and Will, he just handed it over! She opened the box and give a screech. 'A fun'ral piece! You unnat'ral man! I s'pose Statiry ordered ye to fetch this an' have it ready; I see it's made o' durable stuff!' Then she flung it away from her an' yelled for Jeems, and when he come she sent him over to Mis' French's, to fetch Lawyer Fred, that had drawed up her will.

"While Jeems was gone, Statiry tried to calm her, and Will tried to explain *how* he come to be there; but Mis' Phillips put her fingers in her ears an' held 'em there till Fred French come, an' *then* she turned Statiry an' Will out o' the room, as ye might say.

"She had her will altered so's to leave every mite o' her money to Jeems; the int'rest to pay for eddicatin' him, and the whole to be his out an' out when he come of age. She lived two days, but she wouldn't hear no explanations.

"Well, o' course the matter o' that telegraph message was stirred up; Josiah got a good share o' blame; folks said he hadn't showed jedgment, and wa'n't fitted to be in sech a respons'ble place.

"It appears 't the doctor *had* said he didn't think the old lady 'd pull through the night, but nobody suspicioned that Jeems heard him, and that young one never would 've owned up if he hadn't been obliged to by Josiah, Jed, and me!

"Folks said the will might be broke, but Statiry and Will didn't propose to make nor meddle with law. I guess they was wise: in my opinion, it's about as windin' in its ways as pusley, and full as hard to git shet off, if it once gits a holt on ye.

"They took Jeems and moved to Nashuy. I hear the boy's gettin' a firmer fetchin' up, now he's with his pa right along, consid'able firmer, and more of a kind.

"But Josiah, he wilted under the blame folks put on him. His shoulders begun to sag, and he told me he didn't relish a thing, scussly. And the day after the telegraph office was moved over to the Center, he started out to Idyho, to see his brother Seth, so he *said*. I cal'late we've seen the last o' Josiah Gregg in *this* town.''

There was no time for comment, for as he uttered the last words Mr. Holt gave a long sniff, let his chair down from its tilted position, and sprang to his feet.

"If there ain't a breeze springin' up from the west'ard!" he cried, as he craned his long neck out of the door in the direction referred to, "and here's Jed this minute, comin' in the Follet boys' team! The baseball game must 've closed up earlier 'n usual."

Elizabeth L. Gould

Tailpiece
by
Masters

The Basin
by
E. B. Bird

On the Thames at Richmond

A S I paddled up from Richmond
  While the twilight grew,
While the queenly houses
High upon the hills of Richmond
  Faded from my view ;
As I paddled, as I drifted,
  Did I think of you ?

As the arches high and narrow
  That my eye looked through,
Over which the busses
Trundled all the way from Hampton
  Down the road to Kew,
As they vanished in the distance
  Did I think of you?

As I drifted where the river
  Parts and joins anew,
Where the drooping willows
Hid me from the patient anglers
  At their rendezvous,
As the heart of England passed me,
  Did I think of you ?

As I turned at Twickenham Ferry
  Skies were gold and blue ;
Drifting down to Richmond
Past the meadows and the villas,
  Twilight onward drew ;
Then I paused and wrote these verses —
  Did I think of you ?

Charles Knowles Bolton

Mr. Theo. Brown Hapgood, Jr.

SICVT LILIV M INTER SPINAS

Ornament
for Title Page
by
Hapgood

Courtesy of
Copeland & Day

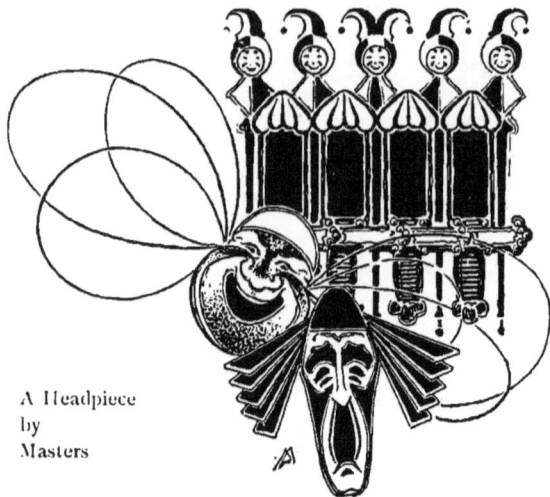

A Headpiece
by
Masters

Theo. Brown Hapgood, Jr., Decorator

HE paths the patient interviewer must perforce plod are unfortunately not generally primrose paths of dalliance, but rather tracks strewn with many thorns. But being particularly lucky myself, I have but to play the comparatively easy task of compiler, and quote from two who ought surely to be very competent to speak. The biographical portion I will cull from a letter Mr. Hapgood himself wrote me in answer to my request for a sketch of himself and work.

" Mr. — — was rushed to death, so I said nothing to him concerning biography. I will, therefore, have to furnish you with facts ; the twentieth of this month (August) I will be twenty-five years old. Born in Boston ; went to Boston Latin School four years, graduating in 1891. Passed my ' exams ' to Harvard, but, as you know, of course, did not honor that institution with my presence, taking instead two years at the Art Museum School of Drawing and Painting. Since then I have been grinding."

Surely a most concise account, though unfortunately almost too brief. Of his work he said nothing, which I regret. I always like to have a man's opinion of his own work, it shows so many things. Speaking for myself, however, I will say that his work is for the most part unsigned, consisting largely of the designing of title pages, the lettering of book-covers, and work of a kindred nature. The minor details, you may say, but the very things that distinguish between perfect and poor results.

Perhaps, again quoting, this time from Mr. J. W. Phinney, of the Dickinson Type Foundry, would be the most interesting thing possible.

George·Fred·Daniels:·Priest

humani
nihil
alienum

A Book Plate
by
F. B. Hapgood, Jr

" I have been much interested in the development of Mr. Hapgood as a designer. Like all young artists, it was difficult for him to choose the school he wished to attach himself to and grow into. For a time he strongly leaned towards the modern Renaissance, and it is only within a year or so that he has turned from his early fancies to the strong, masculine printing of the present revival of the fifteenth century. He has wisely avoided the frivolous and grotesque, and adhered to the best traditions of the old-time ancient schools. While there is nothing new under the sun, a fresh, novel treatment of the simple, vigorous, decorative printing of the antique calls for large, individual talent. Mr. Hapgood is well grounded in the elements of his profession, with a disposition for hard work and an ability to learn and adapt. He will make a broad and substantial place for himself in the professional line he has selected."

And Mr. Phinney's judgment in this case tends to make me look at him with more respect than does anything else for which he can be held responsible.

Blaireau

Cover Design
by
Hapgood

Courtesy
of
The Inland Printer

Immaturity

GREY, grim, they circled pinioned Life and fain
        Would know his heart. Then, radiant, Youth arose
To testify; but like tumultuous rain
They shouted all: " Tush, fool without a stain ! "

Philip Becker Goetz

The Falconer
by
Theo. B. Hapgood, Jr.

NOTES ; BEING, FOR THE MOST PART, COMPOSED OF NOTICES OF BOOKS, WITH HERE AND THERE, MAYHAP, A BIT OF WISDOM.

NEW book is a delight now in a diversity of ways. One never knows, when he picks it up, what novel and surprising features it will reveal. We used once to be pretty sure of finding Mr. Richard Harding Davis portrayed in a multiplicity of poses ; of late, however, we do not meet his awe-inspiring countenance so often. Then, as mentioned in my last, we discovered Mr. Robert Barr masquerading in the dignified guise of Managing Editor of the New York *Argus*. But now from Messrs. Lamson, Wolffe & Company comes, in " King Noanett," the crowning effort in the way of the pictorial portrait panorama.

First and foremost of the group is my friend Mr. Edwin Ruthven himself, cutting all manner of shines as Master Miles Courtney. Now posing majestically in the center of the page, now gallantly leading a repulse, and again praying fervently — probably that the book will meet with my approbation — to say nothing of various other minor performances. Then there is Mr. J. S. of Dale, or rather Mr. F. J. Stimson, as I believe he is now, with a most solemn countenance, as well he may have, for the crime of perpetrating a book of 327 pages is no small one.

And here is Miss Ethel Reed, rushing towards me with outstretched arms, which is surely delightfully thrilling enough to make even the most blasé blush with pleasure. Over in the back, too, is Miss Gwendoline Sandham in a truly angelic pose, gazing sweetly at some one, apparently paralyzed, kneeling before her. But the most delightful picture of all, and the one to which I most often turn, is near the middle of the book and depicts — but then it would be very wrong to say who it does depict, though fortunately I know.

This private portrait gallery printed for public perusal is a large and happy idea. As a matter of fact, I'm tucked away in lots of Mr. Bird's pictures myself, and I assure the gentle reader the thought that you are being gazed upon by thousands of admiring eyes is a very complacent thought indeed.

I await with considerable anticipated pleasure the time when Messrs. Copeland & Day and Herbert S. Stone & Company will venture an illustrated volume, for the delight of seeing these gentlemen performing some heroic *pas seul* will, I am sure, more than recompense for the reading of the book.

¶ I CAME across a curious relic the other day in the shape of a photograph, by Sarony, of Oscar Wilde — " The Picture of Dorian Grey " might perhaps be a not unhappy title. Probably I picked it up when sunflowers were the only flowers that grew, and " Patience " reigned supreme.

Viewed in the sense of pure æstheticism, as I always view things now, it is delightful. The head droops languidly to one side, the eyes gaze dreamily upwards, the long, slightly wavy hair, the lips just parted to give a glimpse only of his pearly teeth — I am presuming, of course, he had pearly teeth — the hands clasped softly one upon the other.

Clad in long silk hose and knickerbockers, patent leather pumps and velvet coat and vest, he leans in a pose of studied negligence against a highly ornate wall. The air of weariness, of ennui, of bored resignation about the whole is distinctly refreshing.

My poor, poor Oscar, to think of '82 and now!

* I HEARD rather a good story some time ago as to the divine inspiration of authors nowadays; and though it is rather old, perhaps everybody has not heard it. Mr. Nicoll, of New York, the gentleman who makes clothes, wanted a poster, or thought he did, which amounts to the same thing. He made known his wants to Messrs. Bachellor, Johnson & Bachelor who forthwith commissioned Mr. Louis Rhead to make one.

The poster was made, delivered to the before-mentioned syndicate, and paid for. Then, however, there came a hitch, the tailor man refused to take it.

But the versatile Mr. Bachelor was nowise daunted, and at once hied himself to Mrs. Burton Harrison and said he wanted a story to fit the poster.

"What kind will it be?" said Mrs. Harrison.

"Oh, any kind. Just call it 'His Lordship,'" said the gentleman.

Probably you have seen the result.

* HAS the end of a realistic novel ever struck you with all its due force and awe-inspiring veneration? Have you ever thought that when you began the first line on the first page that it was but the beginning of the end, that by the end of the last page the majority would be dead, the lives of the others ruined beyond all hopes of recovery? Has it ever overwhelmed you with the horrible truth that realistic novels are all tragedies, that comedies are unknown in the realms of realism?

Has it ever occurred to you that there are no solutions to a realistic problem? that once the problem gets warmed up in its revolution it will knock everything into such a mass of wreckage that when you see it all piled up in the last chapter you wonder how the binding ever stood it?

Have you ever noticed that the main strength of a realistic novel rested in its end? Forming, so to speak, a sharp, stinging cracker at the end of a long, limp whip. As if the author had been careful and sparing of his energy, that he might with a final *coup d'etat* leave the reader petrified with horror.

Have you never overlooked the fact that nothing natural is ever allowed to influence the end of one of this peculiar brand of books?

These are, however, things that every one should know. They are very useful truths to remember.

This has become a realistic age, and to have these branded on one's memory is to be spared many needless disappointments. With these in mind, we can size up the life of the victimized hero from the length of the book; and we will be prepared to find him, on the last page, a blood-curdling mass, or behold him standing on the threshold of a loveless life of misery and woe.

¶ Now that the literary lorgnette has become focused on Mr. Stephen Crane, be as impartial as one can, we must forsooth look at him through the distorting lenses of lionization. Be we never so careful, we feel that in viewing his work we should look through a magnifying glass rather than our unaided eyes of unbiased criticism.

Mr. Crane's first book was a huge joke. His second attempt showed ability and cleverness. His third and fourth productions demonstrate rather clever financiering than additional literary talents. His fifth and sixth — announced — may, on their birth, kill the goose of the golden eggs, whose powers should not be overtaxed, since it can stand but a limited amount.

The late and almost simultaneous appearance of " Maggie " and " George's Mother " very clearly shows the light in which Mr. Crane views his own work. It demonstrates, to my satisfaction at least, that he considers himself but a fad. That he knows to have his ventures reach the port of prosperity, he must launch them when the tide is flood and the favorable wind raised by his " Red Badge of Courage " still blowing. He realizes that "there comes a tide in the affairs of men which, seized upon its flood," and so forth. He is surely seizing time by the forelock to the best of his ability. He knows full well that did he but wait till the wind ceases and the tide turns, his argosies would soon founder in the sea of the unsuccessful.

Evidently the art of making hay while the sun shines was firmly impressed upon Mr. Crane by the projector of the East Aurora School of Agriculture.

But unstinted praise is a questionable blessing. I might say, for example, if I were given to nautical similes, that " Trilby " was blown by it through the harbor of success to destruction on the shoals of oblivion.

As for the two books themselves, " Maggie " should be subtitled " A Sketch "; " George's Mother," " A Fragment."

They both demonstrate Mr. Crane's cleverness in new fields. But had they been succeeded by nothing of more importance, the fact of his cleverness being appreciated is extremly doubtful, or looked at in the opposite direction, not doubtful at all. One never feels an undue interest in the various characters, yet the books are so well written as to be very easy reading. As when coasting a slight descent it is less easy to stop than to go on, so it is with these.

To be sure, there are some very foolish people who assert the absurd claim that fiction should be something else than a vehicle for the writer's cleverness ; but the denial of this laughable proposition would be only giving it unmerited importance. Mr. Crane is a young man whom I admire as one making the most of his possibilities.

¶ EMERGING from the herd of erotic realistic nightmares that have held the reins of popular fancy for some time, comes a strong, healthy romance, suddenly bursting into brilliancy like an incandescent light on a very murky night. Needless to say, Boston turned on the light. " King Noanett " is wholly hers. Its principal scenes are laid in Massachusetts Bay ; it is written by a Bostonian, illustrated by a Bostonian, published by a Bostonian, and it is, like everything thoroughly Bostonese, very good, and something of which one may well be proud. Mr. Stimson has in this, his last attempt, made his first bid for serious consideration as a writer of fiction which will live. From a cursory glance at the various magazines, I should say such consideration was being accorded.

The action of " King Noanett " opens in England, is soon brought to the newly settled colony of Virginia, from thence goes northward to Massachusetts Bay, where the bulk of the book is acted.

Taken altogether, it is a restful book — the direct antithesis of the general run of historic romances. Its tone is mainly low, and sweet, and sad. The regulation pyrotechnics of the ordinary romancer have been frigidly excluded.

It is the story of great loves and sorrows, the story of great happiness and unrequited love. It tells of a love such as I never heard before. Not the flippant flirting of the countess and the courtier, but a love so strong, so pure and passionless, so true, and hence so irresistible, as to be an entirely new element for consideration in viewing fiction ; and an element that must, I fear, be seldom found elsewhere.

Furthermore, it is the character sketching of two nations. There is outlined in Bamfylde Carew — the true, though unintentional, hero of his own narration — the typical Anglo-Saxon, sober, subdued, steadfast. Slow to act till after much consideration, seldom ready with an impromptu speech. And in contrast is painted Mills Courtney, — the hero in the eyes of Carew and the general public, — the fiery, impulsive Celt, ever ready with an oath, a compliment, or a blow : first acting, then thinking.

The plot is excellent and well executed. The incidents are good, and though, perhaps, selected to display to the best advantage Mr. Stimson's knowledge of colonial times and customs, still the very excellence of his descriptions will cause this to be readily pardoned. The denouement is the strongest, the most unexpected and finished thing I think I ever read. I cannot now recall any even approaching it.

¶ ABOUT as flagrant pieces of shameless robbery as I have seen for some time are now being perpetrated in *Truth*. These, judging from the signatures, are sketches by the late Chas. Howard Johnson, although the drawing itself is so bad as to disabuse one of the idea almost at once. On very close examination, however, it can be discovered that what at first sight is the characteristic signature of Johnson is in reality of one Ethel H. Johnson, who makes hers almost identical, with the evident intention of fooling the public.

One might think that *Truth* would be sufficiently honorable to prevent the use of its pages for such a purpose.

¶ COLLEGE life has ever had an apparently irresistible attraction for the maker of fiction. The interval that has elapsed since the alluring adventures of Tom Brown were set in type, and the recent publication of the very stupid chronicling of the uneventful life of " The Babe, B. A.," by the illustrious author of " Dodo," has been amply filled with books on collegiate themes of more or less ability and corresponding interest. Out of this mass of generally mediocre fiction two books that are noticeable by being of more than ordinary workmanship are " Princeton Stories," by

Jesse Lynch Williams, and " College Girls," by Abbe Carter Goodloe. Both are collections of short stories, and of the two, the former is, I think, superior. Miss Goodloe strives too much for the tragic, and has an inclination for "situations" and such. It seems hardly natural that a girl's college could contain so much woe, though of course, never having attended one, I cannot speak from experience, and her less serious attempts ring truer. Of " Princeton Stories," however, we can find no such fault. We feel the atmosphere of Princeton from cover to cover, its eating clubs and cannon, and black and orange stripes. Miss Goodloe's style has been spoken of as resembling that of Mr. Davis, Mr. Richard Harding Davis, and this is to a certain extent, I think, true. Mr. Williams's style is uninfluenced.

C. D. Gibson has illustrated " College Girls " in true Gibsonian style, which is in itself sufficient to warrant a large sale among the young lady Gibsonmaniacs.

Both books are, as I have said before, very good indeed, and well worth reading, and much superior to the ordinary run of their class.

¶ In an old number of *Judge*, which I discovered a short time since, was published the last cartoon of the late Bernard Gillam. By a rather strange coincidence it represented a graveyard of political hopes, and writing this reminds me how many have gone within the year ; those whose places will be long unfilled, Gillam, Johnson, Reinhart, not to mention the greater losses in Field and Bunner. Truly a sad array of genuine worth laid low. " The paths of glory."

¶ I think that, without exception, Mr. Gelett Burgess is the drollest, cleverest man I've heard for a long, long time. His adventures with Vivette, as exploited in " The Lark," and his supremely ridiculous cartoons in the same ponderous publication, have surely furnished more pure enjoyment to the square inch than any similar attempts, their only fault lying in their being so brief, though, perhaps, it is just on that account we so enjoy them. Not content with this, however, he must forsooth turn out something yet more ridiculous. Something to make the antiquated gentlemen writhe in horror,— in name, " Le Petit Journal des Refusées." It is, of course, perfectly manifest that he is the culprit ; no one else could possibly turn out such delicious bits as the following : —

> " I'd love to hunt for angels,
> And shoot them on the wing ;
> I'd love to see them hop around
> And yell like anything."

" G. is for Goup ; I would much rather be a nice Purple Cow than a G-O-U-P."

> " But the Bugaboo, gum, and worm didn't rhyme,
> And the poor little bird had a horrible time ;
> For the gum glued the worm to his little inside,
> And the gastric juice couldn't do what it tried."

But it would be wicked to purloin any more from what will undoubtedly be *the* American quarterly. " Sixteen cents a number, $16 a year." Subscribe at once, before the edition is exhausted.

¶ WE hear from the *The Inland Printer*, of Chicago, that it has arranged with Mr. J. C. Leyendecker, the designer of the first prize *Century* poster, for a series of poster and cover designs for that publication, beginning with the November number. There will be six designs in the series. It is to be hoped they will be more worthy than the prize poster mentioned.

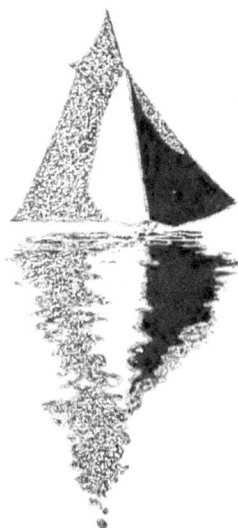

Tailpiece
by
Masters

VOL'I THE NO'III

RED LETTER

BIRD

NOVEMBER

1896

Contents

Art and Literary Societies

The publishers of THE RED LETTER desire a representative in every art and literary society in the world, to look after their interests in these quarters.

If you are a member of any society, and are willing to put in some time gathering subscriptions, on the most liberal terms, they would like to hear from you.

The Red Letter Magazine,

Circulation Department - - - - - - Boston, Mass.

Blanchard & Watts

E take great pleasure in calling the attention of our friends and the public to the fact that on Nov. 1, 1896, we commence our fourth year of business. In the past three years we have distanced all competitors, and to-day have the best equipped, largest, and most modern plant, employ more hands in the engraving business than any one house in New England. We believe our success is due to getting out our work promptly, and giving our customers the best results that can be obtained from the originals furnished. ✠✠✠✠✠✠✠✠✠✠✠✠✠✠✠✠✠

E shall continue in the future, as in the past, to furnish the public illustrations for all purposes as near perfection as possible. We especially call your attention to our facilities for making cuts direct from the object. Our half-tone cuts for illustrating silverware are used by most of the leading silversmiths of New England. ✠✠✠✠

We also make plates, of all kinds of machinery, stoves, bicycles, pianos, desks, and almost every kind of articles used in illustrating catalogues, etc. Publishers of books, magazines, newspapers, catalogues, souvenirs, in fact, anything requiring illustrations, cannot do better than to place their orders with us. A trial order, we think, will entitle us to your kind consideration and your future orders.

Yours respectfully,
The Blanchard & Watts Eng. Co.

Blanchard & Walls

Gentlemen's Fashions

Pictures of People

is a new book, after the same general style of manufacture as Mr. Wenzell's, noticed elsewhere, containing eighty-five of the latest drawings by C. D. Gibson. This, as well as "Gibson's Drawings," the first collection of his work, is offered on the same terms as is "In Vanity Fair." Two more magnificent art books have never been offered.

It might pay you to work a little to secure them

The Red Letter Magazine,

Circulation Department -   -   -   -   -   -   Boston, Mass.

College Men,

as a rule, are interested in athletics. Nearly every one of them endeavors to add to the score himself, or "roots" vigorously when his side "gets there."

"Cinder Path Tales," by William Lindsey, is an ideal book for college men. Its stories, as its name implies, are purely athletic in theme, and intensely realistic and exciting bits of writing, and correspondingly interesting reading. By arrangements with the publishers, we are enabled to give a copy of "Cinder Path Tales" to every one sending us two yearly subscriptions, or one subscription (his own, if desired) and 50 cts. It is an offer no one will regret having accepted.

The Red Letter Magazine,

Circulation Department -   -   -   -   -   Boston, Mass.

Drawing
by
Frank Hazenplug

November, 1896. Volume I., Number 3

The Red Letter

An Illustrated Monthly

" 'T will while away an hour or so with picturings and print." — MARLOWE

When Armies Met

I HEARD the distant summons loud
To battle, from the crested cloud ;
The vaunting trumpet of the gale ;
The rattling musketry of hail ;
The sobbing of the rain — and lo !
The silence of the shrouding snow.

John B. Tabb

" When the Rose Is Dead "

ANTOINETTE LA MARTINE TO JASPER HERRICK.

November tenth.

ON ami, il y a longtemps — it is many, very many years since I last have seen you ; I do not know whether now you ever cast one thought back to the foolish days when Antoinette sang to Jasper only, and Jasper listened and looked pleased. *. Que nous étions jeunes !* Ah, we were young in those days ! And now — *maintenant* — they tell me I am famous, that it is all Europe that listens. They say not only that my voice is beautiful, but that it has sympathy, expression,— *l'âme,* soul,— that it is the voice of one who has felt and known. *Comprends tu ?* Shall you know the reason ? *Écoute moi !* A few hours past I sang to the emperor and his court. They frightened me — those grand demoiselles with the robes, and the jewels, and the beauty ; and the noble, haughty gentlemen with their uniforms and decorations. What could poor little Antoinette do worthy of their attention ? My voice failed me. *J'étais tout embarrassée.* Then, suddenly, I remembered how I sang first, and how for many days afterward, and all that silly, innocent time. And, once more. I sang for you only, and all the gay robes and uniforms faded from my eyes. I was not singing for the emperor, for I thought not of him, but only of my own old girlish happiness. And then the song finished, and I saw them all again, and — *c'est rien,* only now they say I am famous.

It is night, very dark and quiet, and I am alone. One thinks of so many things at night,— *n'est ce pas ?* — all the old things that are passed long ago. The air is heavy with the perfume of dying roses ; they have sent Jacqueminots, and Maréchal Niels, and many more. My rooms are strewn with them. Do you remember the rose-bush that climbed over the little house in the garden, and the small white roses that grew in it every summer? Ah, but they were sweet, sweeter than these great heavy-headed flowers. *Mon ami,* I have been remembering those sunny, far-away days. Somehow, to-night, I can think of nothing beside. I have been wondering where you are, and whether you ever remember, too. Will you not send me some day a little line for the old time's sake ?

Adieu. Thy well-wisher,

ANTOINETTE LA MARTINE.

JASPER HERRICK TO ANTOINETTE LA MARTINE.

November tenth.

Is it strange that I should write to you again after all, Antoinette, or that your face should have been imaging itself to me to-day? They talk of it at the clubs, you know,— eyes, lips, hair, throat,— only they had your hair auburn instead of the glistering brown I remember — in the papers, in the streets, knocking at my ears with all that I have been forgetting — trying to forget, *vois-tu* — and bidding me think of all. Well, I have a sounder memory than the reporter, Antoinette, though perhaps I have more to remember! You granted me so much in your last words to me seven years ago ; you said they were the last, did you not ?

And the meaning of it all is that you sang to them once last week, and that you sing again to-morrow. If Ulysses might deafen his faithful mariners, he would venture from home to hear you. But they are all mad with the siren already ; moreover, Ulysses is faint-hearted, and even — 'tis shameful to own — slothful.

You beheaded the swine with my "*Ständchen*" last week, I hear. Poor beasts, one might have liked to hear them grunt. But for the song? Well, jewels and streaming lights become it as well now, no doubt, as candles and a muslin frock did once. There were roses on the piano, too. Do you remember how their scent tingled and stung? And firelight and — was there something in our eyes ?

" Hör, ich das Liedchen Dingen
Das einst die Liebste sang."

I will grant you I would rather it were by firelight ! But the siren could never be brought to sing it there. — give up the jewels and lights for the muslin frock again ? And I have still a verdant love for salad days and muslin frocks, unbecoming my graying hair, perhaps.

Do you remember my last words to you? Though I never called them my last, as you did yours. *Qui sait !* I have learned that the last word never comes. I would like to wish you something in parting, to prove my friendliness, but there's nothing to wish — " *Hast alles was Menschenbegehr !*"

So farewell,

JASPER HERRICK.

November twentieth.

Mon Jasper: — And you have remembered, and you still think and, perchance, regret a little? Oh, *mon Sien!* And lo, the night, in which I cannot sleep for hearing again your voice and seeing once more your face. You, too, bethink yourself of her whom formerly you called your Antoinette. Does that not mean that our old friendship cannot die entirely, that there are some ties which always — forever — will hold us two together? You recall my face, my eyes and hair? True, years have gone, but believe me, Jasper, I am not much changed. Men still say, as you said once, — foolish boy, — that I am good to look upon. My eyes are still called bright, and my hair has not a thread of gray. *Mais que dis-je!* Gray hair at twenty-five? Surely I need not fear it these many years. What's this talk of jewels and bright lights? What if I am famous? My friend, my friend, know you not that a muslin frock, with a friend to listen, makes a happier singer than all the jewels and lights and strange faces? And my voice is still the same as when first you spoke words of encouragement that set my heart to beating. Do you remember that also? I have learned nothing from all their teaching, only troubled myself with a few long rules, which hinder and do not help. Ah, Jasper, why must this separation last always? Did I say those words were the last? But I was only an ignorant girl, Jasper, and you had grieved me then. I thought you did not care, that it all went for nothing with you. And now, after all this long, long time, your letter comes, and I see that you cared — a little, at least. Forgive me, I was hasty, but I was so young.

Ah, come, and I will sing you the song you used to like the best, and all shall be peace between you and me. And I will wear a muslin frock and forget the rules they taught me, and I will sing to you, as I never have sung yet, — to no emperor — to none of them at all. I care not for this fame, Jasper, except that as perhaps it helped to bring me your letter. *Vraiment*, old friends are always the best and always the nearest to one's heart.

Ah, Jasper, men may talk of the singer Antoinette La Martine as they will. It matters not. Only when you hear it, do you say to yourself that I desire that you come to me, and that I am thy little

'TOINETTE.

November twentieth.

M'amie, will you have yet another little line from the surly Ulysses? I have already growled a second to your own voice, as you know; the whole ocean was between, and who can tell whether we were properly in tune or no? A strange duet, and heaven knows why she made us sing it.

Ah, well, it does us all good to be a little sentimental now and then. And if your wandering memory chances to stray away from the gay robes and uniforms to light upon me — *je vous remercie, Mademoiselle!* 'Tis not because you have the bad taste to despise jewels and gay robes and uniforms; one can't afford that at twenty-five, *c'est autre chose* at thirty-seven! I grant you that plain water is uncommonly sweet to the throat in the morning, after the absinthe at night; but we always return to the absinthe!

Perhaps your morning is to dawn oftener than mine. Ah, child, you have still the light heart of youth; fame, and applause, and love keep it light; I rejoice for you. I was wrong to stretch out my hand to you, 'tis chill and clammy with — why should I tell you with what? You are still the white-frocked girl at heart, child. I had almost forgotten that we do not tell the truth to girls. Twenty-five! Ah, you will learn.

" *Warum sind denn die Rosen so blass !* " Why, indeed? I should have to prove to you that they are. Perhaps you will let me smell of yours one day — the roses that emperors and kings have sent you — and pity the gray-haired man that his are withered and dead. There are always men enough who find the roses fresh and sweet.

But I have you. You have fêtes, and gowns, and lovers to think of, and I keep you from them. Farewell, and keep beautiful and light-hearted.

Absinthe is best.

Yours faithfully,

Jasper Herrick.

Antoinette La Martine to Jasper Herrick.

November thirtieth.

Mon cher ami : — Vous avez beaucoup de bonté. You are truly generous. You remind me of the flight of time. *Mais donc,* I had quite forgotten that though I might remain unchanged, you might have grown gray-haired and fond of quiet. I was thoughtless and cruel to ask you to come — to bestir yourself — without first finding out whether it would be too much of exertion. *Restez tranquille.* By and by, perhaps, when I am tired, too, of all things, I may let you smell the roses as you wish. Now — you are right, there is the absinthe, and 'tis absurd to wait for a comrade too weary to drink.

Au revoir, — when I am gray.

Antoinette La Martine.

Jasper Herrick to Antoinette La Martine.

November thirtieth.

Poor child, you have let yourself make a strange mistake, and I have let you, perhaps. I grieve that we should have thought of each other again at all, but 'tis done. The words I wrote to you last week told you enough. I cannot add to them — nor take away. I blame myself that they were so cold, but *que voulez vous !*

The last word is yet to be said, perhaps; we must say good-by again now. I send your letters back to you. You will like to throw them away, or laugh at them, perhaps How do I know? You are such a child. Farewell.

Faithfully yours,

Jasper Herrick.

Ballantyne Everts

Enter Mrs. * * *
by
Frank Hazenplug

The Development of a Modern Master

FACT of which the chosen are not only aware, but also duly appreciate, is that the *Chap-Book* has fathered and fostered many delightful things that might otherwise have wilted and died under the less artistic and more rational ideas of the less educated editors of more ponderous publications. One of the most pleasing of these delights to the æsthetic mind is the charming work of Mr. Frank Hazenplug. To be perfectly frank, however, Mr. Hazenplug's work has not always appeared charming to even so ardent an admirer as myself. In fact, the first piece of his I now remember, entitled "The Blind," struck me at the time of its appearance as an extremely idiotic bit of design, and I very much fear its deeply symbolical meaning was not properly impressed upon me. I must even shamefacedly admit that the idea the human figure should be some seven heads high was quite prominent among the false gods I then worshiped.

Howsoever, one should not be held too strictly accountable for the errors of his youth, and I therefore trust my later walkings in the true faith will tend to cause to be overlooked my youthful lapses into Philistinic ways.

But since the printing of "The Blind" there has been much over which I have gloated long and admiringly. Mr. Hazenplug's delightfully attenuated maidens are attractive in the superlative degree ; his less numerous, muchly haloed

Drawing
by
Frank Hazenplug

saints are truly saintlike in the agony of their triangular features ; and his rose-trees and potted plants are veritable marvels of forestry and horticulture.

But, seriously, the work of Mr. Frank Hazenplug is deserving of the most careful attention and consideration, typifying, as it does, the most extreme methods in later-day design. Since his " Blind " was created, some eighteen months ago, his improvement has been so constant and rapid that we find in the drawings given in this number of The Red Letter about as exquisite examples of black and white work as it has ever been my good fortune to admire. Mr. Hazenplug's first work was in the *Chap-Book* for Jan. 15, 1895. Two years previous he had taken a three months' course at the Chicago Art Institute, and another three months spent there last winter is the sum total of his art schooling. This lack of study, however, apparently causes him but slight disturbance, since he writes me, " The fact that I have had so little schooling does not make me proud, nor am I deeply remorseful ; if I were, I fancy I might dry my tears, and go to school some more." Considering his little schooling, his rapid improvement is all the more remarkable and creditable in that his work is done entirely alone, and his list of acquaintances includes neither artist nor author.

Mr. Hazenplug was born in Illinois some twenty-one years ago, and has never been out of the State. At the age when most boys were being brought up on stories of adventure and Oliver Optic, he was, so he tells me, bringing himself up on Bertha M. Clay and Dora Thorne. A most peculiar and horrifying diet, surely, and one that is no doubt somewhat responsible for his present style of work. As to the best thing he has ever done there is evidently a differing of opinion, as he furthermore tells me that " the cleverest thing I have ever done, so I've been told, was when, upon being asked my name, I wrote Frank Hazenplug ; however, this is more or less a matter of taste, there being some, I believe, who really admire my drawings." His last supposition, I venture to say, is more nearly correct than his first.

Mr. Hazenplug's work in the field of poster-making has as yet been rather limited, and a short extract from the *Chap-Book* for March 15, 1895, will probably be the most acceptable résumé of it that I can give.

" The first poster signed by Mr. Hazenplug was called, officially, ' The Red Lady ' (by a cheerful calumniator, ' The Idiot Undressing '). Its merit is in the massing, in a small space, of black, red, and white, in a way that will cry to the passer-by from across the street. The drawing is unessential. It is a color scheme with an incidental resemblance to the human form. But in the design for ' Living Posters,' made last December, we have the nearest approach to French methods and ideals in poster-making that an American designer has yet made. A thin, angular, red-haired woman sits on a red chair, in a trailing gray gown, with a broad band of red down her back, and cranes a long neck away from us. She is artificially, consciously ugly. Yet one might as well deny her charms as that of Yvette Guilbert. With the latter we wasted adjectives and vague phrases which should have lasted the year out, trying to explain what is unexplainable. The quality of ' chic ' is an eternal fact, and forces recognition wherever it is found."

Knowing Mr. Hazenplug only through his work, his photograph, and a letter or two, his personality can, of course, be but a matter of conjecture, and hence better not attempted. He has, however, already secured a most prominent place among the ever-growing list of younger decorators and designers of meritorious work, whose existence must not be overlooked when thinking of the future. And granted his work still improve in the measure that it has, or even remain where it now is   though that is unlikely   we have in him a man of the foremost rank and ability.

Richard Gorham Badger

A Poster Design
by
Frank Hazenplug

Courtesy
of
Herbert S. Stone & Co.

A Song

THE sway of the sea
   When the tide sobs out,
Her voice is to me
The sway of the sea ;
Deep death and a free
   To my struggling doubt.
The sway of the sea
   When the tide sobs out.

Philip Becker Goetz

A Love's Cremation

RONDEAU

YOUR billets-doux recall that glen
Where we two plighted troth. And when
I scan this stack of notes from you
I think of rides — and long ones, too,
Of dances : sought by other men,
You waltzed with me. When zephyrs blew,
One starlit night, you kissed me, true,
If these are evidence. I'll read again
Your billets-doux.

Engagements, yea, have I been through,
For I've had sweethearts not a few,
Since last I heard from Ethelwen ——
Oh, woman's wiles are past the ken
Of man — Ah, that fire needs, 'tis plain,
Your billets-doux.

Shireley Everton Johnson

Panel
by
E. B. Bird

The Rose of Mescal.

OW—DY, parson ! "

The broken-winded pinto horse shied feebly, yielding the bridle-path to the snorting bronco terror which had overtaken him. The minister clung fast to the pommel of his high Mexican saddle and turned a mild boyish face over his shoulder.

"Good morning, Mr. Dobbs," he said.

Mr. Dobbs by this time had shot ahead some rods, but he reined in abruptly. The little minister chirruped to his steed, slapped the calico neck smartly with the palm of his hand, and moved on. The two rode side by side — an odd couple — along the narrow trail, through blossoming wild mustard which floated like a golden mist in air above their heads.

"New horse," observed Mr. Dobbs, dashing the perspiration from his forehead. "Nice colt — when I get him broke of a trick or two. He's got a notion of biting. Hi ! "

A jerk on the right bridle-rein brought the gray colt's head straight, but the pinto prudently fell back a step.

"He seems to be in a temper," said Samuel. "I should not think the bit and spurs would improve it."

"Lord, parson ; I mean you can't manage these here hawses with a ribbon an' a lump of sugar ! "

Samuel looked sheepishly conscious.

"I dare say you're right. I don't know much about horses," he confessed.

Dobbs cast a comical sidelong glance at the wheezy pinto.

"No; I shouldn't call you exactly a judge of horseflesh," he drawled. "You didn't get much of a bargain there, parson."

"I got what I wanted," declared Samuel stoutly. "How do you think I'd look on a horse like yours ? "

"Heh ! Nobody'd have a chance to see how you looked ! You wouldn't stay on long enough. But you might just as well ride a clotheshorse as that thing."

As though to console the unfortunate pinto for this harsh judgment, Samuel covertly patted its scrubby neck. By dint of defying public opinion in its behalf, he had acquired a shamefaced fondness for the creature.

"Calico does very well by me. We aren't either of us in any great hurry," he said.

"Goin' to Gilbert's, I s'pose," said Dobbs carelessly.

"Yes, I was," said Samuel Pattee, glancing rather anxiously at his companion. "You, too ? "

"Oh, yes. Gilbert's branding. Only one herd, though. Some of my cattle are mixed up with 'em, I calculate, and I want to find out. Our spring round-up comes

along next week. You must be on hand for the barbecue, parson. There'll be a
dance, too, and we want you to grace the occasion."

"Well, you remember the bargain," said Samuel, not without certain faint qualms
of a New England conscience. "If I go to the dances, you men come to church."

"Sure," said Mr. Dobbs amiably. "Our whole outfit was there Sunday — you
saw us? We had the back benches. And say, parson, it was great — the singing, I
mean. Not but what your talk was straight enough, too. But it was the singing
fetched the boys. There's somethin' about the way you slide out those tunes — well,
I don't know what it is. And as for the Rose, bless her — "

"You mean Miss Gilbert?" said the minister rather stiffly.

"I mean Kate Gilbert, of course. There ain't but *one* Rose, I reckon, in Mescal
County. But that piece you two sang together, chasin' each other up an' down in
that don't-care sort o' way, and then chimin' in at the end — well, say! Did you
hear Micky Briggs applaud? He let himself out afore he thought, but we choked
him off."

"I'm glad you liked the music," said Samuel, melting. "I thought you would.
And I give you just the best I know, the best I can do."

"We know it, parson," said Dobbs briefly.

He gave the prim little black figure a look of half-acknowledged admiration struggling with a strong sense of humor ; quizzical pity dashed with rough tenderness.
This was indeed the general attitude of the Mescalites toward the minister. They
ranked him tacitly with women and "kids" — on the whole, an inferior sort of
human, yet somehow requiring a man to exhibit himself at his best in their society.

"Well, so long. I've got to get to Gilbert's some time to-day, parson, or I'd like
your company."

With a parting chuckle, Dobbs gave the bronco his head and shot away in a tumult
of flying clods and heaven-affronting hoofs.

Samuel contentedly pursued his way alone through the midst of the sun-flooded
mesa rolling in unbroken green to the horizon on one hand, and on the other to the
sweep of purple mountains. A small, stiff figure, he seemed oddly out of tune with
the glory of the March morning, the breadth of the untrammeled landscape, the vigor
of the rollicking wind. But presently he broke out into song, lifting his face and his
voice toward the deep sky. The words were those of a sacred canticle. But the joy
that bubbled over in the thrill and liquid lilt of the melody was of the warm earth, of
springtime, of young love, like the meadow-lark's exquisite brief song rising all round
from the grassy covert. It was the keynote of the scene, and sounding in the lover's
heart made him a conscious part of that vast harmony of earth and sky.

It was love triumphant, for he had not thought of failure ; the irresistible force
which drew him to the Rose of his dreams he held proof of a celestial affinity. To be
sure, a similar force might have been observed in operation all about him, tangling
most of the men of Mescal in bonds at Kate Gilbert's feet. But it was far from Samuel's thought to cavil at or even to take seriously this universal admiration ; it seemed
to him indeed as inevitable and unprovoked as though it had been accorded the royal
flower to which she was likened. A single rose may gladden with color and fra-

grance many beholders; yet it is granted to but one to pluck and hold it for his own!

Descending into the little hollow where Gilbert's house lay, Samuel beheld beyond on the plain an indistinctly outlined mass, in violent internal agitation and surrounded by a cloud of dust. At intervals atoms separated themselves from this body and circled furiously about its edges; or, in a group, made toward an erection at a little distance, which Samuel's experience of a year enabled him to recognize as a branding-pen. The bellowing of the cattle and the shouts of the mounted men, borne on the wind, saluted his ears and warned him to avoid the fray; for the minister's peaceful soul shrank from these semi-barbarous scenes, as privately he characterized much of Mescal's every-day life.

The front of the house, bare to the sun and wind of the prairie, was deserted. Samuel rode around to the back, where a small stream ran between fringes of cotton-wood and willow, and a group of live-oaks spread a broad patch of shade. Under these trees were two long tables made of boards laid on trestles. Down by the brook three men were lying on the ground. Samuel dismounted and was about tying his horse to a hitching-post, when the screen door of the back porch flew open and Kate came down the steps carrying in her strong young arms a tray full of dishes. Samuel dropped the strap and sprang.

"No — you'd drop 'em! I'm real glad you've come along, though; you can help if you want. You're handy, Mr. Pattee, I will say — anybody'd think you were trained to it!"

"So I was," declared Samuel, rapidly distributing black-handled knives and forks around the table. "My mother had six boys and no girls; and she says now men are the better at housework, if you only take them early enough!"

The girl's fresh laugh broke out.

"Your mother's a sensible woman. I've always said I never would marry a man who couldn't cook and sew."

Samuel dropped a knife and looked up at her. She was setting out the cups and saucers, and her coffee-brown eyes met his innocently across the table. Was it? No, it was not the moment, he flutteringly decided. For one thing, there were the three men within ear-shot. To be sure, there were always men more or less in Kate's vicinity, still — The girl herself settled the question.

"Jim," she called, "how's the pig?"

One of the men rose from the ground and beckoned to her.

"You just come here, Miss Kate," he said solemnly.

Kate went, knelt down and bent her charming head over what was ostensibly a heap of green leaves.

"He's done!" she cried, springing up. "M—, how good it smells! You're a *cook*, Jim! When you want a place, you just come to me and I'll give you a gilt-edged reference."

The herder grinned and handled his sombrero sheepishly.

"Them bay leaves are the thing, / think," he said. "Some say onions in the stuffing, but I say no, just a bit of garlic, an' the green stuff — and wrapped in bay leaves. And as to time—" he consulted a silver watch approaching the size of a plate — " we can take him out in twelve minutes."

"Well, then. Mark, you blow the horn, and mind you fetch the men in. Now I'll have to fly. Ma's cut her foot, and she can't walk. Mr. Pattee, you finish putting those dishes around, will you? Ted, you come here and carry out the tray."

She hurried into the house, her crisp pink skirts flaring around her. One of the men followed her; the other took down from a nail in the porch a long tin horn, climbed the knoll behind the house and sent forth a blast, shrill and piercing enough for the trump of doom. This was repeated half a dozen times at intervals of one minute, and ended with a flourish which exhausted the performer's lungs and caused Samuel Pattee to clap both hands over his agonized ears.

Kate came to the door and beckoned to him.

" Ma wants to see you, Mr. Pattee. She's shocked to think I made you set the table ! "

She flashed an irresistible saucy glance at him as she opened the door of the sitting-room. If there had been an instant's delay, it is certain that Samuel would have taken the plunge then and there. But the little minister was not of those who compel circumstances.

Mrs. Gilbert sat in a rocking-chair by the window, with her bandaged foot on a hassock. She was knitting vigorously ; no one, in fact, had ever seen her idle.

" Dear me, Mr. Pattee, isn't this dreadful ? " she said placidly. " So much to do, and here I am laid up, and Kate driving me out of my wits with her pranks. You mustn't mind her, Mr. Pattee. Girls will be girls, and just now she's in great spirits, you see — "

"Oh, I don't mind," Samuel assured her, with the accent of truth. " It's a pleasure, I'm sure, to be of any assistance — and, in fact, I think I'll go back presently — "

" Oh, no, you mustn't. Ted is there, and he can fetch and carry. Our new girl comes to-night, thank goodness. This week everything has just come in a heap, and I was so busy, anyway, I didn't know where to turn, especially with Kate's — "

" Ma, the potatoes are burnt ! " cried the girl, putting a flushed and cheerful face in at the door.

" Dear, dear, that comes of you not letting me sit in the kitchen and keep an eye on things. Never mind, it can't be helped. I guess those men can make out."

The door shut ; and a moment later came a crash of crockery and a shout of laughter.

" Oh, dear, what *is* that girl up to ? My foot — oh, if I could only — "

" I'll go and see," said Samuel, with alacrity. " Perhaps I can help."

" Ted smashed the platter ! " cried Kate at the door. " He washed his hands and he says the soap made 'em slippery."

" Now, Mr. Pattee, you sit still. I won't have you trapesing round a kitchen — the idea ! " exclaimed Mrs. Gilbert. " Those men can wait on themselves. You have a bite to eat here with Kate and me. I want to talk to you, anyway."

" I should be delighted, but I — I'm afraid I'll be in the way. You see, I didn't

Drawing
by
Orville P. Williams

know about the branding, or I forgot. I thought perhaps I could get Miss Kate to run over that duet for next Sunday — "

"Well, perhaps she can, by and by, if she isn't too tired. You have your dinner, anyhow, and then we'll see. There come the men — dear, did you ever hear such a racket as they make? There's more of 'em than I thought for — I hope there'll be enough to go round. I wish I'd sent over and asked Mis' Sewall to come and help. But I've thought all the time the swelling on my foot would go down, and — "

" I hope — it's nothing serious."

" Land, no. Except that anything's serious that keeps me off my feet just at this time! Now, Mr. Pattee, I wish you'd tell Kate to bring in a little something here and come and rest herself. She needn't bother about those men. They're used to looking out for themselves, and, anyhow, her pa can tend to 'em."

" I'll bring her in," said Samuel gladly, and he hurried out.

The men, fresh from washing in the brook, were gathering about the tables, loaded now with great hams and loaves of bread, pots of steaming coffee, and relays of pies and cakes. The addition of the barbecued porker, proudly borne to its place by Jim, evoked a salvo of applause. Mr. Gilbert sat at the head of the table, prepared for battle. He nodded bluffly to the parson, and waved with the handle of the carving-knife toward a vacant place on the bench at his right. But Samuel shook his head. He had caught a glimpse of pink beyond the great trunks of the live-oaks.

Kate was sitting in a swing hung from a giant bough, talking to Mr. Dobbs. Her cheeks were the color of her gown, the braids of her blonde hair were ruffled from their usual smoothness. She leaned her head against the rope of the swing, and swayed lazily, with the tip of one foot on the ground.

" Now, Buck, you go and get your dinner — and you too, Mr. Pattee," she said. " I'm going to cool off, and then I'll have to take ma her tea."

" Your mother asked me to bring you in," said Samuel.

Dobbs retreated, with a humorous glance downward at the resolute figure in the black-tailed coat.

" All right, I'll come in a minute," said Kate, rather absently.

She was not looking at him, but after a moment Samuel ventured to sit down facing her at the other end of the broad seat of the swing. The drooping boughs of the oak tree shut out the view of the men at table, whose vicinity was indicated only by a busy clatter of knives and crockery and an occasional remark or guffaw of laughter. Near by, the stream, running full from the spring rains, swirled noisily around the trunks of the willows, whose long branches swayed in the cooling breeze. Samuel looked at the girl beside him; she was smiling a little; she was most charming. Suddenly he turned pale; something in his throat seemed to prevent him from speaking. She gave a soft note or two of her irresistible gay laugh.

" What are you thinking of ? " asked he.

" Oh, something funny ! I'll tell you, if you won't tell. You won't — sure ? Cross your heart ? "

" My heart," said Samuel, wondering if she heard it beating.

" Well, it's about my bunch of cattle. You know I've got a small herd of my very own. Pa gave me some, and then — some of the men round here — Well, you know, I can't help it if they *will*. They got a notion of branding part of their calves with my brand, and turning 'em in with my cattle. They've been doing that — two or three of 'em — for a couple of years, and you just ought to see the showing the K. T.'s make! Why, they took me over this morning and cut them out of the herd, and land, there must have been five hundred! I tell you I'm a capitalist."

"Well, I suppose that's all right, according to the ways of the country," said Samuel vaguely.

"Oh, I like it," said Kate briskly. "Im going into the business. I've got a scheme. I shall stock a little ranch, and manage it all myself, and — she broke off, laughing in a half-embarrassed way, and glanced at Samuel, the rose deepening in her cheeks. "You know what I said about marrying a man who could cook and sew?"

"Yes," said Samuel, "but you — "

"Oh, I didn't mean all of that. Of course he don't do that sort of thing — I shouldn't like for him to — I was joking. But he don't know a living thing, either, about ranching or cattle, or — "

"Who don't?" asked Sam rather faintly.

"Why — why, Mr. Burtwell. I — I'm going to marry him, you know."

Her happy eyes looked past him with cruel unconsciousness.

"Yes. He's coming out. We haven't been engaged long. He was out here last summer — you must have seen him. He's from Philadelphia."

"I — don't remember."

"Well, I wanted to tell you myself — we've been such good friends, and all. I wanted you to be the first to congratulate me."

She looked up at his averted face.

"And — you see, we shall be married here. And of course I wanted it to be in your church."

Samuel met her smiling eyes squarely. His lips were white, but he put out a steady hand and wished her happiness.

"Yes, thank you, but," said Kate eagerly, "there are some things I want to talk over with you. You know, I meant to give the church an organ, and pa has ordered it — a beautiful parlor-organ it is, like Mrs. Sewall's — and if it gets here in time — "

"Yes, if you don't mind — some other time. I — really, I must be going."

"But you haven't had your dinner!"

"Oh, I didn't intend to stay. I only came over to — I came to — I must go on now really."

"Well, if you must."

She rose and walked on beside him, and he felt that she was looking at him curiously with her bright, wide glance. Suddenly she dimpled and smiled, casting a sidelong glance as they passed the ravaged tables. Out of earshot of the men, she threw back her graceful head and laughed deep and long, a hearty, insuppressible, joyous peal.

out. Two days later there appears a notice in the papers to the effect that Lord Somebody shot himself just before he was to start on his wedding tour. — The End.

I pondered considerably when I had finished the volume, and finally decided that the husband in the dedication was either dead or a myth.

I learn from the Chicago *Times-Herald* that *Mrs.* Henniker is a rising light in English literature, and that she succeeds John Oliver Hobbes as president of the Society of Women Authors in England.   From the same source I gather that "The Spectre of the Real" is "the *joint* production" of *Mrs.* Henniker.   I thought it rather a monstrosity, and wonder what a whole-souled attempt by that lady would resemble ?

¶A PUZZLED subscriber wrote me the other day, and, being wise in my generation, I at once turned the affair over to a learned friend of mine — one who delights in perplexing folks with obvious reasoning.   The letter is immaterial ; the solution is the necessary part of the proposition, and that I print below.   Those still unenlightened will be furnished with colored diagrams on application.

Which is correct, " To-morrow is Sunday," or " To-morrow will be Sunday " ?

Duration is the universal space of existence.   Time is that portion of duration which we measure.   Unmeasured past duration is termed " In the beginning."   Unmeasured future generation is termed " Eternity."

Time is arbitrarily divided into periods of twenty-four hours each.   The next succeeding period to that in which we are at any moment has the general name " To-morrow."   Thus all future time becomes " to-morrow " before it becomes " to-day."

Besides the general name " to-morrow," seven specific names are given in order, to each block or group of seven periods, viz.: Sunday, Monday, Tuesday, Wednesday, Thursday, Friday, Saturday ; and then the series of specific names begins over again.

" Is " indicates present time ; " will be " indicates future time.   " Is " really designates present existence, and " will be " future existence, as, also, " was " designates past existence.

" To-morrow," as applied to or naming a definite space of time, is *present*, although to-morrow, by its specific name of " Sunday," is not present.

That there is a marked difference between " to-morrow," as applied to a distant portion of time, and " Sunday," as applied to the same portion of time, is clearly proven by the fact that " Sunday " may pass along from the future, through the present, into the past, while " to-morrow " cannot do this.   " To-morrow " is fixed, stationary, an ever-*present*, persistent and consistent fact.

" To-morrow " is like a fiddle string.   The bow is " time." The string is to-morrow ; therefore to-morrow *is*.   The portion of the bow in contact with the string is Sunday.   To-morrow is Sunday now, present at this moment.   Draw the bow and *to-day* is Sunday.   At the same time Monday comes in contact with the string, and now, present, at this moment, " to-morrow " is Monday.

If to-morrow is not Sunday now, it never will be.   When the identical portion of time *was* " day after to-morrow " it was Sunday, and it was day after to-morrow before it was to-morrow. When "day after to-morrow" was Sunday, "to-day" was Friday. Therefore, it follows that when to-day was Friday, day after to-morrow was Sunday, and when to-day *is* Friday, day after to-morrow *is* Sunday.

As the period of time advances one stage it is still Sunday, but it has now become "to-morrow," therefore to-morrow *is* Sunday.

Since "to-morrow" cannot advance, it never "will be" anything it is not now.

Mem. — When I say to-day was to-morrow, yesterday, I do not mean to say Saturday was Sunday Friday. The special names always exist and never change. The general names of each period change with each successive advance.

Mem. — Because to-morrow *is* Sunday it does not follow that yesterday *is* Friday. In absolute time there is no present. It consists of past and future. The past is gone. Yesterday was Friday. It no longer exists, and will never exist again. The future we have. To-morrow *is* Sunday. It exists, and will continue to exist until it is passed by to-day into yesterday. Then it, too, will become a "was."

¶ LET those persons who will hold up their hands and sneer when one speaks of the poster as worthy of consideration as a bit of art. The fact remains that it *is* worthy such consideration; and of the truth of this, nothing is more convincing than the books that have been published in honor of the "alluring affiche."

When such houses as Macmillan, Scribner's, and Russell & Son bring out volumes varying in price from $1.50 to $3.00, the poster *seems*, at least, to be more than a very transitory fad.

"Posters in Miniature" — Russell & Son, $1.50 — consists solely of pictures, about 250 in all, and is chiefly notable for the very characteristic introduction and title-page contributed by Edward Penfield. In the former he says : " A poster should tell its story at once ; a design that needs study is no poster, no matter how well it is executed. A poster has to play to the public over the variety stage, so to speak — to come on with a personality of its own and to remain but a few moments. We are a bit tired of the very serious nowadays, and a little frivolity is refreshing ; and yet frivolity, to be successful, must be most thoroughly studied. Some posters consisting of but a few lines, and containing but a few broad masses of color, require a dozen drawings before simplicity and harmony of color are obtained."

All this is, of course, Penfield's posters translated into words ; but since it will be hard to surpass the former, the latter cannot help being good. The book itself shows a desire on the part of the publishers to economize that is very exasperating ; for on one page will be a small bit of a cut, and on the next, one larger than the page itself, which very effectually destroys the symmetry of the whole. Nearly all the cuts have previously appeared in either " The Poster " or " The Echo "; yet, notwithstanding this, it is a very convenient book for the collector to have by him.

Hiatt's " Picture Posters " — Macmillan, $3.00 — is especially valuable because of the excellent historical matter it contains : every one, from the primitive cave-dweller, " who scratched delightful mammals on the borders of his cave," to the creator of an atrocity of last year, has his contribution to the history of the hoarding duly recorded. His reproductions of foreign posters, mostly in half-tone, are also very satisfactory.

Unfortunately, his literary style and critical opinions are not all that one could wish, though these will be largely overlooked in admiring the qualities already mentioned.

" The Modern Poster "   Scribner's, $3.00 — dovetails quite well with " Picture Posters," for where the latter slips down on its literary work the former is strongest, which somewhat recompenses for its paucity of pictures.

" The Modern Poster," in fact, is distinctly a literary work, whereas the others are more properly picture books, and the opinions of the authorities writing are both valuable and readable. The sketch by Bunner on the American poster is perhaps the most entertaining of all.

¶ Since the following letter throws an entirely new light on the matter of Miss Ethel Johnson's signature, as commented on in our last, we are most happy to print it.

EDITOR THE RED LETTER.

Dear Sir : — In your issue of September and October, you make editorial mention of what you are pleased to term " flagrant pieces of shameless robbery," appearing in *Truth*. In justification of our publication of Miss Ethel Johnson's sketches, I beg to say that she is the sister of the late Charles Howard Johnson, and that her signature was designed by him, and used by her during his lifetime on sketches which he disposed of for her. It was his desire that she should never change it. These facts are within our immediate knowledge, and I trust you will be good enough to publish a note of correction in order to disabuse the minds of your readers, both in regard to the conduct of *Truth* and that of Mr. Johnson's sister.

Very truly yours,

P. McArthur,
Editor of *Truth*.

Tailpiece
by
I. B. Hazelton

The Newest Books

DESPITE the fact that the largest part of the books brought out lately are not worthy of very serious consideration, some are. Prominent among these deserving favorites published this fall stands " King Noanett," an American historical novel by F. J. Stimson (J. S. of Dale), with twelve full-page illustrations by Henry Sandham. Mr. Stimson always writes entertainingly, but this time he has surpassed himself. The book has been variously described. Some have called it " a most notable book," others, " the book of the year," but all have agreed that it is a book every lover of the pure and noble in literature should possess.

Although Crawford is, to say the least, rather prolific in his productions, no one can accuse him of ever having turned out a tiresome book. Those marvelous Italian stories of his are conceded to be the best work of his wonderfully facile pen, and "Taquisara," the latest addition to them, is thought by many to be the best of the lot. It is issued in two volumes, much after the style of his famous "Casa Braccio."

Mrs. Humphry Ward is again to the front with a two-volume novel. It is called " Sir George Tressady," and is a sequel to " Marcella," depicting the further adventures of that young lady. Over 70,000 have been sold of the latter, and " Sir George " will probably give her a good run in point of sales.

Perhaps you would like to own one or all of the above-mentioned books. If so, you can have them if you are willing to take a little trouble. We have made arrangements with the various publishers whereby we can offer them practically free ; there is, however, a string tied to them ; you realized that, of course, and the string is subscriptions. Pull the string and the book is yours. If you are interested in THE RED LETTER — and your having this number seems to indicate that you are — undoubtedly some of your friends will also be. " Birds of a feather," you know.

If you will bother enough to find four of them that are sufficiently interested to subscribe for a year, we will send you any one of the books you want. Or, if your courage gives out when you have secured three, their names and fifty cents will bring the book ; or two subscriptions and seventy-five cents will do the same. Or if your friends dwindle entirely away — as friends will sometimes -- send on your own subscription with an additional dollar, and the book is yours.

James M. Barrie is one of the most entertaining figures of the literary world to-day. Among all the writers of the Scotch cult, his works alone will be read in the future· The latest novel from his pen is " Sentimental Tommy." While appearing in *Scribner's* it was the most talked of and eagerly awaited serial of the year. It has just made its appearance in book form, where it is more attractive than ever.

Anthony Hope is always sure of his audience. Since he struck the popular chord

The Red Letter

with his " Prisoner of Zenda," he has played to a most admiring multitude. "The Heart of Princess Osra " is just out, and one need only say Princess Osra, *of Zenda*, to awaken every one's keenest interest. The princess is ever charming in her various adventures and marries all too soon.

" Posters in Miniature" is the latest book on this very entertaining fad. It has a most excellent preface by Edward Penfield, and consists of over 250 very good reproductions of the best of American, French, and English work.

To these books, as well as to the former lot, there is a little string, though in this case somewhat shorter. Three subscriptions and you have your choice. The same is true of two subscriptions and fifty cents, likewise of one subscription and seventy-five cents.

Don't you think the books are worth the trouble? We have another proposition, however, that will be no trouble at all, since you have but to consult yourself.

If you will send us your own subscription, — or if you have already subscribed, that of some friend — we will send you, in addition to THE RED LETTER for a year, a copy of Alice Brown's famous " Meadow Grass," in paper covers. This book has secured more favorable notices than any other published in a long time. Those who have not read it should not miss such a chance. Those who have read it cannot do better than read it again.

The Red Letter Magazine

Boston

Tailpiece
by
E. B. Bird

The Red Letter

An Illustrated Monthly

Edited by Richard Gorham Badger
Under the art direction of E. B. Bird

The subscription rate is one dollar a year. Entered at the Boston Post-office as second-class mail matter. The trade supplied by the American News Company and its branches. Advertising rates on application.

The Red Letter Magazine,

Boston.

¶ THE publishers have no hesitation in saying that they consider the work of Mr. Frank Hazenplug, presented in this number, the finest examples of the " new " art that have ever appeared. And in this connection they desire to say that this is but a forerunner of what future issues will bring forth, until the work of all the younger men will have been presented in the pages of THE RED LETTER.

¶ THE Christmas number will treat at length with Mr. Will Bradley and his work, and the publishers think they can promise something particularly good to admirers of his characteristic style.

The Christmas number will also contain a most entertaining story by Miss Elizabeth L. Gould, whose sketch, " A Village Operator," was one of the features of the October number.

Besides contributions by Mr. Maxfield Parrish and Mr. Frank Bird Masters, it will contain many other attractions, from the front cover by Mr. Bird to the end of the department of " Notes."

¶ THE publishers have to announce that they can no longer fill orders for single copies of number two. The supply of this number was exhausted within three days of its delivery to the News Company, and can now be supplied only with yearly subscriptions, commencing with number one. The number of copies in stock is less than thirty.

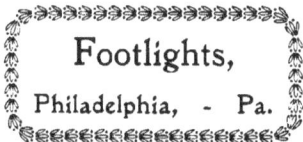

PROF. FARRAND'S
Great Discovery.
Famous Scientist has Found a Positive
Cure for Asthma and Hay Fever.

Among the few really eminent botanists of America, Prof. Farrand, of Vermont, easily stands in the front rank, and a discovery that he has recently made will do much to add to his fame.

After long research he has found a happy combination of herbs and leaves that contain the peculiar health giving qualities of the famous Adirondack region, where diseases of air passages are unknown. Wherever tried this has given great relief, and 93 per cent. of the cases reported a perfect cure of Asthma, some of them seemingly hopeless cases.

This Adirondack Asthma Cure is now offered to the public generally by the Dr. Howard Co., box E 93, of Burlington, Vt., who will mail a large sized box for 50 cents. They do not want pay from those whom they do not cure, and will return the money to any whom Adirondack Asthma Cure fails to benefit. This remarkable offer should be accepted at once by all those who have asthma or other respiratory diseases.

Contents.

HVMPTY   DVMPTY

The Red Letter

An Illustrated Monthly.

" ' *T'will while away an hour or so with picturings and print.*" — MARLOWE.

In an Old Hall

THE fading firelights flicker low
    (Whilst shadows steal o'er step and stair),
And paint with many a ruddy glow
    Fair Margery, musing unaware.

Ah, favored flame, teach me, I pray,
    The trick, if trick it be I seek,
So, when I come at close of day,
    I'll bring that blush to Margery's cheek.

Harold Anthony

The Town Fool's Christmas.

JIMMY JOHN — in his faded green ulster tightly buttoned at the top, but flapping open to show his old overalls — was singing in a high, cracked tenor, as he rode down Packer Hill in the dusk of the short December day.

Old Jess now and then hit a rolling stone and stumbled; Jimmy John pulled her up, without stopping his song. Twice, however, she went on her knees in thesnow. On those occasions Jimmy John dismounted and assisted her to rise, stopping his song for a moment.

Jimmy John was the town fool; there was once in awhile somebody who claimed that he was not an absolute fool; but most of the residents of the little mill town were quite ready to agree with Abner Perkins, the farmer with whom Jimmy John lived, when he said, " He can't read, nor write, nor talk straight ; and he ain't qualified to *vote ;* and if that don't made a fool, I dunno what does."

During the summer Jimmy John worked for his board, and even Abner

Perkins admitted that the town fool was a good worker, "as fur as he knew how." His queer, misshapen figure, in its uncouth garments, was a familiar sight in many a meadow at haying time; and nobody could pick berries better or faster than Jimmy John. But during the winter there was little for him to do. Some distant relatives, who never visited Willowby, paid the sum of two dollars a week from the first of November till the first of April, so that Jimmy John might have his meals and a room (in the shed chamber) with Abner Perkins, when no longer able to work for his board. "My wife don't like havin' him round," Mr. Perkins often remarked, "but those folks ain't willin' to have any o' their kin in the poorhouse, and so we might's well help the afflicted. It's a kind of a cup o' cold water, maybe," he was wont to add piously, drawing forth from a neighbor, who put small faith in his benevolence, the cynical statement that "he reckoned Jimmy John set on the milkin' stool enough to pay for more'n *one* cup o' cold water."

Jimmy John had but one friend in the town,— that was Old Jess. She was an ugly, untamed creature, whom Jimmy had begged from Mr. Perkins when the latter, who had taken her for a debt five years before, proposed in rage and disgust at the end of a month to have her summarily despatched.

"I take her — ride errands on her — work for her eating, keep her myself," Jimmy John had pleaded in his harsh, strained voice, with his dull eyes kindled into giving forth a momentary gleam of intelligence by the force of his excitement. And so clamorously had he pressed his demand that at last Abner Perkins had acceded to it.

Jimmy John carried on long conversations with Old Jess, greatly to the amusement of the Willowby boys, whose open derision sometimes roused the fiery temper that for the most part lay dormant in the town fool's breast.

But on this particular evening there were no boys to be seen on the main street of Willowby as Old Jess fell into it after a final stumble at the foot of Packer Hill. The sound of clear, boyish voices singing gay carols came from the brightly lighted vestry of the Orthodox church.

"Pretty!" murmured Jimmy John, abruptly ending his own song — which would hardly have been recognized as such by any known musical standards — and drawing rein in front of the church. "Pretty, Old Jess! Pretty! Boys singing. Can't say ' Git up, Stumbler!' to you to-night, Old Jess, no, sir! Anyway, I'm a-ridin' you all the time. I'm a-ridin' you, Old Jess. Pretty, ain't it?"

The ears of Old Jess were suddenly laid back in an unpleasantly suggestive manner. As Jimmy John leaned forward, to listen still more intently to the caroling boys, a small fir tree which he had held stiffly upright in his arms slipped scratchily across her neck.

"All right, Old Jess," said Jimmy John, hastily drawing up the tree to its former position. "Jimmy John's tree, Old Jess. Jimmy John's Christmas tree. I heard to-morrow was Christmas, Old Jess. I heard to-morrow was

Christmas, and I got the tree; you know, Old Jess, that's what we've been gettin', you and me. All right, ain't it, Old Jess?"

The animal's ears moved slowly forward, but she pawed the ground irritably. Jimmy John made the strange noise in his throat which she recognized as permission to go on, and of which she quickly took advantage.

She went stumbling on, until the sound of the caroling voices died away in the distance, and the long mill buildings were in sight. Just before he reached them, Jimmy John drew rein again, this time in front of the gate at' the foot of the gravel path which led up to the mill agent's house.

Some large packing boxes stood on the piazza, their shapes dimly outlined in the gathering dusk; but Jimmy John bestowed not even a passing glance on them; his gaze was riveted on a little figure standing at the gate, dressed in a fluffy coat of long white fur, from the high collar of which there rose a little head, crowned with curls that shone like gold, even in that fading light. The face beneath the gold curls was fair and dimpled like a cherub's, and a pair of great brown eyes looked fearlessly up at Jimmy John.

"Angel!" gasped Jimmy John, staring at her in hopeless bewilderment. "You an angel?"

"Why, I'm only Marjorie Tilton," said a voice so sweet that the town fool's idea of a veritable angel was greatly strengthened as he listened to it. "My papa is the new mill agent; he can't come till next week, but mamma and I came this afternoon, and we are getting the house in order, at least mamma is. And to-morrow will be the first Christmas I've ever been without a Christmas tree. Of course we don't know anybody here yet, but my papa packed some holly and evergreen so we can have a *little* Christmas in the windows, mamma and I. Are you taking that nice tree to your little brothers and sisters?"

Jimmy John slid off Old Jess' back and slowly advanced toward the lovely vision at the gate, keeping his eyes fixed on the face from which the two stars shone up at him. In his arms he held the tree, as far away from himself as possible. The child at whose side he stopped put out a little hand and gently stroked the branches of the pretty fir.

"Your — tree — you — angel — your — tree, not — Jimmy John's — any more!" stammered the town fool in a hoarse whisper. "You — angel — Jimmy John knows — he's seen — 'em in pictures — he knows. Your tree!"

As he stood the little tree against the fence, and, leaning forward, touched the shining white fur of the child's coat with his rough fingers, an expression of pity filled the starry eyes into which a look of alarm had begun to creep.

"Will you wait here a minute?" she asked, smiling at Jimmy John, whose whole dull being was filled with strange joy and excitement. "I will come back again."

Jimmy John stared at her in silence, but when she gently repeated her question, he nodded. The little figure sped up the walk and vanished in the

house. A moment later it appeared again on the piazza, accompanied by
two other figures; one of these Jimmy John recognized as that of the village
carpenter, hammer in hand; the other bore a certain resemblance, it seemed,
to his angelic vision, in that it had a crown of golden hair, though it wore a
large white apron.

"He is down there at the gate. See, mamma!" said his angel, pointing
toward Jimmy John's drooping form. "He rode up on that queer old horse,
and he thought I was an angel, and he said the tree was mine. He seems
—he seems a little like poor old Uncle Benny at the almshouse in Banford,"
added the child softly.

"He don't mean any harm, ma'am," said the carpenter cheerfully to the
perplexed mother. "That's only Jimmy John, the town fool. I dunno's
he is a *whole* fool, but he don't know anything hardly. His real name's
James Johnson, but he's always called himself Jimmy John. He lives with
Abner Jenkins, on a farm out beyond the mills, and works for his board. I
heard the boys sayin' this mornin' he'd told some of 'em he was goin' to
have a Christmas tree himself this year, long as nobody ever invited him to
theirs. Our new minister don't hold to havin' a tree; he thinks a Santa Claus
is better, they tell me. But anyway, Jimmy John never sets foot in the
church; he says it scares him, though he'll stand outside sometimes to hear
the singin'."

"Would he do any harm in a person's house?" asked the mother, with her
eyes first on her child's face and then on the forlorn figure at the gate, beside
the little tree.

"Lord bless you, no, ma'am," said the carpenter; "only folks won't have
him on account of his bein' as he is, and then, of course, he ain't ever
dressed fit to go anywhere. I did hear tell once that some of his kin sent
him a suit o' clothes to wear Sundays, but nobody's ever seen 'em on him.
I've wondered sometimes if anything could be made o' Jimmy John more'n
there is, but folks here are all too busy to tackle a town fool's under-
standin'. He oughtn't to be let to ride round on that old hoss as he does,
though; the critter's old as the hills and ugly as Satan into the bargain, and
she'll be the death of him some day; though maybe 'twould be a mercy, for
he don't have any pleasure out o' life, poor soul!"

"Come!" said the mother quickly, and taking Marjorie's hand, she hurried
down the gravel walk to Jimmy John, who shivered as if with fear, but stood
with his eyes fixed on his angel's face.

"Jimmy John," said Mrs. Tilton clearly, "will you listen to me for a
minute?"

The town fool's eyes wavered toward her, and then back to Marjorie, as
if drawn by an irresistible power.

Mrs. Tilton stooped to whisper in the child's ear.

"Jimmy John," said Marjorie, in her sweet treble, "we should like you to come to-morrow night at seven o'clock and see the Christmas tree, and have your presents with us. Will you come?"

"Your tree — you angel," said Jimmy John, with a troubled face, lifting the tree over the fence and setting it as close as possible to the child. "You take it to please Jimmy John."

Three times Marjorie repeated her invitation, and at last some idea of what she meant penetrated the town fool's brain. At the end of another ten minutes he had mounted Old Jess and ridden away, bearing a note to Abner Jenkins in his hand. His face was turned toward the vision which stood at the gate to watch him out of sight. When the curve of the road hid it from view, Jimmy John faced toward his home, giving a strange cry of delight.

"Jimmy John have Christmas, Old Jess," he said, leaning forward to get as close to the ear of his friend as might be. "Jimmy John have Christmas with an angel; you carry him there to-morrow night, Old Jess; you carry him there and stay in the warm barn. You hear me, Old Jess?"

Old Jess stumbled and fell on her knees, depositing her rider at the roadside with small ceremony; but save by this performance, she vouchsafed no hint as to what her opinion of the prospective festivities might be.

Mr. Jenkins's face, when, after an elaborate adjustment of his horn-bowed spectacles, he laboriously perused the note proffered him by Jimmy John, was a study. He looked from the sheet — somewhat damp from its temporary retirement into a snowdrift at the time of the town fool's involuntary descent from his charger — to Jimmy John, and from Jimmy John back again to the sheet.

"Such doin's!" he snorted, at last. "I guess things at the mill 'll be in a pretty fix before long, at this rate! Here, Mis' Perkins, jest you listen to this!"

While Mrs. Perkins listened, the town fool stole out of the room to the shed, and up into the unfinished chamber that served him for a sleeping apartment. He sat down on the hard bed and looked out of the tiny window, across the meadow over which the moonlight was slowly spreading. For a long time he sat there, with lips constantly moving, though no sound came from them. At last he sprang up, and hurried across the room to where an old haircloth trunk stood in a shadowy corner. His hands shook with excitement as he threw back its battered top, and drew forth the only articles it contained — a coat and trousers of a large brown plaid, and waistcoat to match, a shirt once white, but now yellow, and a necktie of brilliant scarlet with yellow polka dots lavishly disposed over its shiny surface.

Jimmy John's dull face took on a glow of something that resembled pride as he fingered these hoarded garments.

"Jimmy John dress for Christmas," he said, over and over again; "please angel; Jimmy John has handsome clothes, handsome clothes and a necktie; yes, sir, a necktie!"

The milking and the eating his frugal supper were alike performed by Jimmy John in a state of unconsciousness ; the fact that the bread allotted him was a little older and dryer even than usual quite escaped his notice. Jimmy John ate his meals alone, in the shed, at any time when it suited Mrs. Perkins's convenience. On this particular evening he supped at half-past eight, when his work was done. Immediately after the meal he hurried up to the shed chamber again and once more examined his holiday attire.

At last he went to bed, with the precious garments piled in a heap on the one chair of which his apartment could boast; the amazing necktie surmounted the pile, and many times during the night Jimmy John put out his hand and smoothed its glossy satin.

The next morning dawned fair and mild, though with a suggestion of winter crispness in the air that made a perfect Christmas day. The town fool's work was over before twelve o'clock, and after a hasty dinner off a few of the toughest portions of the Perkins's toughest turkey, which, after a valiant fight, had succumbed to the exigencies of the holiday season, Jimmy John was free to prepare for his Christmas party.

Cleanliness, strangely enough, was one of Jimmy John's strong points, and if his face was not fair, it was through no lack of soap and water ; if his hands were redder than usual, the ruthless onslaughts of the scrubbing brush were responsible for their hue. The yellowed shirt and the brown plaid suit were donned as soon as the scrubbing process was completed, and at two o'clock Jimmy John stood before his cracked looking glass struggling with his necktie like a country beau.

As he tried in vain to tie it properly with his clumsy fingers, tears of rage and disappointment filled his eyes. At last he tore it off and sat down on the bed in hopeless trouble. Suddenly he picked up the necktie from the floor where he had thrown it, smoothed it carefully and put it in one of the pockets of his coat. He gave one more look at himself and started down the stairs.

Going to the barn, he led out Old Jess from her stall and slipped the worn saddle on her back.

"Jimmy John hasn't any new hat, Old Jess," he said, as he mounted his friend, who, to judge from her general aspect, had been interrupted in disagreeable reflections. "Jimmy John hasn't any new hat, so he don't wear any. No, sir ; he don't wear any old hat with his handsome clothes to the angel's Christmas. You hear me, Old Jess ? "

"Mercy sakes, what are you startin' at this time o' day for ? " screamed Mrs. Perkins, hurrying to the door as she heard the clatter of Old Jess' hoofs going down the road from the barn. But the town fool gave no heed, save to lean forward, urging his ugly steed to quicker action, the pale December sunshine touching his coarse red hair, which blew around his strange face as he rode out of the barnyard and passed from view.

"They'll think we're as big fools as he, I reckon," said Mrs. Perkins in a tone of much exasperation, as she returned to the enlivening society of her spouse in the kitchen.

"Well, let 'em," said Mr. Perkins stolidly, in whose mind the consumption of the ancient turkey had engendered depressing thoughts not wholly unconnected with his own latter end; "folks *are* all fools, more or less."

Jimmy John had no watch, nor could he have read its face had he possessed one, but he knew very well that it was still afternoon, and some hours before the time set by his angel. He turned Old Jess' head away from the village, and rode on to the old, long-deserted graveyard, his favorite haunt of a Sunday. He tied Old Jess to a tree whose lower branches bore witness to former visits, and threw over her a worn yellow horse blanket, which he produced from its hiding-place in some bushes.

He made his way over the ground hemlock and through the tangled undergrowth which choked the old entrance, to his chosen seat, a long, flat-lying slab of slate stone, whose lettering was entirely hidden by moss. Jimmy John brushed the snow from the slab, and seated himself in his usual attitude, with knees drawn up to a level with his chin, and arms clasped around them. Here he sat — now and then getting up to wander about for a short time, and then to resume his old position — until the sun had gone down, and he caught the first glimpse of the moon through the trees.

He stumbled out of the graveyard, and unhitched Old Jess, who had been heavily slumbering under the thin horse blanket, which Jimmy John removed and hid again in the bushes. She seemed even less willing than usual to start when the town fool had mounted, and her eyes emitted vicious sparks, while her ears assumed their most ominous position.

Jimmy John, however, was too happy to take much thought of her, and urged her on down the road, past the scattered farmhouses, past the long mill buildings, till he reached the agent's house. As he rode up to the gate, the door opened, and he saw his angel standing in the brilliantly lighted hall, looking out into the darkness. As he slid off Old Jess' back, Marjorie flew down the gravel path and out through the gate.

"We'd begun to be afraid you weren't coming, Jimmy John," she said gently, putting her soft little hand on the town fool's arm, and lifting the starry eyes to his vacant face; "it is almost seven o'clock, and everything is ready. Let me show you where to put your horse. I suppose she is a very nice horse," said the child doubtfully, stretching out her hand to bestow a timid pat on the neck of the uncompromising Old Jess, who snapped at her fingers with instant energy.

"She Old Jess — my horse," said Jimmy John, surveying his equine possession with disfavor for the first time in their contemporaneous history; "she's cross, Old Jess is; but she's my friend. I ride her all the time; nobody else have her. Look out, Old Jess. Don't you touch Jimmy John's angel. You hear me, Old Jess?"

He caught hold of one floating white ribbon that blew out from his angel's fluffy little gown in the breeze as she led the way to the stable.

Old Jess stumbled after him, apparently intent on biting off his coat tails, which feat, however, she failed to accomplish. When she had been comfortably stalled, though evidently much against her will, Jimmy John turned to his angel, drawing his satin necktie from his pocket and holding it out to her : —

" Angel, tie Jimmy John's necktie ? " he asked in a voice as little harsh as he could possibly render it, and with a look of anxious pleading in his dull blue eyes ; " Jimmy John tried, but he couldn't. You tie it."

" Why, of course, Jimmy John, just as soon as we get in the house where I can stand on a chair, and reach up to it," said Marjorie, patting the town fool's arm reassuringly, as she led him back to the house.

" Mamma ! " she called, as they stepped up onto the piazza, " you are to please wait until I get Jimmy John's necktie fixed before you see him ! "

In the hall she mounted a chair, and while the town fool stood with his head held stiffly erect and his eyes devouring her cherub face, she tied the strip of satin under the yellow shirt collar, in a bow whose loops and ends stood rampant despite the puckered brows and frequent pats which accompanied its composition.

" I think that's a *pretty* good bow, Jimmy John," said Marjorie, surveying it dubiously, with her golden head on one side ; " at any rate, it's the very best I can do," she added, after another minute, stepping down from the chair.

Jimmy John seized the end of her white sash and shuffled along beside her across the hall to a door, on which Marjorie tapped, crying, " We're here, mamma ! We're quite ready now."

The door opened and his angel's mother held out her hand to him, taking one of his rough hands in hers — the left, as it happened, for with the right he held fast to Marjorie's white sash — and bade him welcome.

Jimmy John made no response ; in fact, neither then nor later did he seem exactly conscious of anything save Marjorie. He looked at the tree, to be sure, bright with tinsel and candles, and with a glittering star at its top ; he looked at the wreaths of evergreen and holly in the windows and about the room ; he took the packages Marjorie handed him and held them carefully ; but it was his angel's face to which his eyes turned from everything else. He was apparently delighted with a spray of holly which she pinned on one of his brown plaid lapels, and fingered its prickly leaves again and again.

"Aren't you going to open your presents, Jimmy John ? " asked the child, as the town fool's packages at last slipped to the floor unheeded. He looked blankly at the parcels, and then touched his sprig of holly. " Jimmy John's Christmas present," he said, with the strange look of doubt and trouble in his eyes.

" Let him do just as he likes, Marjorie, dear," whispered the mother, and the child instantly comprehended.

For two hours Jimmy John sat in Paradise. When Marjorie went to the piano and played a gay little dance tune, the town fool, still holding her sash end, listened with all sorts of strange emotions shadowed forth on his face.

" Pretty ! " he said hoarsely, when Marjorie finished the first tune. " Pretty ! " So she played another and another, till her little stock was exhausted.

" I think perhaps Jimmy John ought to start for home now," said Mrs. Tilton, when the last tune was ended. " You tell him, Marjorie." She had been watching her strange guest with a look of deep pity in her gentle eyes, from the corner where she sat.

So the child explained to Jimmy John, and he slowly relinquished his hold on the white sash and started for the door.

" Wait till I get my coat on, Jimmy John," said his angel, laying her little hand on his arm, as he was stumbling out of the house. The sleepy stable boy appeared, lantern in hand, when the town fool, accompanied by his two hostesses, entered upon the scene of Old Jess' captivity.

" I never saw such a horse, ma'am," he began, casting a curious glance at Jimmy John, but a warning look from his mistress prevented any further statement in regard to Old Jess' behavior.

" You must come again, Jimmy John," said Marjorie, as the town fool led out his steed and scrambled onto her back ; " come again, and I will play you some more music."

Jimmy John looked down at her from his precarious seat, with his lips parted. " Jimmy John had Christmas, angel," he said hoarsely. " Thank you,— and her," he added, nodding his head toward the sweet-faced mother. " Jimmy John always remember."

He touched his sprig of holly, and seemed struggling with some further speech ; but Old Jess suddenly started forward, and in another moment horse and rider were out of sight.

" Do you think he had a good time, mamma ? " asked Marjorie wistfully, rubbing her little hand across the starry eyes as if to brush away some shadow. " Do you think he understood about Christmas ? "

" He had a beautiful time, dear, I know," said the mother, putting her arm around Jimmy John's angel, as they entered the house together ; " but I suppose he did not understand very much."

" I don't know as we ought to have done it," she wrote her husband that night, telling of the Christmas festivities. " Marjorie wanted him, and it seemed so pitiful for any human being to be shut out from Christmas, but it would be a hopeless task to try to do much for him. Think of his taking Marjorie for an angel ! Dear little soul, she looked almost like one to-night."

"There's an accident happened last night, ma'am," said the butcher, as he stepped down from his cart at the Tiltons' back door the next morning; "that foolish feller, Jimmy John, he was throwed off his horse ridin' home from somewheres last night, and killed.   I ain't heard all the particulars, but when they found him, the doctor said he'd struck on his head and died instant.   The horse is an awful ugly critter, anyway.   They say Abner Jenkins is goin' to have an end put to her.   She was standin' right beside Jimmy John, whinnyin', when they found him.   Some folks livin' near the road heard her.

"It's cur'ous where he'd been," added the butcher, who, with his back turned, as he opened his cart for inspection, failed to see his customer's shocked face; "but he'd got a sprig o' holly somewheres, they say, and his fingers was clutched so tight round it they had to let it stay.   Somebody told me he had a kind of a smile on his face, too; but I guess that's what the story's gained goin' round.   Nobody ever saw him smile, and I reckon he wouldn't 've known how.   What will you want this mornin', ma'am?"

Elizabeth L. Gould

Rejoicings

THE secret of the beauty of
    December snow; the tender tune
That April breathes I love; I love
    The green upon the crest of June.

I love the high, white August haze,
    Type of the prophet's veil, which still
The hot sun draws upon his face,
    Descending from the heavenly hill;

Love autumn, golden blade and ear;
    September, crimson in her leaves;
October, fleeting on a spear
    Of crispèd grass among the sheaves;

And one first flake of snow.   But clear,
    Each new particular joy above,
The beauty of the whole round year
    I love, I love, I love, I love.

P. H. Savage

Wounded
Anno Domini 1300

A Ministering Angel

HER gentle eye and placid brow
   Reflect the peace that dwells within.
From worldly scenes secluded now,
   She stands forth blameless, free from sin.

When yet a child she entered here,
   Nurtured within the convent's walls;
She early learned to hold most dear,
   Obedience — when duty calls.

Vague rumors of the sin and strife
   That rule and sway the human heart,
The ills and tragedy of life,
   Have reached her, where she dwells apart,

And in the silence of her cell
   She offers up a fervent plea
For those who in their blindness fell,
   Ere yet from mortal sin set free.

Her heart is filled with heavenly grace;
   A sweet and perfect charity
Illuminates the upturned face,
   And proves the soul's divinity.

A ministering angel she,
   Within the cloister's calm retreat.
Fair symbol of that purity
   We worship at our Saviour's feet.

Percy Loring Weed

A Ministering Angel
by
Edward N. Dart

Great Art and Great Heart

HE philologists tell us that language, like the continents, is undergoing a constant wear and tear — what the geologists call a detrition. One of the worst results of this change is the misapplication of big words to little things, and an instance of this is in our daily talk about our great modern painters.

The world of art has produced a very few great masters without fault — men, therefore, of the first rank. Men like Phidias, Titian, Veronese, De Hooch.

It has been slightly more prolific in those great men of the second rank, in whose brilliance there are discernible flaws — such as Tintoret, with his touch of brutality ; Hals, who had all of art except the power to conceal it ; Rembrandt, with his love of low things ; Velasquez, handicapped by his cold Spanish imagination ; Rubens, when he buttressed up his own splendid talent with the only lesser talents of Snyders, Jordaens, and Vandyke ; Angelo, whose sublimity sometimes tottered on the edge of the grotesque.

Men such as these and their like, whether faultless or faulty, have never been approached by any painter of our century. Indeed, the rigid actuality demanded by modern taste makes impossible the existence of such artists, and if one of them should now appear among us, he would be looked upon as a visionary and promptly suppressed.

If I were asked what is the first thing requisite to produce a great painting, I should say, a great man. I beg my readers to understand my meaning distinctly. I don't say a great painter, I say a great man. One of those mysterious human personalities who appear on the earth from time to time, who seem to surround themselves, so to speak, with a kind of aura of magnetic fluid, unrecognizable by the many, and who seem to saturate everything they touch with a strange essence of greatness, indescribable and beyond analysis, but always there and always felt.

I think these wonderful human phenomena are always isolated and come abruptly and unexpectedly, rising suddenly out of the dead level, like mountains in the south of Spain. They never come in avalanches. There doesn't seem to be stuff enough in the universal soul matter of the world to make many of them at the same time.

And so I believe that there never was and never can be a great school of art, but that every school that seems to deserve that name has consisted of one great master at a time, and a host of lesser men whom admiration or emulation inspired to do fine things.

It is a rather melancholy reflection, but I fear it has an historical foundation, that the first great painter of any school has always been the greatest of all, and I sometimes fancy that the earlier the school, the greater was its great man. Who followed Titian and equaled him? Who has ever followed Frans Hals and approached him? Who succeeded Rubens and is worthy to be named with him? Who has lived since Pieter de Hooch, the first genre painter of the world, and ever equaled him in any single quality? Plenty of fine and brilliant painters have sprung up after each of these great masters, but they seem always to have subdivided their genius among them, so that it appears almost like an intellectual law that every great nucleus of art is destined to explode, like Biela's comet, into a shower of meteors.

We moderns, — forgive me, dear reader, but I must say it, — we moderns are merely a heterogeneous assemblage of these meteor showers, revolving in our little orbits, now and then flashing across the sky with a little trail of sparks and vanishing.

Will these little sparks of art ever again agglomerate themselves into a flaming, irresistible mass, or will time fritter them away into mere cosmic dust? To me it seems simply nonsense to talk about a modern renaissance of art. Nothing of the sort has occurred. To the serious thinker the history of art has shown an almost steady decadence from the days of Titian down to this end of the nineteenth century. The art of the Venetians and of Rubens was heroic. The art of the Dutchmen was dramatic. Our art at its best is theatrical.

The Dutch school was the first of the modern schools, and the best. The dawning of the modern spirit had become visible even earlier. When Rubens and Velasquez met in the Spanish court, it was not merely the meeting of two great painters, it was the meeting of two epochs. Rubens was the last of the great old masters, and Velasquez was the first of the moderns. But the Dutch school were the first serious painters of the actual.

Fromentin astonished the Parisians years ago by showing them that they had in their own gallery of the Louvre paintings by Terburg, De Hooch, and Metzu, painted in the modern spirit, and yet pictures that no modern painter could ever hope to equal. The large simplicity and directness and the mysterious method of these little canvases, canvases that some of us had learned to love before Fromentin had made them famous for us, reduced the masterpieces of Fortuny and Meissonier to mere bric-à-brac, and all the methods of the French genre school to the level of tricks of the theater. The vaunted technique of the moderns became by comparison simply superficial and meaningless, less wonderful and less difficult than the feat of a juggler who balances an egg on the end of a walking stick.

Great Pan was dead and there was no more art in the world.

What makes the difference between the art of the great masters and the art of us moderns?

Their technique was better than ours, judging from its results, but method does not make art. Were they more studious than we are? Certainly not. Were more great minds produced centuries ago than in our day? I think not.

Is their something archaic in the nature of art, a certain barbaric simplicity that is lost in our complicated modern civilization?

The idea is a tempting one, but I fear chronology does not bear it out. The finest of the Dutch work, however small the scale, was as great as that of the Venetians. The work of the Venetians was evidently greater than the paintings in Pompeii — as these were finer than the wall pictures in Thebes and Beni-Hassan.

To be sure, if we go back some hundred thousand years, more or less, to the bone etchings of the Esquimoid European, we find a truth of characterization that is utterly wanting in Egypt and Nineveh, but outlines on bone are not great art, but only its childhood.

I believe we have among moderns as much knowledge, as much imagination, as much technical ability, and as much love for our art as the older painters had. And I believe that the only thing we lack is their courage. They were not afraid of their public, and we are afraid of ours.

We are so afraid of our public, and notably of the public of artists, that we do not dare to fully express ourselves, and, therefore, a feverish consciousness pervades all the work of all the modern schools. Modern painters never forget themselves in their work.

The late Thomas Conture said, in his book on painting, that nothing great in art can be achieved without impersonality. I do not at present recall his precise words, nor indeed does it matter, since language was not the medium in which he most readily expressed himself. What he meant was that nobody can do a fine thing while he is thinking what sort of an appearance he is making, what people will think about it, or what his friends will say when they see it in an exhibition.

A fine idea takes possession of you, and you have no choice but to put it into tangible form. It invades and inundates your mind, and there is no room left for little thoughts about yourself. It presents itself to you ready formed and complete, and the putting it into words, or paint, or bronze should be mere mechanical drudgery, which you get through as best you can and as soon as you can. "I have a thousand verses in my head," La Fontaine is made to say, "and I shall have no peace until I go home and write them out."

Your idea is born, and what will you do with it? You dress it carefully in the prevailing fashion, and try to suit everybody, and behold, your idea, that was so great while your brain was carrying it, has become a very little one when it goes out into the world, this world that belongs to the bold.

Marcus Waterman

Drawing

by
Ethel Reed

Prof. Ed. Raymond (Eagan)

A SMALL urchin, with his hands thrust deep down in the pockets of his ragged trousers, stood gazing blankly out over the wide and dreary expanse of made land well known to all residents of Boston's peninsular district as "the dump."

The stump of a half-smoked cigar drooped wearily from the corner of his mouth, as though its weight were too great for the infantile jaws that gripped it. The whole posture of the figure was one of extreme disgust, and he glanced with no kindly eye at a small child of about four years of age, who was tumbling about in the loose red ashes in close proximity to the edge of a bank which sloped away to a dirty, vile-smelling mud hole.

" Well, I'm a son of a gun if I'm goin' to hang round here all day," he soliloquized. " If de ole woman tinks I'm goin' to rastle de kid all de afternoon while she 'n old man Welch takes in de Point and sees de perfesser jump, she's got wheels, dat's all," and a look of scorn overspread his face.

Here his meditations were interrupted, however, by the arrival of a second atom, likewise having in charge a poor, scraggly looking baby.

" Say, Mickey," he piped, " where ger swipe de hopper? Got de mate? "

" Whatcher givin' us," responded Mickey, with an air of offended dignity. " Dis ain't no hopper ; me uncle, de alderman, did de pretty yesterday, but dis is de last one."

" Rats ! " replied the second urchin irreverently.

After a slightly heated argument regarding the identity of the uncle, the conversation turned toward the more absorbing topic of personal grievances, which was discussed and enlarged upon to the satisfaction of both.

Mickey's friend glanced about him suspiciously for a moment, then asked in a low voice if he was " goin' to take in de show."

" Naw," said Mickey.

The eyes of the other boy opened to their widest extent at this reply, but he contented himself with winking knowingly, and saying " rats " again. At this mysterious reply, Mickey became interested at once.

" Say, whatcher givin' us ? What's de game, anyhow ? "

" It's on de dead quiet," replied the other. " Don't give it away, but ' Muff ' Eagan's goin' to do de jump an' queer de perfesser. Goin ' ? "

Mickey's only answer was to seize the younger brother by the arm and drag him to a safe spot between two great piles of rubbish, and his friend, seeing that he had won the day, did likewise ; and the two, after vowing

revenge and sudden death to the smaller children if they should move from
"dat spot," made a sudden dash for First Street and disappeared up an
alley in the direction of the Point.

"Muff" Eagan was perhaps the most widely known young tough in the
whole district, cordially liked by all members of "de gang," and as cordially
hated and feared by the others, most of whom had felt at one time or another
the weight of his powerful right arm or the hardness of his knuckles. He
was a typical young Irishman, tall and well built, with broad, powerful
shoulders and the lung capacity of a horse. Had it not been for the heavy
lower jaw, which lent a rather formidable, bull-dog expression to the face, he
would have been pronounced good looking at once. Not only was "Muff"
popular with his fellows, but it was rumored that several ladies of the district were deeply in love with him. This he neither contradicted nor verified,
but went with whomsoever he pleased, when and where he pleased.

There was, however, one young lady quite different from the rest, who turned
up her pretty nose when his name was mentioned, and remarked, in his
hearing, that he was a "windbag." Now, this was not true, and no one
knew it better than Katie Shea when she made the accusation; but she
was no fool, and there's always more than one way to get what one wants
most.

Katie was a close neighbor of "Muff's," and she was not at all surprised
that evening, as she sat alone on her front door-steps, to have him start over
toward her and ask her to take a stroll up Broadway with him. On her reply-
ing that "she didn't care a continental about Broadway, and that she didn't
want to do no stroll," his surprise was so great that he hadn't wit enough left
to say "he didn't care a durn," or even, "day is others," but turned and
started down B Street towards First Street as though there was a dog at
his heels.

That any girl should not jump at the chance to walk up the street with
him was something that his mind could not grasp, and he made a vow that
"he would have 'dat peach in spite of de devil.'"

He had not taken a dozen steps before Katie called to him and asked, in
a queer kind of voice, "What's yer hurry?"

"Oh, nothing," he responded, his presence of mind returning on the instant; "I thought seein's you didn't feel like goin', I'd go down and get Sadie
McCarty."

This was not much to Katie's mind, for underneath her coldness she had a
very strong liking for the big fellow, and her oddness was only her way of
showing it. He, on the other hand, had heard her say that he was a "windbag," and he would never be satisfied until he had proven to her that she
was mistaken, and then, again, opposition from so pretty a girl as Katie
means a deal to some men.

After Katie had extracted a request that he might sit on the steps and talk

"Oh, nothing," he responded.

Drawing
by
E. N. Dart

with her, the conversation drifted hither and thither, finally ending in her daring him to jump from the tower that was erected for Professor Cummings, who was to give performances every day for a month or more, beginning on Monday of the next week.

Here was " Muff's " opportunity to gain greater fame and Katie, into the bargain, for she had promised to be " his girl " if he would " do the pretty." So, when Monday arrived, he started a full hour before the time set for the jumping, with his tights under his clothes, and his nerve at high-water mark.

Instead of walking, as was his custom, he boarded a Point car on Broadway and laid back comfortably in the seat, with the air of a man who was well pleased with himself.

The day was fair, and as the car turned into Sixth Street, bringing into view the little beach and the pier beyond, crowded with sightseers and pure salt air seekers, Muff dropped off and cautiously slipped between two convenient boat houses and dropped, without being noticed, to the sand beneath. This was easily done, for all the boat houses and lunch rooms are set on spiles, and at high tide the water reaches well up under them. He made his way swiftly along the beach, taking care to keep in the shadow of the overhanging buildings, finally reaching the " Grant House," the last of the row, where he could see distinctly all that was going on.

Yes, there was Katie over at the Pier House, as she had promised, all resplendent in muslin and ribbons, and his heart beat faster at the sight.

Without loss of time he threw off his clothes, and, after placing them out of reach of the tide, he stepped boldly into the water, with a " Here's ter yer, Katie," and struck out for the jumping tower, which was an old spile driver towed over for the occasion ; a large flat scow, at one end of which rose the tall framework in which the hammer plays. At the top an addition had been made of about twelve feet, nice clean wood, a striking contrast to the rest, which was black and time worn, making the drop in all about sixty-five feet.

The professor was advertised to jump eighty feet, so we must take it for granted that the measurements were made from the top of the addition to the bottom of the harbor at high tide ; however, a jump of sixty-five feet into cold water is no child's play.

The tide was almost at high-water mark, and the people began crowding down on the beach just in front of the clumsy craft, eager to catch sight of the object of their curiosity. So intent were they watching the little cabin door that they did not notice the head that was bobbing up and down on the water some few yards astern. So when, a moment or two later, a figure, after stealing cautiously along the further side of the cabin, sprang lightly upon the lower rounds of the ladder and began working its way swiftly upward, the people on shore, thinking that it must be the professor, began to applaud vigorously.

" I thought he was short and light," commented one, "but the fellow that told me must have been off his perch, for this one's tall and black."

" Get on to his shape," said another : but Katie simply sat on the settee in front of the Pier House and looked with all her eyes.

As the applause reached the ears of Professor Cummings, who was having a cigar with the hotel manager below deck, he rose and poked his head out of the door to take a peep. He looked again, and as he did so noticed that all eyes were turned heavenward. He raised his own, then with a yell started for the foot of the ladder, a torrent of oaths and curses pouring from his mouth like so much steam. But what could one voice do against so many? The people neither heard nor saw him. All eyes were fixed on " Muff," who had now nearly reached the top of the extension.

The professor, black in the face with rage, started up the ladder in pursuit, but thinking better of it, jumped back upon the top of the house and cast off the painter of the small boat in which he and the hotel manager had come out. " I'll break every bone in that fellow's body," roared he, then adding, "if the water don't do it for me." So saying, he pushed off the little boat and prepared to " snake him in " when " Muff " rose after his plunge.

But two can make plans, and if the professor's were good, " Muff's " were better ; so, on reaching the top, the latter took a careful survey. A little cat-boat that he had noticed while swimming out seemed almost underneath him now, and had he not been more or less used to heights, he would have sworn that she had dragged her moorings.

After fixing the direction in his mind he turned his attention towards the shore. At such a height the whole Point, with its factory chimneys mingled indiscriminately with the roofs of car sheds and dwelling-houses, lay like a panorama before him, and as his eyes rested upon the great golden cross that adorns the " Gate of Heaven " Church, he involuntarily crossed himself. The people beneath him looked like so many little black and white spiders, and seemed so directly under him that he found himself vaguely wondering what would become of him if he should jump too far out and land on the beach ; then with a smile at himself for fearing to cover a good seventy-five feet at a single bound, he raised his hand above his head as a salute to the anxious watchers. Just as a little white handkerchief waved for a moment on the Pier House piazza, he carefully launched himself forward into the air, then in another second he was shooting with the swiftness of a cannon ball toward the dark green surface of the water. At first the rapidity of the descent dazed him, but as his mind recovered its action he seemed to see both land and water rising to meet him with terrible quickness. He had just time to straighten himself out when the flat of his feet struck the water with a report like a pistol, and he went down, down until his feet touched the smooth, sandy bottom without a jar. His first thought was, " I must make dat cat-boat or, by de holy! I'm scooped"; so he struck out boldly, keeping well below the surface in the direction he thought was right.

It was well for him that his lungs were large, and that he had filled them well before the start, for even as it was, the quick descent and plunge into the cold water had nearly shaken the breath out of his body. His contract was not yet fulfilled; so he pushed himself forward with his powerful arms like a miniature tugboat. He strained his eyes for the first shadow that he knew the hull would cast through the water, but everything looked light and of an even color.

His head seemed as though it would split, and there was a noise in his ears that rivaled the boiler factory close by his home. His lungs ached with the pressure of the water, and a strange thrill shot up his spine and then down again. "I might's well be done up one way's another," he thought at last, "and I've got to get some air." But just then, right ahead, he saw the welcome shadow, and, with his last effort, he reached the further side and bobbed out of the water up to his armpits.

His head grew light and dizzy as his great lungs filled with air, and he gasped like a fish, swallowing, as he did so, quite a quantity of water. This did not last long, as he was an expert swimmer and used to staying under water for quite a time, but as he looked back over the big rudder of the cat-boat he noted the distance with surprise. " Well, dat's de longest turn I ever did under!" he exclaimed mentally. Then, as he noticed the excitement caused by his non-appearance, a grim smile played across his face and he said aloud, " Well, dat feller's queered all right, and I gets Katie."

It was an easy matter, with his head above water, to reach the shelter of the Grant House piazza, making a wide detour, keeping the hulls of yachts between himself and the shore, sinking to his lips behind one every now and then to avoid being noticed by those who were rowing about in small boats. Once he was nearly run down by a large sloop, but he dived under her un-noticed. Only once he thought he would be discovered, as quite a number of people had collected on the float in front of the hotel, but again he took a roundabout course, came up behind them, and as they were all gazing intently in the direction of the spile-driver, he arrived under the protection of the piazza without being seen. Fifteen minutes later he was where only the hardiest policeman would dare follow, and he heaved a great sigh of relief, for if they should, who could find or catch him in his own haunts?

Katie did not return home for a number of hours, which rather took the edge off his happiness; but when she did come, her eyes were red and swollen from crying, and when she caught sight of him, the look on her face suggested that she saw a ghost.

" Muff" sprang up. " What's chewin' you, Katie?" he asked; " has any one been gettin' gay wid yer?"

" O 'Muff,'" she hiccoughed, " I thought you was drowned."

"Well, Katie Shea," began "Muff," but then he softened as he saw how glad she was to see him. "See here, Katie, how der yer suppose I could queer de rung unless I was drowned?"

Then Katie saw. "Well, you did it all right," she answered. "He was so scared he dassent do the jump, and the people didn't want to see him, anyhow."

That night they promenaded B Street arm in arm, as proud as two turkeys.

"Say, Katie, did any bloke get on to who was drowned?"

"No; and they ain't found the body yet."

So they parted until Tuesday early.

With the next day came the finishing touches to "Muff's" reputation when the postman handed him a letter bearing the stamp of the Grant House. It ran as follows: —

Dear Sir: — I am on to your game, and I don't deny that it was a clever one. Professor Cummings will not jump again, and if you want the job at three dollars a day, call and see me to-day at half past four sharp. So large a salary must necessarily be kept quiet, and you must also change your name to, — well, call it Prof. Ed. Raymond.

Yours truly,

F. A. ——.

Care of Grant House,

So. Boston.

To "Muff" Eagan, Esq.

Puffed with pride, he went over and showed the letter to Katie. "Say, Katie, what do you say to goin' down to Patsey Coyne's and havin' a broiled live lobster an' a —"

"I'll go you," said Katie.

It was not until after "Muff's" jumping season was over that the story leaked out, and even later when "Muff" realized that the enormous salary paid him was surely the best stroke of business that the shrewd manager had made for many a day.

G. C. Willey

"DREAMS"

FRANK A. NANKIVELL

Percival Pollard
by
F. A. N.

Notes & Christmas Numbers

", AFTER all, you know, there is something very funny in all this talk and excitement over the poor Bacchante. Nowhere else in the world could such a scene occur; it is thoroughly Boston*ic*. One can fancy a foreigner passing through town the past week and writing to his compatriots an account of the discussion regarding the statue, and his expression of wonder concerning the whole affair.

¶ HAVE you ever built "estates in the newspaper"? The architectural directions are very simple. First, you should be slightly dissatisfied with your present condition in life; not very much so, but just enough to vaguely wish for better times, perhaps for a home of your own, if you have none, or for a larger one, if you can already call some roof yours. Second, you must buy a newspaper and read the " For Sale " advertisements until you come to one that strikes your fancy. Then just stop and dream about it, fit it up, lay out the grounds, make improvements, — anything. But, never, *never*, go to look at the place. If you do, you will return, disheartened, to dream no more : as long as you stay away you can rely implicitly upon the description given in the paper, and it will seem so much more real and possible than a mere imaginary home which is all in your head. The fact that such a place actually exists somewhere besides in your own mind, even though it be only in the mind of the one who wrote the description, will give you confidence in it. These " newspaper estates " are the most satisfactory substitutes imaginable for the old style " castles in Spain."

¶ THERE was a most amusing sketch in a recent *Punch*, which, àpropos of the visit of Ian Maclaren and Mr. Barrie to this country, may well be brought to notice. It appears that a Londoner had assiduously applied himself to the study of Barrie, Crockett, Stevenson, and Maclaren, and, after having, as he supposed, mastered the Scotch dialect, sallied forth, very much as a schoolgirl who has learned the French language in a " finishing school," to converse with the natives. His first encounter brought forth wonder ; his second, scorn ; and his third, anger and the suspicion that he was crazy. He returned to the murky atmosphere of his own city and declared that all Scotch dialect stories were a " fake."

At one time the Anglo-Saxon firmly believed that English was to be the universal language ; but if the waves of dialect are to continue to sweep over us, the probabilities are that the tongue of the " canny Scot " will be the court language of the world.

¶ With the " Zoo " in our midst, the "lion-hunters," for when Boston is so justly famed, will doubtless be relieved of the anxiety attendant upon maintaining their reputation as celebrity providers, since genuine lions can be rented at any time for a dinner party or tea.

¶ The man who can read "The Damnation of Theron Ware " without swearing, throwing something across the room, or kicking the dog, must be made of pious clay, or lack a sense of decency. Well done ? Of course it is well done, but why need it have been done at all ? A pathological discussion of a cancer or other loathsome disease may be well done to the point of perfection, but it is hardly the thing to be foisted upon the unsuspecting man who buys a book with which to while away an hour. Its sub-title should have been " A Study of Morbidity," and it should have been published by some society for psychological research as a monograph on a diseased intellect. It is no offense against morals, for true art is a thing above and beyond morals ; it is purely and simply an offense against good taste, and as such, unpardonable.

¶ The cover for Christmas *Harper's* is rather disappointing, and although designed by one of the foremost artists of brush and pen, we prefer the work of Merson and Church in former holiday issues.

¶ The design for the cover of the December *Century* is the work of a Boston artist, Mr. Theodore Hapgood. It is a fine piece of conventional design, showing careful work. The usual lettering at the top is strengthened by a holly design, with a scroll in the center, in the lower half.

¶ It is seldom that Boston sees a more novel or better constructed play than Mr. Jones's " The Rogue's Comedy." Mr. Willard's style of acting is remarkably in accord with the spirit of the play.

¶ John-a-Dreann announces that it " is very desirous to receive contributions from all who have written anything that they think would not disgrace them if printed."

We trust that this all-embracing request will not meet with so many returns that the editor will be swamped, but " his blood be on his head," he has unsealed the jar from which shall rise the giant.

¶ Why does not some enterprising publisher offer a prize for the best essay or piece of literary criticism, submitted to him ? We have had prizes offered for the best detective story, the best romance, the best fish story, the best tale of adventure, etc., etc. Now that it may be safely presumed that our literature is quite sufficiently stocked in these various directions of literary endeavor, would it not be well to make a slight effort to turn the attention of authors and the reading public in general to the good old forms of writing that are so little in use to-day? The end of the century has produced fiction *ad nauseam*, but very little in *belles lettres*.

Book Notes

" Dreams, books, are each a world; and books, we know,
Are a substantial world, both pure and good.
Round these, with tendrils strong as flesh and blood,
Our pastime and our happiness will grow."   *Wordsworth*

THE tendency of the time has been to overestimate the
part played by the unusual and abnormal in literature.
We hear far too much about the "novel of the problem," and such excrescences on the healthy growth of
literature as "Jude" and "The Damnation of Theron
Ware" receive more prominence thant heir importance
warrants, while far too little is said about the sane
and wholesome productions which, after all, will represent to future generations the literature of our century. In spite of the mushroom growths of
scorbutic type which pass through the glory of five editions and into obscurity
in three months, in spite of the enormous financial success sure to follow a
"hit," — often secured at the expense of the artistic soul,— in spite of the
tempting spectacle of a multitude of readers eagerly awaiting the author
who will consent to write down to them, in spite of all this, there is a vast
majority of writers who still write for art alone. This class of writers is
the class to whom future readers will look for the interpretation of life at the
close of the nineteenth century, and they will not look in vain. After the
problems that belong so much more truly to the legislator and the sociol-
ogist than to the layman have been exploited in all their noxious phases,
and the public, weary of mental "slumming," return to a normal condition,
the writers who have labored faithfully at their art, firm in the conviction
that purity and virtue are more than names, will reap their just reward.
Among the writers whose works are free from the scrofulous taint so preva-
lent in some quarters is Mr. Bret Harte. Messrs. Houghton, Mifflin & Co.
have just brought out a collection of short stories by this very breezy and
virile writer, called "Barker's Luck and Other Stories." The stories have
mostly appeared before in the magazines and are now collected and published
uniformly with the rest of Mr. Harte's works. They have the usual range of
this prolific writer, and together constitute a very cosmopolitan volume.
"The Indiscretion of Elsbeth" is the slightest of the sketches and is hardly
up to the average of Mr. Harte's work. We believe that it first appeared
in *The Ladies' Home Journal,* which may account for its lack of flavor.
"Barker's Luck" and "A Mother of Five" compare favorably with any
work that the author has ever done. (16mo, $1.25.)

Sympathy and fidelity are, perhaps, after all, the rarest artistic gifts. To be able completely to obtain the " point of view," and then to so reproduce it that others may in turn achieve it, is art indeed. Alvin F. Sanborn, in his "Meg McIntyre's Raffle and Other Stories," published by Messrs. Copeland & Day, has succeeded in picturing with marvelous accuracy the life and incidents of the streets. Mr. Sanborn's types, we feel, are more than types, they are actual individuals ; and after he has brought them before us to show us their nature and character, we feel sorry to lose sight of them, and must, perforce, wonder and speculate on their future careers. " Baucis and Philemon " is treated with a tenderness and sympathy which shows the author at his best. The subject is somewhat conventional and lends itself so readily to false sentiment that Mr. Sanborn's delicate treatment makes it especially noteworthy. Unfortunately, the same faults exist in this book that brought forth so much adverse criticism upon " Moody's Lodging House." They are much less marked, but still we cannot help wishing that Mr. Sanborn had left certain things unexpressed ; the realistic side is not made more secure by their utterance, and the book would be much pleasanter reading had they been omitted. (16mo.)

Through the courtesy of the publishers we have been furnished with the proof-sheets of the forthcoming volume of verse by Francis Sherman, entitled " Matins." (Copeland & Day.) A lover of Rossetti, whom Sherman much resembles in form, or an admirer of Morris, cannot fail to see in this Canadian poet a representative of the school to which the two above-mentioned writers belong. His work is that kind concerning which no neutral ground can be taken ; he is either intensely charming, and a poet of the highest and best, or he is no poet at all. His verse is marked by strong individuality and absence of the conventional, and it is easy to see that he is a man about whom the most diverse opinions will be held. Two of his longer poems, " The Rain " and " Summer Dying," are most typical of his poetry at its best. Prophecies are hazardous, but Mr. Sherman will most certainly gain wide recognition. (Octave.)

¶ The most artistic specimen of the book-maker's art that has reached us this month is " Penhallow Tales " (Copeland & Day). The contents of the book are to be classed with the contents of perhaps fifty other books of precisely the same nature. " The Satyr's Head " is the only story in the book that possesses marked qualities of any sort, and it is distinctly a strong bit of work.

The Red Letter

An Illustrated Monthly

Edited by Harry Draper Hunt
Under the art direction of E. B. Bird
Managed by H. W. Stephenson

The subscription rate is one dollar a year. Entered at the Boston Post-office as second-class mail matter. The trade supplied by the American News Company and its branches. Advertising rates on application.

The Red Letter Magazine,

Boston.

<><><><><><><><>

¶ THE RED LETTER aims to represent the best work of the younger authors and artists. Contributions will receive careful attention.

<><><><>

¶ OWING to unavoidable delays it was impossible to publish Mr. Bradley's work in this issue.

<><><><>

¶ THE January number will contain an illustrated article on H. L. Bridwell, and other special features.

<><><><>

¶ THROUGH the courtesy of Messrs. Copeland & Day we are enabled to publish one of Miss Ethel Reed's illustrations for the forthcoming volume of verse by Louise Chandler Moulton, entitled " In Childhood's Country."

<><><><>

¶ ORDERS for single copies of the first three numbers of THE RED LETTER can now be filled.

Number One . . . .   15 cents.

Number Two . . .   . 25 cents.

Number Three   . . . . . 15 cents.

STEARNS
IS THE
VOGUE

E.C. Stearns & Co
Syracuse. N.Y.
Toronto. Ont. Buffalo.
San Francisco N.Y.
Paris, Cal.
France.

The Red Letter:

For January
1897 ❧ Vol·1 ❧ No·5
Price 10¢

"I will while away an hour or so with picturings and prints"

Contents

PROFITABLE ADVERTISING

A Monthly. Fully Illustrated.
The Advertisers' Trade Journal.

Devoted to the interests of publishers and advertisers. Full of practical, profitable ideas. Tells what you want to know about advertising. Pays advertisers (write for rates). Is of great value to the subscriber.

KATE E. GRISWOLD,
Editor and Publisher,

Price, $1.00 per year.
Send for sample copy, 10 cents.

No. 13 School Street, Boston, Mass.

Three-sheet Poster
by
H. L. Bridwell

The Red Letter

An Illustrated Monthly.

"'T will while away an hour or so with picturings and print."—MARLOWE.

Genius

WE stand before the uttered thought as those
  Who alien gaze upon a written wall;
  Some day a stray word, sun-like, lifts a call:
Thenceforth we breathe above eternal snows.

Philip Becker Goetz

Mrs. Lawson's Conversion

AS I sat by the foot of Lawson's bed and watched the peaceful candle-light glinting from the small crucifix that lay on his breast, my foolish self-reproach, and even my pain, partly left me. I could not have foretold this; it was only natural that in wandering a few days from village to village I had sent back no address. So while I had sketched peasant merry-makings, and had listened to sweet legends and sad Breton folk-songs, and had danced burly dances, only a priest had soothed his death. After all, perhaps it was best so; for my distracted bounds from skepticism to mysticism, and from mysticism to skepticism, would have disturbed the quiet in which he was happy.

At last, just before his death, he had fully expressed the gentle spirit that he loved. Day after day, leaving the rugged capitals and dark archways of the town, he had climbed Mont Dol; and seated beside a pool,—the great footmark that Saint Michael stamped when he jumped to his island rock,—he had painted his vision of the rich fields, the quicksands, the tide, and the warrior angel's monastic fort. Thus through an opalescent revery he had expressed the beauty that was in him.

Then he had lain ill a few days under the thatched roof whose ridge-pole, covered with moss and flowers, he had often sketched in the sunlight; and suddenly he had died, silent and alone, except always for the priest who held the crucifix above his eyes. On that he had gazed as he smiled the smile which I saw now; and, as the priest said, he had partaken of sacrament. This son of English Dissenters had received extreme unction, dreaming, half dazed by the glittering crucifix, thoughtless, vaguely comforted.

Imagining things thus, I waited by the foot of his bed. It was hard to tell when Mrs. Lawson would arrive. She had not answered the telegram Belhomme our host—still *our* host, I thought with a little shudder—had sent. She had not answered, so she must have started at once, and should have arrived before this.

I picked up the torn *indicateur* from the floor, and followed cross references from time-table to time-table. There was the train, and there! No; then she would have arrived at three. Perhaps the inventive old lady had planned to save time by branching off at Vire. "Vire, Vire," I said to myself; but, weary and sleepy, I looked for it in vain. "Vire, Vire," I muttered. The name mixed with the twitter of the birds whose dark shadows fluttered in the watery green light that leaked through the blinds. "Vire? But perhaps she took the Havre boat," I went on. "I must look that up. The Havre boat ——" I imagined it making fast to the dock, the gang plank run out, the people landing; and to see more distinctly I shut my eyes.

.   .   .   .

Why, there were Robertson and Peters,—how funny that they weren't off shooting in the North,—and Jenks, Jones, and, of all people in the world, old Belhomme! Oh, certainly! He was carrying her bag. Poor, shriveled, little old lady. That faded brown dress didn't make her look any more harmonious than usual! How pale she was; she must have been seasick; she staggered ludicrously. "I really ought to help her!" I exclaimed. But somehow I couldn't move.

Then I seemed to wake in a Dissenting chapel. "I oughtn't to have gone to sleep in such a place," I rebuked myself. "Good heavens! why did I come to this varnished little shop, when the only religion I can stand is the Greek incense and golden robes, or—an agnostic lecture? What horrible, utterly horrible singing! And it's such bad taste letting that ill-dressed youth rush up to the priest—the minister, I mean—in the middle of meeting. Oh, it's Belhomme's telegram! Don't be alarmed, I beg you, Mrs. Lawson," I said, laying my hand on her little dry, folded ones. But she heard the boy whisper her name, and whirled up the aisle. She tore open the telegram. How firm she looked! Her lips, though, were blue,—a dull blue. "I think I should try making it with cobalt and a little lampblack," I said to myself. " But how that carriage rattles. I must tighten the bolts!"

.   .   .   .

I stood up, suddenly, wide awake. The candles had guttered a good deal, and were very short; it must be late. I looked at my watch : five-thirty! All day I had slept, and had dreamed heartless dreams. Poor Lawson,—how calm he looked, how peaceful! No wonder that I had felt so little horror that I had let my head rumple the sheet there beside his knees. But his eyes were more hollow now. His mother should have seen him while he was altogether lovely.

While I was still gazing the renewed rattle of a cart and loud talking in the kitchen made me start again. It must be she, and I had not met her. "Mais, madame, puisque je vous dis qu'il est mort, mort, mort!" old Belhomme vociferated.

And Mrs. Lawson's voice answered cheerily : "Bore? Yes; I understand. I knew being ill would be an awful bore to him, so I brought these."

"Mais, madame, je vous en prie!" the old man expostulated, following her up the short stairs.

I must meet her in the entry. But as I pulled open the door she tripped toward me, two yellow and green storybooks in her hand, and pushed me lightly back into the room.

I trembled, and my ears throbbed. I noticed only that her face became as pale as in my dream, and her lips just that horrible blue. Her yellow and green storybooks crashed to the floor. With her hands stretched out in the conventional gesture she stood still. At last, however, she turned firmly round, passed me unnoticed, and saying very precisely to Belhomme, "I beg your pardon, sir," shut the door in his face.

Though she pulled my chair to the head of the bed and sat down vigorously enough, her dried little body soon began to tremble so fitfully that the chair legs rattled on the uneven boards. While she gazed at Wilfred her face became horribly bloodless—pale as paper; it seemed lifeless, except that her mouth, jerking down at the corners, made and unmade a wrinkle, sharp as a knife mark, that set me quivering. In my helpless sympathy I even longed to slink away; but as her chair blocked the door, I stole into the dimmest corner and sat on the floor, my throat choked against my knees.

After a very long time I saw that she trembled less and was less rigid, and I heard her sob naturally. At last she even stood up, and, looking calmly into his face, stooped to kiss him.

Poor mother! That coldness made her moan and tumble forward on her knees, praying aloud. Soon, however, she was again almost silent. Gradually her lips stopped moving, and she stared blindly upward, unconscious.

"Wilfred!" she suddenly cried. The sound changed to a moan that rose and fell like the full cry of some animal. It softened till the lowing of a cow in the shed overcame it, then it swelled and reverberated woefully. That primitive, almost animal, cry filled me, shook me to the very soul.

"Mrs. Lawson! Mrs. Lawson!" I begged, and, jumping to my feet, stood helpless.

But now she was silent, conscious; her eyes saw again—for the first time saw the crucifix.

She stared tensely at it; she frowned, and her quivering lips became set as religious horror awoke in her. She snatched the image from her son's breast, and dashed it on the floor. The Romish candles, which made his smooth, black hair glisten so brightly, she took from above his head and angrily set down, two by two, about the crucifix.

Then she stood still. For a moment the candles lit the under side of her chin and the end of her nose, and cast dark shadows in the hollows over her eyeballs, so that her face looked like a skull.

"Philip, Philip, tell me, Philip, did he—did you—" she asked. "did you lead him to that?" And she pointed to the glittering crucifix.

"I wasn't here! I didn't even know till last night," I pitiably stammered.

She struggled to her feet, and with her longest strides tramped up and down. Faster and faster she tramped. Her eyes seemed dead. "Is she insane?" I whispered to myself. But little by little, walking more slowly, she became calm. Altogether quiet at last, she opened the door and called,—

"Sir! sir! Pray come here."

Old Belhomme guessed that he was wanted, tramped up the stairs, and came to the door puffing.

"Mon Dieu, mon Dieu," was all he could say when he saw the desecrated figure of Christ. "Mon Dieu! Mon Dieu! Mon Dieu!" and he waved his clasped hands up and down.

"Be quiet, and listen," said Mrs. Lawson.

"How did you dare put your popish images and heathen lights by him?" she went on, pointing furiously toward her unworried dead. "He didn't want them. He didn't! Tell me," she moaned, "tell me, if you know anything."

Belhomme was helpless.

"Mrs. Lawson," I expostulated, "I assure you, Mrs. Lawson, our host can't understand you. Really, he meant no harm. It was merely his notion of respect."

"You said you weren't here. You know nothing about it," she snapped, desperately. "Then how can I find out? Promise,—promise on your honor, Philip,—tell me truly what he says."

That made it hopeless. I promised, really half amused. Poor little lady, to her this was a matter of life and death.

"Ask him," she said, "did Wilfred Lawson die a member of the Romish church?"

"Est-ce que Monsieur Wilfred Lawson est mort en bon Catholique?" I freely translated.

"Mais oui, assurément! Monsieur l'abbé me dit qu'il est mort comme un saint. Madame, peut croire qu'en vérité ——"

"Quick—what does he say? what does he say?" Mrs. Lawson interrupted.

"Really, perhaps, after all, he doesn't know," I answered, while Belhomme rattled on, smiling, and turning out the palms of his hands.

"Philip, tell me," she cried.

So I translated, word for word: "Madam, he died peaceful and blessed, in everything succored by the reverend priest."

"Thank you; you may go," she said to Belhomme, and shut him out.

"Philip," she said, in a solemn voice, "you saw me dishonor Wilfred's religion; you must witness my reparation."

One by one she took the candles from the floor, and began ranging them about his head.

I couldn't contain myself. "His religion!" I exclaimed. "How do you know he had any religion,—except worship of beauty?" She went on placing the candles. "He was no Catholic," I persisted. "Because an old priest comes through the fields with a tinkling bell and all the peasants take off their hats,—because he holds up a crucifix and comforts a speechless, dying man,—do you think all that makes Wilfred a Catholic?"

"You can never convince me," she answered, undisturbed, —"you can never convince me that he was—like you. I've heard skeptics talk before. Wilfred belonged to the Romish—to the holy Catholic Church!" ·

"Poor little mother!" I thought. How she had always followed him. How she had obeyed all his whims,—had even let him leave her. And now she must obey even her false imagination of his wish! False? Really false? Perhaps, though, she was right; perhaps she came nearer to his spirit than I thought. Surely, now there was a deep tenderness about her; for when she had carefully placed the last candle, she took up the crucifix and kissed it, and kneeling at her son's feet, she held it above her in both hands and gazed at it lovingly. At last she laid it on his breast, and, making a clumsy sign of the cross, said,—

"Come, bring me to the priest."

Henry Copley Greene

Vale, 1896. Salve, 1897

LAST night we laid him down to rest,—
            So
                Silently.
He was our friend, our very best.
            But
                Yesterday.
Now all is changed, for with the morn,
Another friend to us is born :
And, like the world's ingratitude,
We say, in tuneful, happy mood,
        Good-by, Old Year,
            Good-by !

We walk his chamber of the Past,—
            So
                Silently.
We think of joys that did not last
            But
                Yesterday.
The chimes that rung his dying knell,
A Jubilate, loud, did tell
Of joys to come—a New Year's birth !
We join the pæan upon earth,
        Hail, glad New Year !
            All hail !

A twelvemonth hence, and you must sleep.—
            So
                Silently.
A twelvemonth hence, and we must weep
            As
                Yesterday.
For you, like him, must soon grow old ;
Your cherub wings, that now enfold
So much of promise,—joys to be,—
Must droop ; and we shall cry to thee,
        Good-by, Old Year,
            Good-by !

Your name with cypress we shall twine,—
So
Silently.
And quaff from Memory's sweet wine
Of
Yesterday.
For New Years come, and Old Years go :
Life is a pageant, and a show,—
A twelvemonth story, quickly told ;
Then hail the New ! God speed the Old !
Hail, glad New Year !
All hail !
                              Grace Le Baron

Mr. James's Young Men

THE other day comparing real men with men of fiction, I found myself wondering to what extent modern novelists are to be trusted in their portrayals of the character masculine. In turning over this subject my mind naturally reverted to Henry James, who, as a man and a student of character, ought to be correct in his drawings of men.

Strangely enough, the strongest impression remaining with one, of Mr. James's young men—for I had young men chiefly in mind—was far from agreeable. I had a vague remembrance that many of them were snobs, that others were prigs, and that there were very few who would have been really interesting in flesh and blood. Before deciding that Mr. James's analysis should lead us to determine that his young men are like most young men, I resolved to seek again the companionship of Roderick Hudson, and Hyacinth, and Winterbourne, and the many others of half-forgotten memory.

Now, men of fiction, like men of real life, are not easily grouped in fixed classes. The best of them has his faults, the worst, his virtues. Mr. James himself inclines as little to paint a perfect saint as an unmitigated villain. Yet, certain types repeat themselves so regularly in his stories, that his young men might easily be arranged in four or five groups. All the men in the same group, without being precisely alike, have characteristics so similar that they are at once recognized as closely related.

First of all, there are the young men of genius (or talent, if you will), among whom Roderick Hudson stands readily at the head. Few of Mr. James's creations are so thoroughly alive. Chafing under the limitations of

Northampton Society, already half-spoiled by the few women who know him well, he appears at first too volatile to profit by Rowland Malet's generosity. Sentimental enough to engage himself to Mary Garland, on the eve of his departure for Europe, he still succumbs to the wonderful beauty of Christina Light, whom fate sends in his way.

"What does Miss Garland think of your departure for Europe?" his benefactor had asked. "Oh! she thinks what I think," he answered; and this attitude of complacency continues to be his attitude, not only toward the devoted Mary, but toward his mother and Christina as well. With all his genius and nervous energy, transplanted to the enervating atmosphere of Rome, Roderick does not strike his roots deep enough. After great successes he becomes idle, desultory, fantastic, moody; he even sinks into dissipation. There is a woman behind it all. He philanders with Christina, and thinks less and less of Mary, waiting for him under the Northampton trees. He is the supreme egotist, and Christina herself exactly characterizes him : "You have never really faced the fact that you are false."

He is the egotist whose egotism is more hurtful to himself than to any one else; whom women despise even while they pet. As Mr. James says, he "never saw himself as part of a whole—only as the clear-cut, sharp-edged, isolated individual, rejoicing or raging as the case might be, but needing in any case absolutely to affirm himself." So young to die, to meet so tragic a fate, yet what in a longer life would he have accomplished?

Poor Hyacinth Robinson, too, is to be placed among real men ; poor Hyacinth, with his dark memories of his murderess mother, with the cloud of a shameful origin hanging over him. With his fine feelings, with his soul of an artist,—who knows what height he might not have attained under better auspices? Yet he, too, is a philanderer, finding solace for hours, otherwise lonely, in the society of Millicent, the bold London shop-girl.

"Are you afraid," he asks indignantly of the good woman who has brought him up, "are you afraid of my marrying a girl out of a shop? Do you think I would marry anyone who would marry me? The kind of girl who would look at me is the kind of girl I wouldn't look at?" Pretty pride for a poor little bookbinder !

A peer's daughter said that Hyacinth had "charming manners," and an Italian princess thought it no waste of time to confide in him. He grew to like the princess exceedingly, and he had "hitherto supposed that when a sentiment of this kind had the energy of a possession, it made a clean sweep of all minor predilections." Yet, like most of Mr. James's men, he can oscillate gracefully between two women. He can listen to the aspirations of Princess Cassimissima, and he can find pleasure in walking about with Millicent, "with her Sunday gown, and little airs, and silver bracelets." "It's a pity I have always been so terribly under the influence of women," he sighs frankly. But Hyacinth does no woman any harm. His is a pure and upright soul, and he falls a victim, not to passion, but to a superfine sense of honor. He kills himself rather than fulfill a vow in which he has no heart, made to the Nihilists with whom he has dealings.

Felix Young, the cosmopolite American,—American only in name and blood,—belongs in the category with Roderick and Hyacinth. Frivolous, penniless, shabby, according to his own account, with his philosophy that life should be enjoyed, that it should be regarded as an opportunity rather than a discipline, he seems human, and he has a charm all his own.

" In Bohemia I always passed for a gentleman," he says naively; " I always respected my neighbor's wife." He hesitates long about offering himself to his cousin Gertrude, lest he should seem " disloyal" to her father, who has offered him hospitality.

" Hospitality? an abuse?" exclaims that father in bewilderment when Felix expresses this fear to him ; and thus a distinction between the American and the European way of looking at these things is strongly marked. Had his suit for Gertrude been unsuccessful, Felix would never have killed himself. He might have had a sore heart, but he would have made the best of it. He would have gone off to Europe to paint pictures, to do what he could to dull the pain, and he would not have been slow in finding consolation.

Peter Sherringham, though a diplomat with the prospect of an exalted career, is almost as much alive as Felix, or Hyacinth, or Roderick. His love of beauty, his love for the theater, his latent Bohemianism, might have played sad havoc with his future. Wandering around Paris on summer evenings with Miriam Rooth, helping to place her on the stage, what would have become of him if she had accepted his love? He knows himself that she is neither fish nor flesh, that " one had with her neither the guaranties of one's own class nor the immunities of hers." But after many heroic efforts to suppress his passion, he does not hesitate to offer her everything,—himself, his fortune, and the prospect for her of being an ambassadress. His cousin Betty, whose tenderness for him Peter, like the rest of the family, must realize, does not draw him away from his dark-browed Miriam. Nevertheless, he has undoubtedly a feeling akin to surety that if Miriam's laughs of scorn are enduring, he can rely on Betty. Certainly in the end, when Miriam has married the other man, he finds that he loves Betty. Taking into consideration the latter's artistic temperament and talent for sculpture, one can prophecy for them a life as nearly Bohemian as is consistent with a diplomatic career.

Betty's brother and Peter's cousin Nicholas occupy a place on the borderland between conventionality and the less clearly defined realm where Roderick, and Hyacinth, and Felix abide. It is true that he has talent, and that he paints portraits which are quite wonderful as the work of a man who has had little instruction, of a man who has held a seat in Parliament. In spite of his reluctance to be under obligations to anyone, in spite of his declaration in favor of freedom, one suspects him of reflecting too deeply on his mother's query, "What freedom is there in being poor?" There is hardly a doubt that he will marry Julia, hardly a doubt that he will follow his mother's advice and "go in for a great material position." Then what of Art, of Bohemia, of freedom?

A second interesting group is made up of those rich young men whose virtues almost equal their wealth. For none, or almost none of Mr. James's bad men are rich; and none, or almost none of his rich men are bad.

Think of that model of virtue, Roger Lawrence, who, despite his good income, is rejected by the woman of his choice. Does he sit down and bemoan his fate? Far from it. He adopts a friendless little girl, and has her trained in all the arts and graces. He nurses his capital, speculates a little, and soon has a fortune. He nurses his affections, too, and rigorously represses them when they stray too vigorously in the direction of a seductive Peruvian Teresita. When his fortune and his ward are both well grown, he believes that his hope is near fruition. If Nora herself at first rebels at the thought that she has been carefully brought up merely to be the wife of a good and rich young man, she soon sees the error of her rebellion. Roger and she are doubtless forever happy.

Rowland Mallet, the patron of Roderick Hudson, does not find an outlet for his surplus income by adopting a little girl. He takes an infant of a larger growth, and occupies his mind and employs his money in opening opportunities for the young American sculptor.

Rowland, with his sensitive conscience, is never quite clear as to his duty. "I am clever enough to want more than I've got. I am tired of myself, my own thoughts, my own eternal company." At this his penetrating cousin Celia cries out, "What an immense number of words to say you want to fall in love." But Rowland is always uncertain how deeply he is in love. He never was quite sure whether or not he had loved his cousin Celia. In his soul he becomes positive of his passion for Mary Garland. But she is betrothed to the unworthy Roderick, and Rowland merely says to himself, "Remember to forget Mary Garland."

"There are certain things you know nothing about," Roderick had once exclaimed petulantly to Rowland.

"What are they?"

"They are women principally, and what relates to women," replies the wise Roderick. Yet, for years and years after Roderick has been laid in the tomb, Rowland, secure in the love of Mary Garland, could show that he knew how to win and keep a good woman's love. For who can doubt that Mary returned his affection.

Robert Acton, another rich young man, is a little less aggressively virtuous than the two just described. His sedate family, because he has traveled as far as China, consider him rather a man of the world. He inclines to take the humorous view of things, and though fond of books, is also a student of human nature. In his younger years he had thought that it would be a great deal "jollier" not to get married. But advancing age brought wisdom, and he even thought seriously of marrying the flippant Baroness.

He devotes himself neither to a youthful ward nor to a talented protégé. He helps the time pass quickly for an invalid mother, and he is ever at the service of an imperious younger sister. He has one point of superiority over most of Mr. James's young men. He does not, in our sight, at least, think affectionately of more than one woman at a time. We are told, it is true, that some time after the Baroness' return to Europe he married "a nice young girl." Yet this was decidedly better than breaking his heart over the morganatic wife of a petty German prince.

Gordon Wright is one of the most provoking of the good and rich young men of our group. With his thirty thousand a year income, he feels that matrimony is not to be lightly entered into.

"I want to marry with my eyes open. I want to know my wife. You don't know people when you're in love with them. Your impressions are colored. . . . I object to being fascinated."

He subjects the woman of his choice to the critical judgment of his friend Bernard Longueville. He proposes to her a second time, in the face of that friend's adverse judgment, and he finds her still obdurate. In spite of his intention not to be fascinated, he marries a silly flirt, whom he considers simple and tender. Though he has a brief disillusionment, he finds his happiness in returning to his former opinion.

Ralph Touchett, though the richest of all Mr. James's young Americans, has neither a ward, a protégé, an invalid mother, nor a love affair to look after. When his father dies he has sufficient employment in taking care of his own miserable health. "A certain fund of indolence that he possesses came to his aid, and helped to reconcile him to doing nothing." He permits himself the luxury of an unexpressed love for his cousin Isabel, and does her a false kindness in getting his father to will her a fortune of several hundred thousand dollars. Ralph had a keen sense of humor, but this was a rather poor way of showing it. "I hope I shall live long enough to see what she does with herself," he had said at the time he persuaded his father to make his will in Isabel's favor. He lived to see his cousin the victim of a fortune-hunter, and his sense of humor did not come to his rescue when he made the pathetic admission, "I believe I ruined you."

Caspar Goodwood and Christopher Newman are men of a different type from the other rich young Americans portrayed by Mr. James. The former, though he has a moneyed father, has also had a hand in producing wealth himself, and in his imperious pursuit of Isabel, he shows a force and vigor which would have been impossible to Roger, or Gordon, or Robert, or Ralph.

Christopher Newman, though a genuine man, has not—to my mind, at least—a very clearly drawn individuality. In his relations with women he is certainly honest, and he is as obtuse to the attractions of the dubious Parisienne, Noémie Nioche, as he is appreciative of the virtues of Madame de Cintré. His ideal woman "must be as good as she is beautiful, and as clever as she is good." When, therefore, he has found these qualities embodied in Madame de Cintré, we wonder that he does not drag her from the convent where she would bury herself.

The group that one likes the least, perhaps, among all these young men, may be called the critic class. There belongs Bernard Longueville, the artist, with his theory, " One can't be in love with two women at once, but one may perfectly have two of them, or as many as you please, up for competitive examination." He is willing to accept the duty thrust upon him by Gordon Wright of inspecting Angela Vivian, whom the latter would like to marry. He studies her carefully during his friend's absence in England, and decides against her. When after three years he meets the girl again, it is a pretty turn of fate that he should find that he has been in love with her all this time himself. It is more, perhaps, than he deserves that the girl should respond to his love.

Longmore, with his sympathy for the greatly abused Madame de Mauves, is hardly a cold-blooded critic. One feels, however, that curiosity as much as admiration leads him into the society of the unhappy lady. " Are you really as unhappy as I imagine you to be?" he ventures to ask ; and later, after he has declared his admiration for her, he meekly accepts his dismissal. The Puritan element is hard to eradicate from a man's blood, even though he may have spent several years in Paris.

Littlemore and Waterville, who are spectators of Mrs. Headway's Siege of London, would prefer silence to speech about the pushing lady from San Diego. Littlemore, with years of European experience, could tell the respectable women from others at a glance. Waterville was often puzzled. " Countesses looked so superficial, the others so exclusive." But both are slow in accepting their duty of warning the susceptible Sir Arthur Demesne about the real character of Mrs. Headway. " All I've got to do is not to marry her myself," is Littlemore's excuse, and Waterville's attitude is much the same.

Of all these critics, Winterbourne is probably the most annoying. It is difficult to feel that he might not have saved Daisy Miller from the consequence of her indiscretions, or rather from the indiscretions themselves. But it is more amusing to him to hold those unchaperoned interviews with her. It is easier to be a critical spectator than an honest friend. A pretty girl is always worth flirting with, even though she may have bad manners, superfluous flounces and jewelry, and a careless and underbred mother.

To a great extent the men whom we have considered are Americans, and young,—at least fairly young. Though we may not have liked them all, hardly one of them can be called bad. For the men of bad character one must look to such creations as the Europeanized Osmond, or the French M. de Mauves, neither of whom, by the way, is exactly young, and several others of less definite personality. But the foreign men whom we approve are more numerous than those whom we dislike: the volatile Valentine, with his "Oh! the women, the women, and the things they have made me do;" Count Voglestein, with his perturbation about the social status of the beautiful Pandora Day; Count Valerii, an Italian, who is really fond of his wife; Gabriel Nash, with his volubility and idealism, and his little system for leading a truly æsthetic life; even the bold and self-satisfied Paul Muniment,—have some attractions. Lord Lambeth and Lord Warburton are noblemen of habits so irreproachable, of minds so bright, and of wealth so large, that Bessie Alden and Isabel Archer, in refusing them, seem almost superhuman,—at least in these days of international marriages.

Maurice Glanvil, the young Englishman who runs away from Fanny Knocker, because, as he says, "I don't care a bit for money, but, hang it, I must have beauty," is almost admirable in his disregard of mercenary considerations. He is a happy contrast to the American, Morris Townsend, who really would marry the unattractive Catherine Sloper, if only he could be sure that she would add her father's wealth to the fortune left her by her mother. With the worldly cleric, Herbert Lawrence, and the inflexible minister, Mr. Brand, we come almost to the end of the real men depicted by Mr. James.

There are, to be sure, a number of nonentities of more or less vitality, like Clifford Wentworth, Basil Dashwood, Eugene Pickering, little Mr. Rosier, Mr. Bautling, Basil Ransom, and others, who serve their purpose, and whom we are not intended to carry too deeply in our minds. The heroes, or figures, in the majority of Mr. James's later stories, have no life, and it is doubtful if they were meant to be breathing personages. They are subjectivities to be comprehended only by people endowed with special psychic power. The average reader will not be offended if he is not counted in this special class. He will turn rather to the books of Mr. James's better years, and whether he decides that the young men there portrayed are snobs, or heroes, or simply average men, he will find them at their worst or at their best highly entertaining.

Helen Leah Reed

Architectural Study
by
E. N. Dart

A Rising Illustrator

ART as presented in our century,—and illustration has undergone such extraordinary growth and development during the last decade or two, that as compared with the illustrative work of forty, or even twenty-five years ago, the advance that is apparent seems little short of marvelous. It is only when we take up a copy of the popular illustrated magazines published, say in the early forties, and representative of the choicest artistic talent at that time procurable, that we realize to the fullest what tremendous progress the art has made. With the ever-increasing demand for illustration, both in periodical literature and journalism, there has come forward a rapidly augmenting company of young artists whose claim to the title might have otherwise failed of recognition, or, at most, have met with local appreciation only, had it not been that work in black and white offered them a medium by means of which they could with comparative ease bring their talents prominently before the public.

In the leading periodical publications devoted to art and all that pertains thereto, there have at various times appeared articles, critical and otherwise, concerning the lives and works of many of the better known illustrators of the day; but as yet little has been said or written of one who, although one of the youngest illustrators in the field, possesses talents and versatility that must eventually bring him into the front rank of his craft.

It has been said that artists, like poets, are born, not made; and in Edward Nelson Dart we find the truth of this saying well exemplified; for, like many of the greatest artistic geniuses the world has known, the direction of his life work was manifest at an early age. We have all read of the famous circle of Giotto, and the immature efforts of the youthful Benjamin West with his father's barn as a canvas; and, indeed, of a hundred similar instances of the small beginnings of many a painter who, in after years, was to rise to fame and fortune as a master of his art; so that we should not, therefore, be surprised to learn, and, indeed, may consider quite legitimate, the fact that Mr. Dart won recognition as a skilled draughtsman of

elephants at the precocious age of five. His penchant for the fine arts becoming more and more pronounced, we find him at eleven commencing serious art study in the evening drawing school of North Adams, his native town, and entering enthusiastically into the work of the local Art Students' League. During the six or seven years of his study here in the several branches of freehand and mechanical drawing and design, he received invaluable assistance from his instructor, Mr. Arthur W. Scribner, who was quick to recognize the powers of his pupil and aid in their development, and it was he who first prophesied the young artist's future success.

In 1891 Mr. Dart came to Boston and entered an architect's office, where he soon showed pronounced ability in the mastery of architectural detail and technique; and it was here that he obtained the thorough knowledge and fine appreciation of the principles of construction, which in his later work has stood him in such good stead. With the few months spent in architecture closed Mr. Dart's preliminary art study; and to one familiar with his work it is doubly astonishing that with a comparatively restricted education in his chosen profession, and without the advantages of foreign study, he yet stands head and shoulders above a multitude of others who have had far greater opportunities. Of his work, much of which has appeared in the *New England Magazine*, *The Boston Herald*, and other local publications, it is only necessary to say that aside from that of a purely architectural character, it is in the main of a serious, thoughtful nature. His women are dainty, well-dressed persons, who, you are certain, can engage you in pleasant conversation, and his men are hardy but gentlemanly types. In delineating the ideal, Mr. Dart is particularly felicitous; as will be readily conceded by those who have seen his illustration of the "Ministering Angel," published in the Christmas number of THE RED LETTER. He has a ready grasp of needful essentials in monochromatic work, and his illustrations invariably possess an air of suggestiveness. Mr. Dart's ambition is to not only win distinction as a high-class illustrator, but to achieve success also as a portrait painter.

Percy L. Weed

Illustration
by
E. N. Dart

A Pioneer in Artistic Poster Work

THE man who introduces the artistic into an industry which has hitherto been entirely utilitarian, does a service to art no less than the man who paints a great picture. The days of the hideous in advertising are distinctly of the past, and no longer are the artistic sensibilities of the public offended by the glaring crudition of fifteen years ago. That this is so, is due in no small degree to the work of Mr. Bridwell.

"H. L. Bridwell was born near Cincinnati some thirty years ago. His early inclination for drawing, which he writes us was inherited, was not indulged until after he had received his school training, and spent two additional years in varied pursuits. In the early eighties he became connected with the famous Strobridge Lithographing Company, and has remained with them ever since."

The foregoing scanty facts are all that we have been able to wring from Mr. Bridwell in regard to his life. His work is more public property.

At the time Mr. Bridwell became associated with the Strobridges, purely decorative posters were almost unknown, and the lettering and ornament upon pictorial posters were entirely of the hard, mechanical sort, mostly copied from lithographic show cards. He at once began to design the posters by which he is now so well known; and his departure from beaten tracks was noted and commented on favorably by the magazines. His early work shows the influence of the black and white pictorial drawings of Pyle, Abbey, and others; but the characteristics of his later and more widely known posters were present in sufficient quantity to stamp it with the strength of individuality which is so truly his own.

The difficulties of one-sheet posters are few compared with those of the twenty-eight sheet posters, which form the bulk of his work. To secure strong effects, readability, and balance, much must be included, and somehow embellished, that is usually objectionable from an artistic standpoint.

Mr. Bridwell's ideas of art in general, and poster work in particular, can be given best in his own words.

" I have no theories to describe nor any scheme of artistic nature in the world personally. What I aim at is *simplicity* and *clearness* of design and crispness in execution; a design with extremely few elements, and those strong ones. Beyond this, I try to never repeat myself. I do not like eccentricity when it goes into ugliness, to attract attention. Art is to make people cheerful, and not to remind them of hospitals and asylums."

The most famous of Mr. Bridwell's posters are doubtless those of three sheets, and also those of one half sheet made for " The Rivals," as given by Joseph Jefferson and his company of stars in the spring of this year.

Others are, " The Mandarin," " Sothern," " Trilby," " Della Fox," " Beerbohm Tree," " Kiralfy's Spectacles," " Frohman's Companies," " Romeo and Juliet," " Palmer's Companies," " Felix Morris," " Nat Goodwin," " Voyage of Luzette," and " Wm. H. Crane."

Harry D. Hunt

Three-sheet Poster
by
H. L. Bridwell

Impressions in Southern Spain

BY A LANDSCAPE PAINTER

WROTE the following sketches with the hope that I might occasionally show the reader a pleasant picture, or perhaps make him smile. If I am ever so unlucky as to make him think, I entreat him to accept my excuses. I have said very frankly what I like and what I don't like. If the reader disagrees with me, I hope, for all that, we shall be very good friends. *J. W.*

SOME INTRODUCTORY ABUSE

DEAR D. : I promised to write you some letters from Spain, and I owe you an apology for so long deferring it. The truth is, I am somewhat of the opinion of De Amicis, that one should write his experiences on the *nihil nisi bonum* plan, and there is so little good to be said about Spain that it is scarcely worth the postage. It has finally struck me that if I were to write you a few pages of hearty abuse of the country and the people, I might thus get rid of some of the bile I have been accumulating for the last three months, and so put myself in condition to be passably amiable thereafter. And you will please understand that I intend to be as abusive as I possibly can.

. I wish at once to correct the statement that traveling in Spain has become safe. We are told that the railroads and the *guardia civile* have scattered the brigands, and that the brigands are now forced to keep hotels.

The brigands are not suppressed, since the European papers are now full of the horrible murders committed by the brethren of " the black hand " in Malaga and thereabouts.

This civil guard consists in part of a very active, and, I believe, very daring, mounted patrol, which keeps the country apparently safe. I have seen one of these fellows, in his handsome uniform and plumed sombrero, ride alone into Granada with three or four prisoners following him on foot, shackled together and chained to his saddle. I thought at the time what a prize he would have been for a French painter in search of a new subject for the salon; and very handsome and picturesque he looked, with his plumes waving and his rifle carelessly slung across his back. I also wondered how many reals he would take to let his prisoners escape. I might as well say here, that however brutal or dishonest we may consider the Spaniards to be, no one can accuse them of being cowardly. I think them by far the bravest of the Latin races.

The duplicity of the Spaniard is historic. Their utter want of moral sense, especially among the better class, is something amazing; but the magnificent rascality of a Spanish innkeeper is of the nature of a disease. It is a monomania.

As I was leaving one of the largest and most honest hotels that I know in Southern Spain, one of the men employed in the house asked if my bill had been paid. I replied that I had paid it the evening before. "Never pay in advance, Señor," he said, "or you may have to pay twice."

"But," said I, "I took a receipt."

"That," said he, "makes no difference in Spain."

Of course when I speak of Spaniards I don't mean the Spanish Moors, who still form the bulk of the working classes over large districts. These latter, as for instance in the province of Murcia, are a warm-hearted, jolly, rather honest people, hospitable and not ungenerous. But conceive of applying either of the above epithets to a true Spaniard! Please recall your own experience of the country, and try to imagine to yourself a generous or hospitable, or, heavens above, a jolly Spaniard! Do you remember them at the Alhambra hotels, sitting for hours before their thin Bordeaux wines,— Val de Peñas not being good enough for them,—with the corners of their hypocritical mouths drawn down to their chins? Did you ever hear one of them laugh? I never did, nor even see one smile, except it was to cheat his neighbor out of a real,—how I love the word,—a real, a royal—the king's own coin—twopence halfpenny.

I think the Spaniard is, and always was from the days of the Incas to now, a parsimonious, superstitious barbarian. There is no nation of any race or color which ranks with them for ignorant, selfish brutality. The history of Spain is like the history of a marauding herd of wild animals.

You wouldn't believe how much better I feel after letting fly my real opinion of these people. There has been such a lot of humbug written about the country that it is a great comfort to knock it about a little, a very little; for you must understand that I might write a volume without fully expressing myself.

The late Professor Clifford was not only a singular combination of a poet and a mathematician, but he seems to have been one of the most genial and kind-hearted of men. In his published letters he gives a much worse account of the Spaniards than I do. The ladies of his party, walking alone in the streets of Granada, were stoned. This could not have happened merely because they were walking alone, as Professor Clifford suggests, for I have often seen Granadine ladies without any attendant. Probably it was because they were strangers, or wore bonnets, or more likely because they were in Spain. I don't know any other country where such a thing could happen in peaceful times and in the public streets of a principal city.

Professor Clifford also states, if I remember rightly, that the Spanish post office officials steal the letters to get the stamps, a real being quite a temptation to these gentlemen. This might account for the fact that very few of the letters posted by me in Spain ever came to hand,—a thing that has never happened to me in any other country.

There is one eminent Spanish trait that I don't feel I have yet done justice to. The sober Spaniard, as somebody terms him,—I dare say it is Washington Irving, whom may God pardon the woe he has wrought to the Anglo-Saxon traveler and the hotel to which he has been godfather,—the sober Spaniard is sober because he is too economical to be self-indulgent. The Spaniard is the stingiest man in the world.

A number of friends have told me that the Spanish gentleman never invites foreigners to his house, because of his jealous sensitiveness, and all that. Don't believe it. He is about as jealous and just as sensitive as the poor brute of a bull whom he mangles and maltreats for his one amusement.

The whole hill of the Alhambra is a monument to Spanish parsimony, past and present. Why, no sooner had they driven away that harmless, good-hearted, poor devil of a king, Boabdil el Chico, the last good king that ever was in Spain, who ran away and got himself killed on another continent in another man's quarrel,—no sooner had they dispossessed this little Moor than we find the Catholic king and queen driving a pitiful bargain with Christopher Columbus for the possession of a continent of which all three of them perfectly knew the existence, haggling like shopkeepers, letting him out of the door, and calling him back as he crossed the threshold to finally come to terms. From the hill of the Albaycin you may see the very spot where the queen's messengers overtook him. Was there ever such a picture of a stingy, lying, beggarly, twopenny halfpenny king and queen?

If you wish a companion picture, look at Carolus Quintus pulling down half the Alhambra to build up his hulking bull ring of a palace, which he was too poor to finish,—an architectural abortion which still stands there in spite of the earthquakes that were his pretext for leaving it off. I will tell you by and by what the present Spanish king is doing with the poor remnant of this poor Alhambra.

The Spaniard is the most obstinate of all known creatures. What he was in the days of Isabella, what he was in the days of the Inquisition, he is now, and always will be until he is wiped out by a recolonization of his country.

As he trimmed his beard in the days of Boabdil, so he has trimmed it to this day. The portraits in the Generaliffe bear me witness, not to quote the work of Titian and Velasquez. From the Castilian noble, with a head like a mummy, to the Grenadine peasant, with a face like a pug dog, they have not changed a feature in four hundred years. Buccaneers and beggars they were and are, and of all beggars the most offensive. I would rather a hundred times meet the ragged, cowardly ruffian of a French peasant, with his loaf under his arm and his insinuating whine. "C'est tres sec, M'sieur," than the persistent, shrill iteration of the Spanish beggar, "Señorito, uno chavetto! Señorito, una cosetta!" followed by his thin smile of thanks, "God will repay it to you in health." Well, even a centimo's worth of health would be a desirable blessing among the influenzas, and chills and fever of Granada.

I have always considered, Horace to the contrary notwithstanding, that every opera should begin with a chorus. The resources of my establishment not permitting such a display, I have treated you instead to as loud a blast as I can command, and I wish you may like it half as well as I do. I would like to blow away some of the cobwebs of romance that Irving, and Gautier, and De Amicis have woven about this land of prosaic begging and stealing.

The other day, strolling about up in the native town here,—for truth will out, and you see I am writing from Africa, and not from Europe, praise be to Allah,—I met a great broad-shouldered, six-foot Arab, marching along among his neighbors, lifting up his voice and weeping heartily, like a child, wiping the running tears with his brown knuckles. How do I know what he was crying about? Perhaps there was a dead baby in the little white cabin, or perhaps his wife had beaten him about the head with her slipper, because he had brought her kunnafeh with honey of the sugarcane, instead of kunnafeh with bee's honey.

Do you know, the honesty of the man's grief was a perfect luxury to me. Here was something unaffected and straightforward. I was out of Spain at last. Thank God, here in dusty Oran every now and then an honest man stalks by in a ragged burnous. The sun pours down on the many-domed mosque below my window, and, hark! at this very instant, up there in the green and white tiled minaret against the dark-blue sky, the sweet-voiced muezzin sings his plaintive prayer to a God in whom he believes.

Vane usted con Dios.

(*To be continued.*)

ORAN, October, 1882.

NOTE.—The above letter was written under circumstances that will explain themselves sufficiently to any traveler in Spain. I retain it, from a painter's feeling that any strong impression, even if incomplete, is worth preserving. To sum up the matter, the Spaniards are brave, industrious, frugal, independent, irresistibly charming in manner, treacherous, cunning, heartless, and politically ungovernable. They have a more reckless bravery than the Italians, more personal charm than the French, and more thrift than ourselves. On the other hand, the Spaniard seems to me to be without the logical directness of the French, the patience of the Italians, and the "enterprise" of the Americans.

1897.

¶ One of the most discouraging signs of the times is the dominance of the commercial spirit in art and literature. To this can be charged the vulgarity of much present-day work. A man does not write less than his best because he has a taste for that sort of thing, but because that seems to be the kind of work that brings the greatest return. The public seize upon the medium because it is so alluringly spread before them, and so artfully advertised. The artist lends his skill to their demand for more, and author and reader, reader and author, continue to react on each other until one wonders at the end. Trading upon reputation is done to-day as never before. A man hits upon an ingenious plot, a striking situation, and forthwith a work is put upon the bookstalls that meets with success. His name becomes blazoned in light, publishers besiege him with requests for "more," enterprising journalists interview his groom, and tell whether he takes one lump of sugar or two in his coffee. Money is spread before him; he has but to reach out his hand to enjoy every luxury. He writes fast and furiously, everything, anything; the public buy eagerly, until suddenly they find that he is not the great artist they had imagined from his first book, — and he is cast aside. Another man leaps into his place, and the farce is again played. No one seems to gain wisdom by the experience of others, and especially is this true of the momentarily successful author. Not content to refuse the present for the future, and make his position secure, he will continue to write rubbish as long as he can trade upon his name, forgetful that a name is but poor capital at best.

All this has been said and noted many times, but the extent to which authors of some just pretense to a substantial claim on the attention of their contemporaries have been tainted by the commercial spirit, has been passed over in silence.

It is becoming more and more the custom to make a single new story the excuse for a fresh volume. Perhaps two or three new stories appear in the magazines; the writer at once selects enough more to make up a volume, and a "new book by Mr. ——, the famous author," is announced. His admirers hasten to purchase it, only to find that they are the victims of a fraud. This is as distinctly "obtaining money on false pretenses" as any method known to the police courts. No wonder that *fin de siecle* literature is marked by degeneration!

¶ *The Chap-Book* has been casting some very pertinent jibes at *The Bookman.* Fie, little boy, remember the respect due to gray hairs, even if they are a mark of prosiness !

¶ *The Lark* says, " A Profit is not without Honour save in Boston."

¶ In spite of the fact that one doesn't believe in superstitions, it always gives a little feeling of recklessness to tempt fate by disregarding the warnings of the omen-wise. A lady of my acquaintance says that she never feels quite so daring when she braves a real danger, as she does when she starts something on a Friday, or sits at table with thirteen.

¶ *The Chap-Book* announces an important change in its size and form. Henceforth it is to assume a place with the many. Alas, that this should be ! From the time when it began to print the work of that inveterate hack, Mr. R. Harding Davis, we foresaw the end. " It wishes to invite criticism as a literary and critical journal of the first rank." Doubtless its wishes will be granted, and the " criticism" will be forthcoming. Next, we expect to see *The Lark* take up the function of a homiletic review. God save the mark !

¶ A KNOWLEDGE of the world makes a man either charitable or cynical ; therein lies the difference in men.

¶ " Yes, he's a good fellow, but —— " " Yes, she's a nice girl, but —— " After that " but" comes the real opinion. It doesn't matter much what the first part of the sentence is, it is always the qualifying part that sticks in our minds and influences us in forming opinions. Why should this little, minor, qualifying clause be the most important member of the sentence ? It is always so, even when the qualification adds to, rather than detracts from, one's character. " Yes, he drinks, but he is a good fellow." " He is a good fellow, but he drinks." Which sentence gives us the better opinion of its subject ? Oh the power of qualification ! May those who criticise me put the bad points first, and follow them by the soothing benediction of the good ones !

¶ *The London Times* has been devoting space in its columns recently to " The German Band Nuisance," and one of its correspondents gives the following simple but efficacious method of silencing these torments. He says that " when a brass band struck up opposite his house he sent his page boy out armed with half a fresh lemon. The boy stationed himself in full view of the performers and proceeded to suck the lemon, making contortions of his face the while expressive of the sensation produced by the intense acid. In a short time this spectacle produced a sympathetic contortion of the lips of the bandsmen, which rendered it impossible for them to continue playing their instruments. They abruptly stopped the performance and went away in disgust."

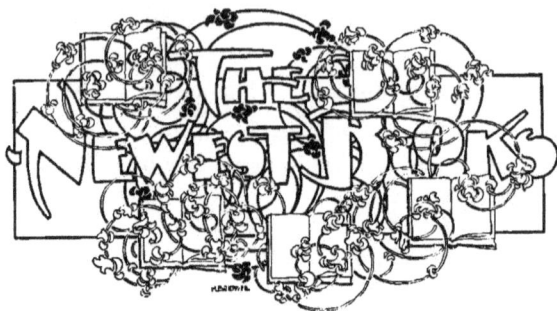

¶ "IN the Quarter." "The Latin Quarter" of Paris is the Mecca of all young artists. All who have spent a period in this fascinating place, and all who hope to do so, should read Mr. Chambers' novel of student life. (F. Tennyson Neeley, $1.25.)

¶ DR. NORDAU makes Herr Bärwald say of "The Comedy of Sentiment": "The story is typical. It might serve as a warning to others. It has such an edifying moral—veracity forever!" In this book Dr. Nordau has traced the story of a man and a woman who care very little for each other, but who make impassioned love for 278 pages, and separate by mutual agreement at the end. The author has very cleverly analyzed the mental conditions that accompany such an unusual state of affairs, and has succeeded in infusing interest into an uninteresting subject. (F. Tennyson Neeley, $1.50.)

¶ IT does not take one deeply versed in literature to distinguish the sex of an author, especially when that author treats of the illicit relations of the sexes. "Life the Accuser," by E. F. Brooks (Edward Arnold, N. Y., cloth, $1.50), needs not to be twice read to reveal the woman's point of view behind it. The story is the one that has been told so often in late years,—the wronged wife, the seduced girl who is kept from the lover to whom in all reason she belongs, the unhappy love affairs of several innocent people who are thrown entirely out of balance, apparently, because the straying husband married before he met the heroine, and so forth. Yes, it is the old scene: the stage-setting is the same, but somehow the actors are different, and therein lies the interest of the book. The analysis of motive and the construction of character save the book from mediocrity, and give it a degree of life.

¶ JOEL CHANDLER HARRIS is sure of a permanent place in literature, because of his wonderful knack of story telling. His new novel, "Sister Jane," is an agreeably written tale of old-time Southern life. The portrayal of character is decidedly the strongest side of the book. Its plot is weak, and lacks unity. (Houghton, Mifflin & Co., $1.50.)

❧ MAGAZINE readers have of late often had their attention attracted by the quatrains of Philip Becker Goetz. His verses, always marked by seriousness of purpose and beauty of expression, have appeared at intervals. A dramatic poem by him, his first extended essay, is just published. Although somewhat tedious as a whole, touches of much beauty occur.

> " For as night,
> Opposed to purple west, rises from the sea,
> So sorrow comes from gladness, lighting so
> A thousand stars, else ever undescried !' "

(Peter Paul Co., $1.25.)

❧ MR. LE GALLIENNE has given us in the " Quest of the Golden Girl " (published by John Lane, the Bodley Head, and sold for $1.50), a most charming nineteenth century idyl. This most un-English of the English writers is always delightful, in prose or in poetry, and his modern " Sentimental Journey " should be read by all who love a ramble through quiet country lanes and the hospitality of quaint country inns. An occasional touch of cynicism, always graceful and never mordant, adds to the flavor of the book.

❧ TEACHING the art of writing by lectures is as easy as giving swimming instruction on dry land. As far as it may be done, however, Arlo Bates has succeeded in " Talks on Writing English." Mr. Bates is admirably fitted for the task he has assumed : poet, novelist, journalist, and professor, he has had experience in all the lines of literary work, and speaks with the security of a man who thoroughly understands his art. (Houghton, Mifflin & Co., $1.50.)

❧ THREE little volumes of verse have reached us from Copeland & Day this month : " Gold Stories of '49," by " A Californian "; " A Boy's Book of Rhymes," by Clinton Scollard ; and " More Songs from Vagabondia," by Bliss Carman and Richard Hovey. " A Boy's Book of Rhymes " will be enjoyed by all boys from ten to fifty years old, for its charming little sketches in verse and its thorough sympathy with the things that make a boy's life worth while. The vigorous verse in Carman and Hovey's book makes one long to be off on a tramp :—

> " Loafing under ledge and tree,
> Leaping over boulders,
> Sitting on the pasture bars,
> Hail fellow with storm or stars."

The Red Letter

An Illustrated Monthly

Edited by Harry Draper Hunt
Under the art direction of E. B. Bird
Managed by H. W. Stephenson

The subscription rate is one dollar a year. Entered at the Boston Post Office as second-class mail matter. The trade supplied by the American News Company and its branches. Advertising rates on application.

The Red Letter Magazine,

Boston.

¶ THE RED LETTER aims to represent the best work of the younger authors and artists. Contributions will receive careful attention.

¶ THE special features of the February number will be illustrated articles on Florence England and Maxfield Parrish, and the second installment of Marcus Waterman's series on Spain. Mr. Pendleton will contribute a story entitled "Mrs. Black's Sixth Sense."

¶ ORDERS for single copies of the first three numbers of THE RED LETTER can now be filled.

Number One	.	.	.	.	.	15 cents.
Number Two	.	.	.	.	.	25 cents.
Number Three	.	.	.	.	.	15 cents.
Number Four	.	.	.	.	.	15 cents.

Mason & Hamlin

FRANK WOOD, PRINTER, BOSTON

The Red Letter:

For February
1897 · Vol·1 · No·6
Price 10¢

I will while away an hour or so with picturings and printing

Contents

Contents for January

FLORENCE PEARL ENGLAND

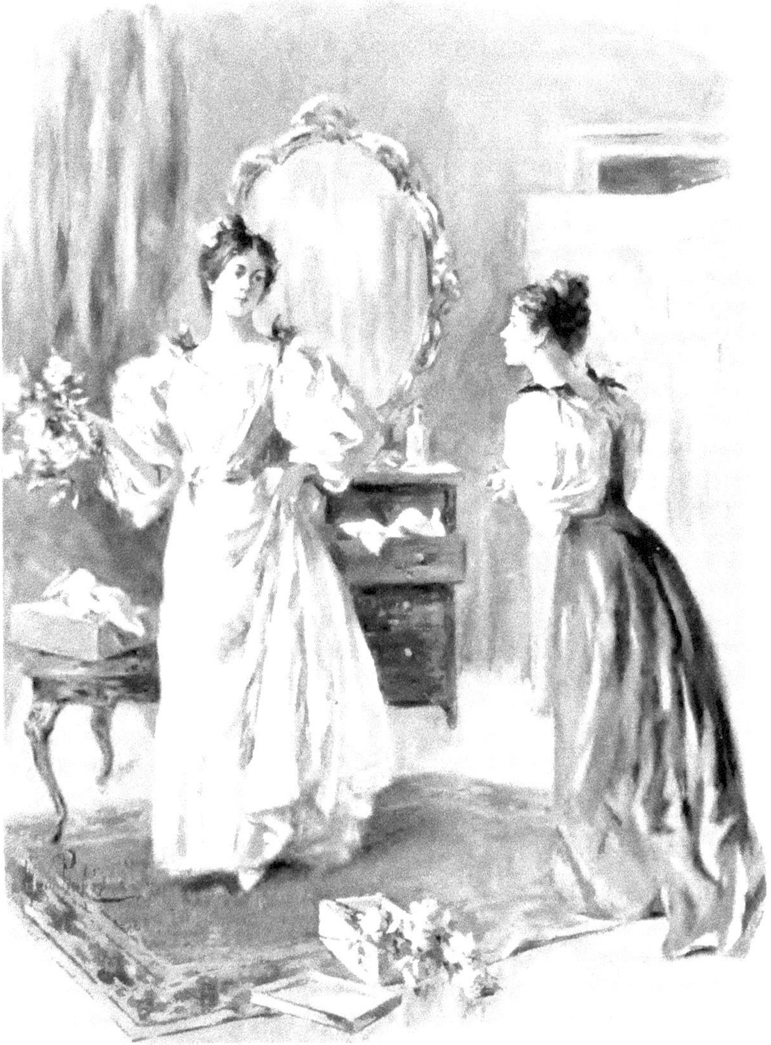

Permission of Lippincott's

The Red Letter

An Illustrated Monthly.

"'T will while away an hour or so with picturings and print."—MARLOWE.

At Sunrise

DARK-MANTLED Night, the star-eyed and the dumb,
Flees when she hears the sun god's chariot wheels;
When at her throat, from out his hand, there comes
A javelin of light, she dying reels,
And her heart's life-blood, as it ebbs away,
Dyes crimson the white garments of the Day.

S. Raymond Jocelyn

A Butterfly Net

MY host Arnold and I were smoking on the terrace of his place in Kent.

It was a perfect night.

Snatches of music and an hum of voices came from the drawing room, fountains plashed below, and a wakeful bird twittered in the great elm near the house.

"It is a good time for your story," I suggested. "You say Mrs. Arnold does not enjoy hearing it, and we are not likely to be interrupted."

"While the Bishop holds the company with the tale of his ride to Islington? Yes; he is good for an hour, at least. Well, have a cigar;" and setting himself in his lounging chair, Arnold began.

"It is two years ago this winter that I decided to go over to Arizona for a rare specimen of Yucca moth, found only at the head waters of the Colorado. My entomological hobby has led me into some strange corners of the world, as you know. But when a man attains my position in a science,— I say it with modesty,—a good deal is expected of him; and there is little I would not do for the glory of the Arnold name and the enriching of the Arnold Museum.

"Two years ago I was just thirty, and the only butterfly I had not studied was the butterfly woman. The great American desert was the last place I should have thought of finding one in. if I had had any thoughts on the subject. The first thing I did when I boarded the Mariposa. a little stern wheeler that kicks her way for three hundred miles up the Colorado, was to fall over a pile of luggage on the deck,—a small arsenal of guns, rifles, and ammunition. I was burdened with my leather cases and portfolios for specimens. sponges. chloroform bottles, and butterfly nets. In these days we do not transfix our victims with pins, and let them die by slow degrees of torture. A drop of chloroform on a sponge in an air-tight vessel does the business as thoroughly, and a good deal more humanely and expeditiously. While I was struggling with my scattered belongings, I heard a girl's voice at my elbow : 'Don't bother with my traps, please : I will have one of the guides stow them away presently,' it said. Looking round in the moonlight.—the Mariposa leaves her wharf at Yuma in the evening,—I saw a dainty bit of femininity in a Lincoln-green leather hunting skirt and leggings, a pale yellow suéde shirt. and a big *sombrero*, decorated with trout flies and leaders. A cartridge belt served her for a girdle, in which gleamed the silver mountings of a revolver and a hunting knife.

" At the moment she looked more like a lunar moth than anything else. with the little rings of fair hair escaping from under the rim of her hat. the healthy pallor of her cheeks heightened by the moonlight and the faint shadows beneath her eyes. A lunar moth adrift in a sirocco would have seemed less out of place than this exquisite creature. abroad on Arizona's savage river.

" I soon discovered that she was a mighty hunter, whose appointment with a mountain sheep and a cinnamon bear, in the Cum-pa-huit Cañon. four hundred miles up the river, was long overdue. She was barely five feet two. and weighed less than a hundred pounds, but her wrists were like steel, and she had the suppleness of the panther. Of course our acquaintance progressed rapidly. Her party consisted of her mother, Mrs. Sinclair. her big brother Tom. and the guides. It was surprising how soon this small creature's contempt for my sober science began to bother me. It mattered nothing to her that a half dozen Universities had tacked degrees to my name. and that I might have constructed raiment from my medals and orders as glittering as the wings of my moths and butterflies. She considered me, from the first, a lunatic, at large in Arizona with a butterfly net and a bottle of chloroform : and I went further. after a few days in her sprightly company. and. like old Dogberry, ' wrote myself down an ass.'

" 'And so you're an entomologist.' she said, regarding me much as I should have examined a new grub. 'How funny ! I used to know an entomologist.' There are not many of my profession whom I have not met. so I asked her his name.

" 'Dickie Jones, of Yale, the captain of the football team,' she said demurely. 'Don't you know him? He is awfully scientific. You should see his horrid daddy longlegs and spiders tacked up all over his rooms in Durfee. And his butterflies,—tiger swallow-tails, he called them. Of course the Yale men wouldn't have them there, so he gave them to a friend in Princeton, who wore them all around his hat at the last Yale-Princeton football game. And Princeton won! Dickie is in India now. I hope to get over there and shoot a Bengal tiger, yellow with black stripes, you know, just like the dear boy's butterflies.'

" Although this conversation occurred early in my acquaintance with Miss Sinclair, I could have cheerfully choked Dickie with a spongeful of chloroform, and impaled him on a hat-pin in my museum.

" 'Don't go to India,' I urged. 'You have to shoot tigers in a jungle, you know,—and a jungle is a beastly place.'

" 'Oh! then you know something about them?' she asked, her pretty brows lifted in surprise.

" 'Yes,' I said. 'I did India for tarantulas.'

" 'And have you ever seen a tiger?' "

" 'You always see a tiger if you're out for a tarantula,' I replied. 'It's the fellow after the tiger who gets the tarantula.'

" 'Of course you've never shot one,' she said, with some scorn in her voice.

" 'Why, no,' I said, slowly. 'I was on the Arachnids, you know.'.

" She gave a little shudder. 'Ugh!' she exclaimed. And then she smiled, as if reassured by a thought. 'I suppose its better than having the Arachnids on you,' she said.

" When we got better acquainted, she confided to me her pet scheme for illustrating the alphabet with stuffed animals; an Aard wolf for an a, a babale for a b, a dhole for a d, down to the quagga and the zebu. Of course I had seen them all in their habitats, and told her so.

" 'And I dare say you've stumbled over a Tasmanian devil, too,' she exclaimed, ' when you were in hot pursuit of a darning needle!'

" I related a story of my adventures in Abyssinia, when I came near getting a zebu for a zebub. A zebub is a big fly that makes it lively for the zebu.

" ' I thought I had a little fly
My silken net within,'

she improvised, quick as thought, adapting the language of 'Sylvia and Bruno.'

" ' I looked again; it was an ox!
Imagine my chagrin.'

" 'Oh, but you don't need a net for the zebub!' I cried, triumphantly. ' He is a clumsy insect, awfully slow, and easy to catch.'

" Then, by Jove, she asked me demurely if there 'was an English as well as an African zebub?'

" She knew very well that there was, and that I was that wretched bug. A man is at a tremendous disadvantage when he falls in love with the first girl he has ever had more than a casual acquaintance with. The life I led on that Mariposa! I began to pity the poor insects with which my museum in Kent was frescoed. It was the old story of the moth and the candle. I suppose it was poetic justice that having gone out into the wilderness to slay moths, I should myself have been made captive.

" Day by day the country around us grew more wild and solitary. I say solitary, but it was alive with Indians, and the shores of the river blazed with fires at night and echoed with hideous noises.

" One day a party of Indians came on board the boat, as they often did, to show their blankets and bead trumpery. Mrs. Sinclair was an enthusiastic collector of Indian curios, and all but one of the creatures had gathered around her.

" Miss Sinclair was sitting alone on the other side of the deck, reading. I heard a little scream, and saw her pinned in a corner of the deck shielding herself with her hands from a young brave, who was bending over her, his hot breath on her face. Quick as a flash I had reached him and knocked him down. He picked himself up, with a slow smile that showed his teeth, but had no mirth. · There's your Tasmanian devil, Miss Sinclair,' I said, as he slunk across the deck.

·" The captain seemed disturbed when I told him about the affair. · It's the season for the Indian snake dances,' he said, · and bad whiskey goes with snake dances. You have to handle these vermin with gloves.'

··· I should prefer it.' I replied, flicking the dust from my hands with my hankerchief. I mention this trifling incident because it has everything to do with my story. It was natural enough that by the time the boat reached her last landing, I should receive an invitation from Sinclair to join their camping party; and as I was hopelessly in love with his sister, and took no pains to conceal the fact from any one, least of all herself, I seized the opportunity it afforded me to be with her.

" I fancied I rose a peg in her favor when she discovered that I could use my fists as well as a butterfly net.

" It was odd," my friend Arnold said meditatively, as he stopped to relight his cigar, " that for the first time in her life Miss Sinclair missed her shot at both the cinnamon bear and the mountain sheep. I can only account for this, and the fact that I brought them down, each in a single shot, by the explanation that the stars were fighting for me as they did against Sisera. It piqued Sylvia, for so I always called her in my thoughts, that a mere murderer of moths, a butcher of butterflies, a killer of caterpillars, should outdo her in her own field. I enjoyed her pretty petulance, and perhaps I should have been more than human if I had not enjoyed, too, my small triumph.

"When I invited her, with a spice of mischief, to join my moth hunts, she shook her head dolefully and said : 'No; the only bugs I could catch are the scarabs that you find in the museums of antiquities. They can't be scarce or shy, judging by the exhibits.'

"I told her she was the bravest little girl I had ever seen. 'You would walk right up to a bear's jaws,' I said.

"'Yes,' she replied quickly, 'that's just what I have done. Walked up to his jaws and shot over his head!'

"She was pretty nearly right. The shot she had at the bear was an easy one. But who can fight fate?

"'I shall get something out of this expedition,' she declared to me the night following the day I had killed the mountain sheep. 'You shall not have all the glory,' with a glance at the tree where the bear's hide hung. 'I believe that I am on the verge of a discovery,' she added.

"'Nothing,' she said, 'escaped me;' and the next day, when Mrs. Sinclair met me at the flap of her tent on my return from a moth hunt, crying excitedly, 'Where is Sylvia? Did she go with you? She has been away from camp for two hours, and neither Tom nor the guides have seen her,' I recalled Sylvia's remark about discovering something.

"'My God!' I cried to the guides, who stood around the camp fire. 'Don't you know the dangers to a woman abroad in this trackless country?' and for an instant I staggered with the weakness of fear. Scattering the men in different directions,—Tom was already in search of her,—and without stopping to relieve my pockets of my bottle of chloroform, my sponges, and my butterfly net, or to pick up a revolver, I plunged down the trail which I knew by a lover's instinct she had taken,—a trail which Sylvia and I had found a few days before, leading to some cliff dwellings. I had gone two miles, perhaps three, when I heard sounds,—voices rising into a strident chorus, dropping into a hideous yell from a single throat : 'Ai-ay, ai-ay; hyah, ay-ah! Ay-ah, ay-ah, ay-ah!' And then I recalled what the Captain had said about the Indians and their snake dances. That it was the season for the latter, I knew, and at once I associated the shouts I heard with some such festivity. God help anyone at the mercy of those fiends! You know the unearthly noises of which the common tomcat on your back fence is capable? Join to these the baying of a pack of hounds following hard the track of blood, and the wild, worrying cry of a tiger as she mouths and mangles her prey at midnight, and you can get some faint idea of the clamor that gained in volume as I climbed the cañon. It transpired that Sylvia had traveled this trail less than an hour before, determined to search the village of cliff dwellings which we had discovered together for something which should make her Arizona journey memorable. Throwing a rope over a projecting boulder, she had pulled herself up to the fifth story of a tower, and through a loophole into a square chamber leading to a narrow passage. This she entered on her hands and knees. It was quite dark. Her hands came in contact with what felt like tapestries, faintly moving in a ghostly wind. The dust of centuries rose in clouds around her. At the far end of the passage a light gleamed like a star. Nearing the light, a confusion of sounds reached her,—shouts and yells, the crash of cymbals, the rythmic tread of marching feet. What she saw in another instant must have frozen her blood. She had stopped on the verge of a cliff, a sheer fall of a hundred feet. Below her, in a rocky basin, fifty or sixty painted savages were dancing around a heap of squirming, writhing snakes. A fire burned in a ring about the snakes, from which one and another of the Indians seized brands, waving them above their heads. Foremost among the dancers Sylvia saw the young savage whom I had punished on the Mariposa. His lithe, copper-colored body glowed with the heat and the oils with which he was anointed. He took up the refrain, to which the others replied. Sylvia must have realized her danger, and drawn back within the shadow of the passage, but not before the Indian had caught a glimpse of her fair hair and the flutter of her skirt. He left the dancers, unobserved, and ran to the foot of the cliff at the same instant that Sylvia, flinging herself upon her face, tried to pull herself back to the tower, hoping to gain the ground by the way she had come. Midway her head came in contact with a rock, evidently detached from the wall of the passage since she had last traversed it.

" It completely blocked her exit.

" In agony she ran her hands over the rock's smooth surface for a crevice. There was none. Below, she fancied she could hear the Indian's quick breathing and the soft smiting of his moccasined feet upon the cliff, as he nimbly scaled the height.

" ' Help! help! ' she cried, wildly. ' I am lost! ' She beat the rock with all her strength, bruising her head and her hands in her frenzy. Then something seemed to give away in her brain, and she fell forward, mercifully unconscious, clutching the ghostly tapestries. She did not hear my shouts, poor child, nor feel the tremor of the wall as I flung myself against the rocky barrier that separated me from her. Hurrying along the trail, half maddened by the unearthly uproar of the Indians, I reached the foot of the tower, and, looking up, saw the rope and Sylvia's scarlet handkerchief, lying like a cactus blossom on the rim of one of the tower's portholes.

" ' She is in there,' I said to myself, and a sickening wave of horror surged up from my heart, choking and blinding me. In another instant I heard her faint cries. ' I am coming, I am coming," I shouted, pulling myself up by the rope, and with difficulty dragging myself along the passage. I came to the boulder, and for an instant hope died in me."

Arnold paused, and by the light of the fusee which he had struck I could see that his face was pale, and his hands shook.

"It was only for an instant," he went on, recovering himself. "All I cared for on earth was divided from me by that cursed wall of rock. 'Sylvia! Sylvia!' I cried, putting my mouth to the wall. No answer came from the other side. The strength of a dozen men possessed me as I tore at the boulder. It moved slightly. Then, with my shoulders against it, and my feet braced upon the opposite wall of the passage, I made a final mighty effort. The stone slipped aside, disclosing, in the faint light, Sylvia lying along the passage, unconscious, and an Indian's head just appearing above the edge of the cliff. I had no weapons, nothing but the butterfly net and the bottle of chloroform. In an instant I had made a desperate resolve. Saturating a large sponge with chloroform, and fastening it securely in the meshes of the net, I tossed it lightly over the Indian's head as he raised his shoulders to the level of the floor of the passage. Then I twisted the handle until I had drawn the silken cords of the net tightly around the creature's throat.

"The whole thing was done so quickly, and the Indian was so completely off his guard, that he made no resistance. His hands were occupied with holding himself up by the cliff's edge, the fumes of the chloroform choked him, the wet sponge filled his mouth as he opened it to yell. Although his eyes were blinded, he instinctively pulled himself up into the passage. I drew myself toward him, and jumped upon him like a tiger, bending his head back and completing the work of partial asphyxiation. The Indian gurgled and struggled as he battled blindly with me, before he succumbed to the strange power of the chloroform. I baptized the sponge again liberally from the bottle. Limp and apparently lifeless, turned upon his face, his nose buried in the sponge, it was not difficult to bind the thongs of leather from the Indian's scanty dress firmly around his arms and legs. Then tearing down the blankets which had hung in their place through those uncounted years, awaiting their last service, I tied them securely over the brute's face and around his throat. How I managed to get back to the tower with Sylvia, and down the rope, I do not know. Less than a week afterward we were all on board the Mariposa again, homeward bound; and from the fact that Sylvia finished a letter to my father which I had begun, you can gather that I made fair progress in my courtship. The letter began in my handwriting:—

'ON BOARD THE MARIPOSA, Feb. 2, 18—.

"'DEAR DAD:—

"'I've got the moths. [That was my announcement. Then followed in Sylvia's Gothic characters:] 'One fluttered around my net for a long while before I caught it. It is called a "Sylvia Genus, Puella Americana, habitat Washington Square, New York." It will bear transplanting to Kent. Indeed, I may safely say that it will do well wherever I am, whether in Kent or Kamschatka. It is devoted to its captor. Funny, eh? Not so funny when you learn that I saved it from deadly peril at the risk of my life, and that for a month I have lighted its sky with a flame of gracious service. But gratitude is not love. Sylvia loves me. Will you not love Sylvia for the sake of

Your affectionate son,

ANACREON ARNOLD.'"

．　　．

The Bishop's and Arnold's story ended simultaneously. There was laughter again in the house, a little space of silence, and then Mrs. Arnold's voice called through the window,—

" Anak, Anak, come and sing Sylvia."

" It is her favorite song." Arnold said to me. " Do you care to come in and hear it?"

" I will listen to it here." I replied; and a moment later I saw my host standing beside his wife, his hand upon her shoulder, as she played the accompaniment to Schubert's delightful song:—

> " Who is Sylvia? What is she,
>> That all her swains commend her?
> Holy, fair, and wise is she;
>> The heavens such grace did lend her
> That adored she must be.

> " Then to Sylvia let us sing,
>> That Sylvia is excelling.
> She excels each mortal thing
>> Upon this dull earth dwelling;
> To her, garlands let us bring."

Mary Wakeman Botsford

THE
MASK
AND
WIC
CLUB
UNIVERSITY
OF
PENNSYLVANIA

A Clever Master of the Grotesque

ROTESQUENESS in art work requires the saving grace of a masterly execution if it is to be classed under Art with a big A. Readers of THE RED LETTER for last December will recall the frontispiece, " Humpty Dumpty," with its humorous suggestiveness and its marvelous execution of detail. More striking still was the cover of the Christmas *Harper's Weekly*, marked by the same vivid humor and cleverness in the production of effect by limits. Both drawings were signed Maxfield Parrish, and both were characterized by the same originality and strength.

Mr. Parrish has done a great deal of elaborate fresco work, and in this line of work is best known by his delicacy of color and graceful line drawings. In poster work he has won so many prizes that he is called the " American Poster Competition Winner." His best-known posters are those designed for H. O., Columbia Bicycles, and the *Century*, although seen only as exhibited by their owners. The work by which he is most widely known is, of course, the cover work he has done for *Harper's Weekly*, *Bazar*, and *Round Table*. His work is always characterized by the same men with attenuated members, decidedly irregular features, and a world of expression in their bead-like eyes and pursed-up cheeks. Mr. Parrish can suggest more by a few dotes and dashes than most men can convey by the most elaborate portrait work. Taken out from the drawings, a series of the mouths, eyes, and noses of his men would look like a shorthand alphabet, but in their proper places they are the most expressive features imaginable.

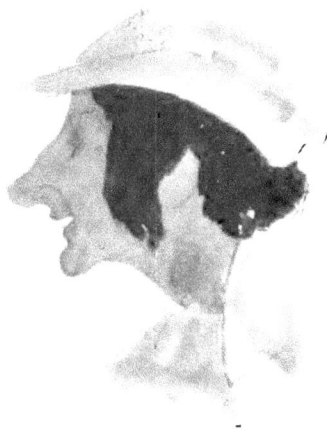

In the series of illustrations of Mr. Parrish's work herewith produced, the cover for the " Journal of the Edwin Booth Shakespeare League" shows his decorative power; the cover for the " Mask and Wig Club" announcement his characteristic figure drawing; the initial heading this article his careful working out of detail, and his impress of individuality on every stroke of his pencil, even in his trees and rocks; the sketch of a head set in the text, his cleverness with the grotesque; and the illustration of a silver lamp designed by him for the yacht Merlin, his contributions to the industrial arts.

Maxfield Parrish is in his twenty-seventh year. After attending Haverford College for some time he began his art study by a three-year course at the Pennsylvania Academy of the Fine Arts. Since that time he has busied himself in varied lines of work, always with success and increase of power. Of himself he says, simply, " Painting is my bent, the decorative, perhaps, more than the realistic or literal." Although eminently successful in whatever work he has undertaken, it is mainly in the future that we look to see Mr. Parrish's best work. A young man, his work has the faults of young men, and at the same time their freshness and crispness.

Harry D. Hunt

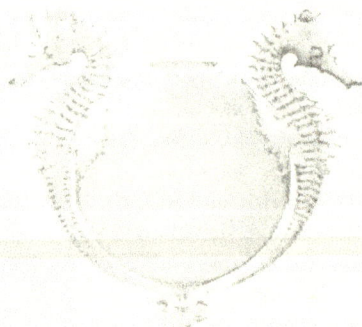

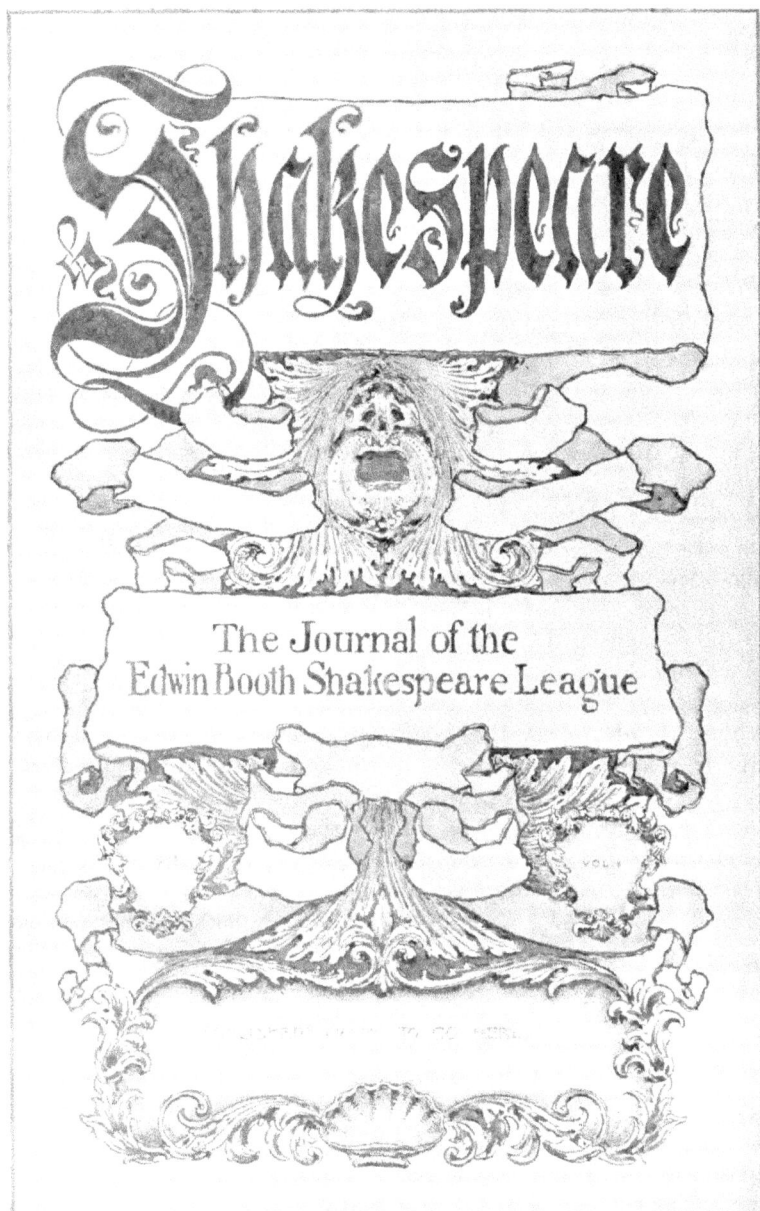

The Journal of the
Edwin Booth Shakespeare League

The Passing of the Savoy

T what is known as a " professional matinée," the other day, there sat together members of a box party, two young English people, who recall, to students of the arts, two widely differing exponents of black and white.

They were the son of the late George du Maurier, and the sister of Aubrey Beardsley.

Young du Maurier is a member of Mr. Tree's company of players; Miss Beardsley is an actress in Mr. Arthur Bourchier's company. Who shall say New York is not cosmopolitan?

About du Maurier, what is there left to say? His more genuine admirers, the followers of his sketches in *Punch*, have been overwhelmed as by an avalanche by the horde that flocked to the worship of " Trilby." As a pestilence " Trilby " has ceased, and not even the sight of Mr. Tree as Svengali has been able to fillip it back into life; but as an artist du Maurier will ever have a claim on immortality, in that his sketches, angular and often monotonous as they were, gave us a vivid and accurate picture of a phase of British society that was in actuality even more angular and more monotonous.

In the case of Aubrey Beardsley, his sister's presence here comes at a peculiarly appropriate moment, in that in some sort there is just come the end of another epoch in this curious young artist's career. The *Savoy*, the London periodical into which for exactly a year past the curious have delved for evidences of just what new eccentricities in black and white Mr. Beardsley was showing, has just ceased. It did this, moreover, in a fittingly novel manner. Two months before it died it calmly announced that with a certain issue, on a certain date, having then been alive one year, it would disappear. As against the " we are here to stay" tone of many publications hereabouts, followed presently by unexplained and continued silence, the method of the *Savoy* is decidedly pleasing.

To recapitulate the rise to prominence of Aubrey Beardsley were to re-tell too much that has been told. As far as concerns the *Savoy*, however, it may be said, that after Mr. John Lane's decision that Beardsley was too dangerous for the Yellow Book, seekers after Beardsley drawings were for a time left mourning. Mr. Leonard Smithers, however, presently came to the rescue with the *Savoy*. Mr. Smithers was the publisher; Mr. Arthur Symons, known as the author of " London Nights," and much other literature of the sort roughly called decadent, was the editor; and Mr. Beardsley was the Art director. It was first published as a quarterly, but only two such issues appeared. Some haze of success must have appeared on the horizon, for the announcement came that the periodical would appear monthly, instead of quarterly. The complete set, therefore, consists of two quarterly issues and six monthly.

As to the present health and industry of Aubrey Beardsley there could be no greater proof than this final, parting number of the *Savoy*. The entire art of the number is by this artist; it consists of no less than fourteen drawings, some of them full-page size. When one remembers the almost painful amount of detail that Beardsley now weaves into the draperies and backgrounds he is now wont to use, the quantity of labor implied by this is considerable.

In the interview that I had with Miss Beardsley, it was pleasant to note the affectionate enthusiasm with which she regarded him and his work. We spoke, of course, of his illness; that illness which many a sensational writer depicted so vividly here in America, that the public at large is somewhat of the opinion that Beardsley is dead.

"Yes," said Miss Beardsley, "he was dreadfully ill, poor fellow. It was in Brussels. I nursed him through it. But we really thought he was going to die, you know. And it was pathetic to hear him talk, and talk of what he was going to do when he got well,—all manner of big things! —when not one of us ever thought we would see him well again. He was very cheerful all through it. When he was convalescing he used to amuse himself reading some of the obituary notices that had been printed in American papers."

"And now?"

"Oh, he's getting on nicely. He's living in Boscombe, near Bournemouth. He went to town once or twice, but he couldn't stand it; it's his lungs that are affected, you see, and the London fog is death for him. So he stays up in the country, and works away steadily. His publisher, Mr. Smithers, has a book coming out, 'Fifty Drawings by Aubrey Beardsley,' that's to have all of his best work in. Aymer Vallance, a dear friend of his, has done an iconography of his work from the very beginning, and that's to go in this book. Then there are book covers, and such other things, coming out constantly."

"Does he ever think of coming to America?"

"O yes; he's often spoken of it. He's very curious about everything over here. He envied me a little about that, I think. It was through him, you know, that I got such nice engagements. He knew Mr. Tree, and got me an engagement in the Haymarket company; from there I went with Mr. Bourchier. Aubrey used to act, too, when he was at school. I dare say you can still find people in Brighton who saw him in amateur theatricals not more than ten years ago."

Remembering some of Mr. Beardsley's work, I felt like asking Miss Mabel if her brother were not still essentially an actor, in black and white; but I felt that it would be neither polite nor fair. You can't expect a sister to see anything but the good in a brother.

Besides, Beardsley is so original a force in modern black and white, so perpetually new, so never the same, that one may even forgive him the suspicion of posing. What one must find it harder to forgive is the ease with which the general public nowadays, understandingly, applies the word Beardsleyism to everything it does not appreciate. Heavens, some of the sketches to which I have heard that word applied !

Percival Pollard

Isaiah VI. 13

"**A**S a teil tree or an oak,"
   So the ancient prophet spoke,
" Whose heart is in them when they shed
   Their leaves ! " The prophet now is dead ;
But on a girl his mantle falls
And·heartens other funerals.

December stood in confidence,
   Winter long had pitched his tents,
When she and I together came
   Along a way without a name,
And there she bade me lift my head
The while those verses old she said.

A little oak above the snow
   I saw within the meadow grow,
A sturdy tree, not over high,—
   Some several inches more than I !
His leaves were gone, but in the air
His branches other beauty wear.

About him little whips of wind
   A wreath of winter sunlight bind.
The snow upon his feet is cold,
   But in his heart is more than gold,
And light that only winter knows
Springs up to blossom on the snows.

P. H. Savage

A Clever Young Illustrator

AMONG the younger Boston artists whose work in black and white has lately attracted considerable attention, Miss Florence Pearl England easily holds a high place. *Life, Truth, Puck, The New England Magazine, The Ladies' Home Journal, The Youth's Companion,* and many other well-known periodicals, have all had illustrations of hers within the past year or two, and she was the illustrator of one of the books published for the recent holiday season by the Lippincotts.

Miss England has lived in Boston only eight years. Although of New England descent, she was born in Milwaukee, and her early life was passed in the West. Her father, Rev. George A. England, was a well-known chaplain in the regular army, and until she came to Boston, Miss England lived chiefly at military posts. Her fondness for drawing showed itself very early. She could draw before she had learned to write.

Miss England received a good general education, largely under the supervision of her father, and studied and worked at her art in a somewhat desultory way before she came to Boston. There she studied for a time at the Cowles School, and later entered the School of Drawing and Painting at the Museum of Fine Arts as a regular student. She took the full course in much less than the usual time, and completed it in '93. Her chief teachers were Tarbell and Benson, and her work both in drawing and painting was ranked among the best work of the School.

Her winters since she left the Art Museum School she has spent in New York, studying part of the time at the Art League. Miss England's early

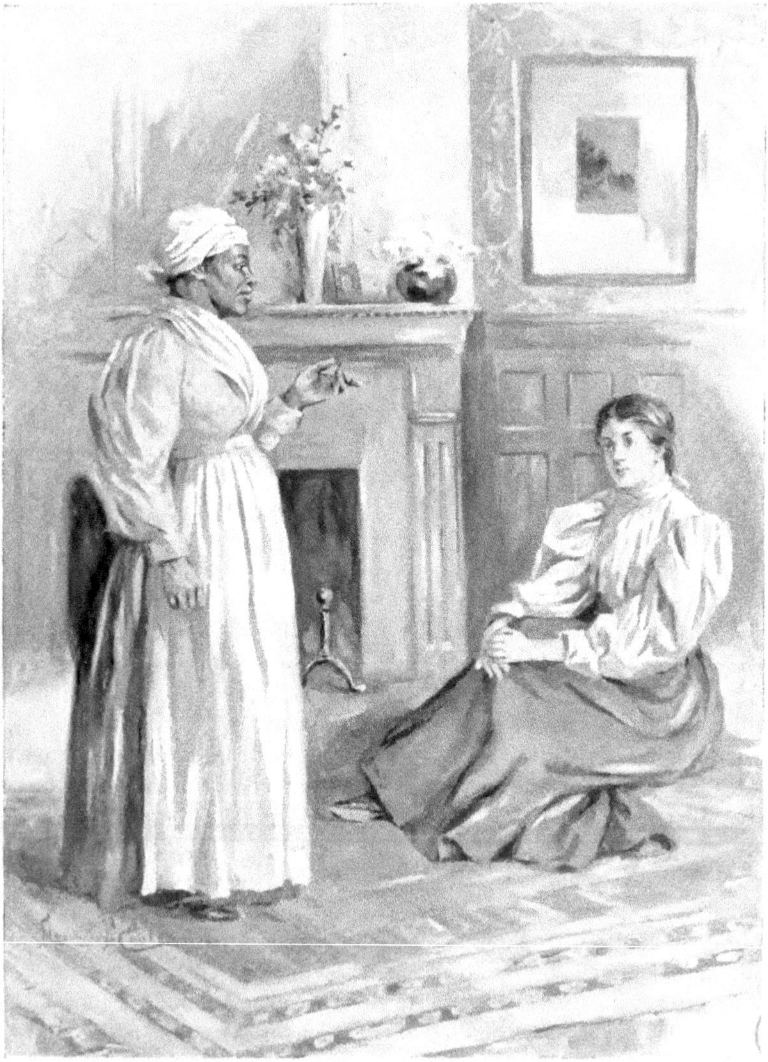

Permission of Lippincott's

color work was highly praised, and she hopes in the near future to resume it. But her greatest inclination has always been toward illustrating, and she has been glad to respond to the calls that have come to her for work in this line. Her special fancy is for drawing pretty girls and women, and she says that she would be contented to draw pretty faces and figures from morning to night. Sometimes she has been able to give herself free scope in this direction. Last winter, for example, *Puck* published a series of her graceful figures of young girls, sometimes in illustration of a bit of society verse, or more often without text or comment.'

Miss England has yielded herself very little to the poster fad, although she did a very charming poster of a Puritan girl for the Christmas '95 number of the *New England Magazine*, which was also taken as the design for the cover of the same issue of the magazine. The *Nickel Magazine* published an effective poster of hers the past autumn.

The most extensive pieces of illustrating thus far have been the drawings for Miss Helen Leah Reed's "Miss Theodora," a novelette which ran serially in 1895 in the *New England Magazine*, and her illustrations for Miss Amy Blanchard's "Betty of Wye," published this season by J. B. Lippincott & Co.

As Miss England is blessed with a keen sense of humor, has a good knowledge of literature, and is a careful student of human nature, her characterizations are true to life. In illustrating a book or a story she catches at once the author's meaning, and she seldom fails to please author as well as readers. She believes herself to be more realistic than imaginative, and it is true that she always works from a model. At the same time there is enough imagination in her work to take it out of the realm of the prosaic.

In the matter of technique she is a painstaking and careful draughtsman. Her pen and ink work is clever and effective, but her wash drawings are also highly praised. Since the publication of her first work, two or three years

ago, Miss England has shown rapid improvement. It is safe to say that if she continues to manifest the same energy in her chosen field, it will not be long before she has a leading place among our best illustrators.

Finally, for the personal word which is always expected, Miss England is of more than medium height, with a slender figure, and the blond complexion and golden hair of the purest Anglo-Saxon type.

Impressions of Southern Spain

II

GRANADA

SPAIN is a pie in which the plums are a hundred miles apart. To any Jack Horner in search of the Spanish picturesque I would recommend the following itinerary :—

Go first to Gibraltar. Run across the border and look at Algeciras. From Gibraltar take steamer to Tangier. From Tangier go to Oran and Algiers. From Algiers to Marseilles, and thence to Paris or Italy, as you think best.

If, however, you must travel through Spain, and especially if you have a few words of Spanish, take my advice and travel second class, always supposing that you are merely a man. If you are a man and his wife and a guidebook, making progresses from one English-speaking hotel to the next one, with the singular idea that you are seeing the country, I have no advice to give you. Follow the extraordinary directions which you will find printed in your Murray and your Bradshaw's special; be enthusiastic when you are told, and be very careful not to weep before the wrong picture, and go your way with God, as one says in Granada.

If, then, you are simply a man, and have wit enough to know that seeing the world includes seeing its inhabitants, travel in the second-class carriages. You can make yourself perfectly comfortable; the difference in expense is very great, and you will find, as I have (this is in strict confidence), that the second-class travelers in this world are sometimes more agreeable company than the first. How many kind words and kind attentions I have had from these good-hearted people! How pleasantly they pointed out to me the sights from the windows, and helped out my little Spanish with endless good nature! Never shall I forget a cold night journey to Madrid, into which I was surprised at half an hour's notice, and the good Samaritans who shared their lunch with me, and would not take "*gracias*" for an answer; and how jollily we finished together, first, their leather *botta* of Val de peñas, and last my leather *botta* of dry montilla, which, by a miracle of luck, I happened to have; until in the early dawn we saw the new comet rising, tail foremost, over the eastern horizon. How different was this jolly picnic, in this jolly low company (for I have reason to suspect that my companions really kept a shop in Madrid), from another night journey that I remember long ago in the Marseilles express, when my carriage was taken by storm by a large Englishwoman with two followers and a dog, who filled the whole compartment, and pushed me into a corner and looked pins and aromatic vinegar at me the whole night long, because the cushions smelled of tobacco. At four o'clock that November morning I ceased to be a conservative, and from that time I have had a fancy for riding second class. So it happened that I rode from Malaga to Granada with a lot of kind people, who took pains to tell me when and where to look out at the magnificent gorges through which the road bores its way; and so it was that instead of hurrying blindly through that wonderful mountain, a quick cry of "Mira, mira, Señor!" always prepared me for each new picture. You see, I must except these Malaguenos in my abuse of the Spaniards, and very glad I am to do so.

The landscape of Spain is very peculiar but very extraordinary, and upon the whole I think it is the grandest in character that I have ever seen. Doré, of all men, gives me the truest impression of the rugged mountain scenery; but the open landscapes, with the wide, desolate plains, the vast chains of far-off desolate mountains, a whole world of pitiless steel-gray patched with rust colors, formal rows of distant gray olive trees growing out of the ashy earth, great herds of goats and mules browsing where nothing is to be seen but sand and pebbles,—all this is unpaintable and inexpressible. No man could ever have rendered the character of this on canvas, unless it was Rousseau in his great days, before he succumbed to the pressure of the age, which converts art into an industry.

I have always thought that the best way to see any country was from the windows of a railway carriage; and the Spanish railways, with their ten mile an hour trains, wandering up and down like a turnpike road, around this mountain and through that one, and across the dreary, burned-up plains, give one an endless series of strange landscapes, with plenty of time to study them.

At a couple of hours distance from Malaga the railway climbs half way up a mountain range, and then pierces the summits in a series of a dozen or twenty tunnels. Between tunnel and tunnel one finds himself in the heart of the strangest conceivable mountain scenery.

Enormous cliffs, nearly perpendicular, ragged and eccentric forms, which would be proper enough in a broken boulder, but which seem wildly improbable on this tremendous scale, great cañons splitting the mountain asunder and going suddenly down out of sight, between whose walls you catch quick glimpses of the peaceful plain far below, and little level towns beside little trickling rivers, and then another shriek of the engine and another tunnel.

Everywhere the colors are the same. There is nothing but rock, dark gray rock patched with great masses of iron stains, varying from ochre color through all shades of dull reds to brownish purple. Grass I never saw growing in Southern Spain, either in the mountains or on the plains, except once in a little side street in Murcia,—where the women were kneeling beside the open aqueduct washing linen. I have often seen it for sale in the markets, carefully tied up in little bundles like asparagus.

I think it is this lack of any greensward that gives the dreary look to the landscape, especially when one emerges from the mountains upon the open plains. To see the naked land stretching mile after mile, looking like vast ash heaps, where the nearest approach to anything green is in the straight rows of little grayish olive trees and blackish fig trees, the first pollarded into the shape of cabbages gone to seed, and the latter twisted and gnarled into serpentine lines writhing in an apparent attempt to draw sap out of the sunbaked ground,—all this, which is really the height of cultivation, gives one the impression of utter barrenness and desolation. Imagine a stretch of twenty miles of this dead gray plain, with here and there a mountain abruptly rising out of it like one solid rock, and some vast range beyond, jagged and fantastic, yellow, and orange, and red, and ashy gray, and over this the dry, burning sky under which the soil shrivels and cracks, and you will get some notion of the material of a Spanish landscape. But no words can give an idea of the vast distances, and the great masses and wild forms.

When you get beyond Loja, a little old brown town inhabited by brigands, and bullfighters, and other evil-disposed people, the plains are con-

verted into great rolling gravel heaps, under which the mountains are
sometimes buried nearly to their ragged summits. Here your hat will be
blown out of the window, for you have insensibly climbed another mountain, and the wind rushes across in sudden, irresistible gusts. I sincerely
hope you will have another in your satchel with which to make your entry
into the ancient city of Granada.

Before we enter the hotel omnibus, with its gayly harnessed mules, its
indifferent driver, who grumbles because he has to wait for your baggage,
and the fat, red-faced young man in the corner who says, "Me guide;
speak English; parlez vous francais, monsieur?" I wish to say a word
of friendly warning to the landscape painter.

This grand scenery which has been gliding past us all day is grand,
above all things, because of its monotonous tones, its vast distances, and its
enormous scale. It is utterly unpictorial and unpaintable. Reduced to
the scale of your canvas it would lose all its interest. The plains would
become a dust heap, and the mountains broken lumps of mouldy Dutch
cheese. Go and look at it if you like, but leave your colors behind, unless
you wish to paint the little whitewashed, gray-tiled farm houses, with
their picturesque laborers and rows of mules against the dazzling walls, on
which their shadows fall like silhouettes cut in black velvet. To do this,
which can be more easily done on the other side of the Mediterranean, you
must make a pilgrimage on a mule or with a knapsack, and live among the
people whom you paint. You will find them suspicious, avaricious, half
fed, and dirty, and you will do well to provide yourself with a package of
Persian powder and certain other medicaments with which your apothecary
will supply you.

Every town in Spain has its own distinctive coloring. Malaga is a pink
and sky-blue city. Murcia is dust colored. Cartagena, where—since the
bombardment—they have built cement factories, is of the universal color
of brown cement.

Granada is one of the white cities, with gray-tiled roofs and old churches
here and there that make yellow-brown spots in the town.

Granada, the old town, is built on steep hills, and like all cities so built
is far more picturesque than the cities of the plain. The new town, like
all the new Spanish towns, is cheap and uninteresting. Formal stuccoed
fronts, with large windows and no projections but the iron balconies, and
certain plaster of paris renaissance scrolls over the doors and windows,—
there you have a picture of the whole of modern Spain. Tall, square
edifices built of sticks and stones, mud and plaster, and barbarously daubed
over with distemper color. So little idea have these people of the relation
of weight to strength of material, that the heavy tiled floors laid on rows
of round sticks, often settle in the middle in a hollow like the gutter of a
Roman street. One never sees this fault in true Moorish constructions,

although built with very similar material. The very house in which I am now writing, although built by the Arabs centuries ago, has its walls without a crack, and its massive floors as firm and level as when first laid. The true Moors are in this, as in other matters, vastly more intelligent than the Spaniards. Indeed, I am tempted to believe that these latter are intelligent exactly in proportion to the mixture of Oriental blood.

The Grenadines, in most cases dark haired and dark eyed, are the most eminently Spanish of all the southern Spaniards. They have none of the roundness of form and face which characterizes the Spanish Moors. They have long faces, high, contracted foreheads, long, pointed noses with a decided downward tendency, and a chin as long as the typical English one. Only in place of the broad, square, English jaw, they have a narrow, pointed one, which gives the whole head a somewhat foxy appearance. The under lip is full, and almost invariably protrudes. The well-known portrait heads of Velasquez conserve this type perfectly, and although the royal household, which he has doomed to immortality, were of the blondest of blonds, in their features and in their pasty complexions they might pass for Grenadine Spaniards of to-day.

In form the Grenadines are square-shouldered, broad-chested; thin in the flank, with a pelvis as contracted as that of a tiger. They are of very low stature, the limbs short and finely formed, the hands and feet very short, broad, and fleshy. The foot of a woman of Granada, although not large, has much the shape of a ham.

The women are square-shouldered, long-waisted, narrow-hipped, short-legged, wear heels four inches high, invariably make up their faces white, and always use the mantilla. It is rare to see one pretty, except that their eyes have a somewhat Oriental expressiveness, and their hair and eyelashes are magnificently thick. One occasionally sees blonds with hair of a coppery gold, but although one guesses them to be Spanish, from their pallid, colorless skin, they are marked exceptions to the general type.

It is very interesting to me to notice the difference in type in different provinces of the Spain of to-day; not merely because I believe race history to be thus most exactly recorded, but especially because the railways, which are revolutionizing the country, will soon break down and generalize all these distinctions.

I beg pardon for having nothing interesting to say about Granada. The little I have to tell has at least the merit of not being in the guidebook. Granada has all the disagreeable features of a poor city infested by tourists. The town itself is so poor that being unable to pay its gas bills (I was told that the accumulated indebtedness amounted to fifty thousand *douros*, or dollars, but Allah is all-knowing), the gas company has cut off the supply of gas, and the streets are now (1883) badly lighted by petroleum lamps. The rate of living is so low that *centimes* are more used than any other coin, and the gift of one to a beggar begets a smile and an oration of thanks. One buys figs, the only eatable fruit, at a few *centimes*. The kilo and labor is so cheap that one finds in a hotel ten times as many servants as guests, and in a shop five times as many clerks as customers. And yet if you go into one of these shops, where apparently not a *peseta's* worth of business is done from morning to night, they make nothing of asking you ten times the real price for the commonest articles, while at your elbow you hear the natives haggling for *cuartos*. I do not speak of these shops which are idle three quarters of a year, lying in wait for the rich Englishman. Such is the curiosity shops (*antiguedads*), where they calmly ask you twenty, fifty or a hundred *douros* for an old rag or rug, or a broken fan.

" These Spaniards," said a very polite Jew whom I met on the road to Granada, " have no idea of the value of time or of money." I think they are like all other very poor people, who seem to be keenly alive to small values, but whose imagination makes no distinction between hundreds, thousands, or millions. Any of these dazzling sums equally represents to them immeasurable wealth. When by any accident they come into possession of one of these inconceivable amounts, they throw it away with more recklessness than would the most prodigal millionaire. As I seem to be digressing into very general remarks, I will add one other which I have found to be as true of Granada as of other towns. You are better served, bargain more pleasantly, and get more for your money of a Jew, than of any other dealer whatsoever. It is not for nothing that a race is born traders for fifty generations.

I can finish what I have to say of Granada in a very few words. With two exceptions one hardly sees anything of national costumes. The people look as if they were dressed by American " clothing stores." The one exception is the lace mantilla, the other, the priests. The streets are as full of priests as of beggars. With their black flowing robes and curious hats, with the broad brim tightly rolled at the sides, they are not unpicturesque ; but the expression of their faces is terribly repelling. Long features, hard lines, and a stern scowl mark this class of men, who have at length lost the support and the respect of the people. One asks why the Jesuits do not take care of the beggars. Alas ! the poor men have a hard time to support themselves. Devotees have become rare, and people bargain for a mass as they do for a pound of potatoes. And yet these forbidding-looking priests are after all only a type of the people. You have only to shave a Grenadine to discover a Jesuit, just as by shaving a Murciano you find a bullfighter.

I have only one more remark to make about this most irritating town. If you walk through the main streets you are annoyed by hundreds of beggars. By taking care to load your pockets with copper coin you can manage to get on, but in the neglected and picturesque parts of the town you are mobbed.

I have never in my life seen such an accumulation of misery, and filth, and clamorous hunger. Old and young, blind and lame and maimed, cling to you and block your way. Dirty, one-eyed children stop their play and join the crowd with outstretched hands and incessant, shrill cries. The thing is terrible and utterly repulsive.

I don't suppose I am very hard-hearted. I know that if I have any sous in my pocket I can't pass an Arab beggar with his patient, silent demand. The simple gesture with which he kisses the gift and points upward is a whole poem, and if it were not a mere touching bit of nature would be a wonderful piece of art, worth vastly more to see than the little that one pays for it. But these beggars of Granada are like a frightful nightmare. They are beyond all human sympathy. Your pity is smothered in disgust.

ALGIERS, January 7, 1883.

Mrs. Black's Sixth Sense

JUDGE BLACK was Government appointee over one of the circuit courts of a Southwestern State. His district comprised several counties, and he made periodical visits to the chief towns of each; but the most important cases usually came before him in the town of Red Bank, where he resided.

The events whereof the following is a record took place in the course of the trial of one Mark Gibson. The accused was a man of wealth, and, in a local sense, of high social position. His crime— for there appeared to be absolutely no doubt of his guilt—was the murder of a young woman whom he wished removed from his path in order to make possible an ambitious marriage. So much for this case, into the shocking particulars of which it is not necessary to go further.

At seven o'clock on the second day of the trial (the examination of witnesses was still in progress, the evidence becoming more and more damaging) Judge Black sat at supper with his wife in their home. They were alone, having no children, and there being no guests.

" If the guilty are not punished, what protection is there for the innocent? What is to become of society—of weak, helpless women?" the Judge's wife was saying.

" Yes, of course," responded the Judge, with the air of one not greatly entertained by a repetition of trite axioms.

Judge Black was a fine-looking man of middle age, large of build and a little stout, with iron-gray hair, intelligent gray eyes, and an honest face. His wife was slender, delicate looking, and by no means handsome. Her hair was dark, coarse, and straight, her face absolutely without color, and a little sallow. Her eyes alone rescued her from being hopelessly plain.

In spite of the dark bluish patches usually to be seen beneath them, and although they appeared to be of no pronounced color, they impressed most observers as being not only beautiful but of incomparable intelligence. They seemed, as it were, the windows of an intense, luminous soul, compelling attention, respect, and homage. They seemed to compass at a glance the true inwardness of everything.

" I was not surprised when I heard of Mark Gibson's crime," Mrs. Black continued. " I knew what sort of man he was."

" How could you know except from idle report, and one can never be sure of that?" rejoined her husband, judicially.

" I don't mean that," was the quick response. " I mean what I felt when he came near me. I could tell what he was, and couldn't bear to be near him that evening he was here last fall."

" Surely he behaved himself as a gentleman should."

" Oh, yes! I don't mean that. You don't understand me. It wasn't anything that he said or did ; it was what I felt in his atmosphere. I can't explain it, but it was as clear to me as day that he was utterly without principle ; that he was bad,—capable of anything."

As she spoke, Mrs. Black's eyes seemed to be orbs of bright light, burning with the intensity and enthusiasm of the soul within.

" I'm afraid you allow your imagination to carry you too far," commented Judge Black, uneasily.

" It was not imagination," was the earnest rejoinder. " I can always tell what people are. I can't explain how I know, but I know. I have never been mistaken in a man's character yet."

" Surely, Clara, you are not serious?"

" Profoundly so."

A servant now entered to bring in a dessert, and the conversation was suspended. It was not the first time that Judge Black had been startled by his adored wife's vehement assertion of what he regarded as impossible. He recalled how, one day soon after their marriage, she had declared in company, in the most natural way in the world, that something or other was "as blue as the word Julian." It was noticeable that after hearing this curious comparison made the company stared, grew sober, and the conversation was quietly diverted into another channel.

"What possessed you to say such an absurb thing?" asked the Judge— then only a young lawyer—as soon as he was alone with his wife.

"But, Arthur, the word Julian is blue," insisted Mrs. Black, with annoyance. "All words with the 'oo' sound in them are blue."

"You are jesting."

"Indeed I am not. All words have color to me. So have all musical sounds. Haven't they to you?"

"Certainly not."

"How strange. Sit down at the piano and try me. I'll tell you the color of every note you strike,—or at any rate the color it suggests to me. There is for me some variation of color connected with every chirp of a bird, even."

"This is unnatural. I fear you are not well."

"Dear me!"— with a serene smile. "Why, I have been so all my life, and glad I am, too. What a privation it must be to live without such an exquisite, delicate sense."

This supersensitive appreciation of color harmonies to which the average man is blind, could do no harm, but Mrs. Black acknowledged to a still more remarkable acuteness of perception likely to prove dangerous in case it should elect to play her false; viz., the discerning or "sensing" of the characters of her acquaintances from what, for the want of terms, may be called their moral exhalation.

According to the scientists, there is a physical exhalation proceeding for several feet around from the body of every man or animal. When two persons stand face to face, therefore, these exhalations touch, as it were interlace, and each person feels more or less sensibly something belonging to and of the quality of the other. This may in a measure explain the common experience of attraction or repulsion so often immediately felt by either person or both, and altogether without rhyme or reason, so far as the intellect alone is concerned. Mrs. Black claimed, though not in set terms, that there was a moral or spiritual exhalation as well, as plainly indicative to her of a person's inward quality as a cloud in the sky is indicative of rain. How much of mere imagination, how much of reality entered into this, the chronicler cannot attempt to say. But it is a fact that, so far as is known, her intuitive perceptions never led her into errors of judgment with reference to the character of others.

She was a woman of no little culture on literary and musical lines. In America such persons are found now and then in the wildest and most remote regions. She read and loved all the best things in the masters of verse, and when she came suddenly upon lightning flashes of genius, all mayhap within the compass of half a dozen words, she could not sit still for joy, and would give vent to her feelings in tears and low delighted laughter suggestive of an innocent child. She had been known to declare that there were passages in Chopin and other masters, the victorious upward leap, as it were, of maddening waves of harmony, that filled her for a whole evening with a fiery, inextinguishable joy.

It was on the evening of the third day of the trial that, after eating heartily of his supper (people dine at midday in the Southwest) and smoking a cigar comfortably in his wife's sitting room, Judge Black retired to look over some papers in an adjoining apartment which was his home office. The two rooms communicated by large double doors, and these were rarely closed. Without moving, Mrs. Black could see her husband as he sat down under the lamp, and note every expression on his face as he opened and read a letter awaiting him on his desk.

The watchful wife observed at first a look of great surprise; then came a muttered imprecation and every evidence of lofty indignation. This stage was shortly succeeded by deep, impenetrable revery. As Mrs. Black sat there, watchful, anxious, wondering, a strange thing happened. It was quite unaccountable that she should have fallen asleep under such circumstances, and yet she decided afterwards that she must have fallen asleep and dreamed.

In the dream the actual scene witnessed with her waking eyes remained. She still sat in her chair and the Judge was before her, seated at his desk. But as her eyes rested on him there was gradually outlined before her absorbing, piercing gaze a faint, filmy, circular haze, filling about one third of the office, and apparently radiating from the Judge as a central point. This was not all, for presently the dim outlines of two dark forms were seen above and a little to the back of the head of the musing man. The dark forms grew more distinct and became two human, or rather inhuman faces, for they were hideous, malevolent, devilish. At the same time Mrs. Black noted with horror the growth of an unusual expression in her husband's eyes—an expression of lustful cupidity.

"He is being tempted to evil!" she whispered, with certain conviction and in breathless suspense.

"Pshaw! what am I thinking of?" muttered the Judge a moment later, with a start. "Not for worlds—not for worlds! What insolence to attempt to ——" The letter was suddenly thrust noisily away from him on the desk.

And the watchful eyes that saw everything took note that now the evil forms had receded, and were almost lost to view at the very circumference of the dim, encompassing haze, and that their former place was occupied by two other faces, bright and beautiful, and most wondrously luminous as to their eyes with tenderness, goodness, and love. Gazing upon which changed tableau, the watcher shed tears of joy.

But after a little time Judge Black suddenly reached forth his hand and drew the letter to him. In the same moment the bright faces began to recede and grow dim, and the dark, malevolent ones to swim surely forward. The Judge read the letter again, and yet again, cupidity returning to the expression of his eyes and intensifying, while the evil faces bending about him became so clear that they could be seen to look toward each other in hideous, leering triumph.

A bell rang in the lower part of the house, and Mrs. Black awoke with a start. A moment or two later the Judge rose to his feet as a servant appeared, announcing the name of a visitor who desired to see the master of the house.

"What have you been crying about, Clara?" he asked, while passing through the outer room where his wife sat immovable.

She did not answer. She looked weak and ill, but as soon as he was out of sight she ran hastily to the desk in the study and searched until she found a letter, written in a disguised hand, with neither date, signature, nor address, which read thus:—

"Considering the state of public sentiment, it is practically certain that the jury will render a verdict of guilty in the case of Mark Gibson. If Judge Black will commute the sentence expected to follow to imprisonment for life, he will receive in payment ten thousand dollars in cash. If on entering the court room on Thursday next, he will signify consent by immediately taking out his hankerchief and putting it to his face, that night at twelve o'clock the money will be placed at his door in a leather bag by a messenger, who will ring the bell twice and then retire.

"If Judge Black should refuse to accept this offer he may live to regret it. Mark Gibson has powerful friends, and desperate measures may be resorted to if necessary. A word to the wise is sufficient."

Mrs. Black appeared to be in a very serious frame of mind while breakfasting with her husband next morning. The Judge thought that she gave utterance to more serious and moral reflections than he had heard from her during six months past. She remarked that the great thing in life was not to have riches, or honor, or power, but to have honesty and incorruptible integrity. To appear to be right was immaterial; to be right was the only thing. She affirmed that every woman of the right sort would gladly live on a crust the year round rather than be immensely rich and know that her husband could be corrupted. To care for principles, not riches,—that was the great ideal.

"Yes, of course," echoed the Judge, unsuspecting but rendered serious.

For these remarks were not made too urgently, or in a way to suggest to Judge Black that his wife knew of his great temptation.

"Take your case, Arthur," she proceeded, outwardly quite calm, though filled with dread. "I'd rather see you shot down in the streets by the angry relatives of that man Gibson, for instance, than see you pronounce an unjust sentence through fear of them."

"Don't think of such things," was the quick reply, with an inward shudder.

"For what is there left for a wife to love," she persisted, her bright, intense gaze full upon him, "if her husband loses his manhood, his sense of justice, his courage and integrity? Robbed of all this, he is only a beast in the form of a man."

Judge Black concurred, but none the less was he on trial again that night and the night following. From her place in the adjoining room the wife watched, in growing anxiety and suspense, the varying expression of her husband's face as he read and reread the letter, alternately refusing and consenting.

The trial of Mark Gibson had drawn to its close. The counsel for the defense had delivered the last stirring appeal, and the prosecuting solicitor for the State had made the last terrible summing up. As the jury were retiring to consider their verdict, Judge Black allowed his eyes to scan the court room while he wondered which one, or several, of the relations and friends of the prisoner had sent him that insulting and threatening letter. Whoever they were, they had up to this time watched him in vain for any sign of an acceptance of their proposition.

The court room was crowded with all classes of people. The best male elements of local society, the laboring man, the better class of negroes, the riffraff of both races,—all who could squeeze in and find a place were there. Many in the crowded seats, the twelve men of the jury, even some of the lawyers who had to do with the case, were chewing tobacco. Cuspidors were conspicuous everywhere, but the sawdust sprinkled over the floor presented palpable evidence that unless these happened to be in the right place at the right moment, comfort (or indolence) was never sacrificed in their interest. A perceptible odor of fluid tobacco pervaded the whole place.

After the jury had gone out there was a hush of expectation, broken only by low murmurings. The friends of the prisoner stared at the impassive, impenetrable Judge with less and less hope in their faces and more and more anger in their eyes. The prisoner himself looked straight before him with an air of light indifference, as if surely confiding in his youth, and strength, and the power of influence and wealth. There was no suggestion of fear or contrition in his clear-cut, handsome face and cold, cruel eyes.

In less than half an hour the jury returned, with the expected verdict of "Guilty."

Few there were in that motley assembly, made up of all the elements of a crude, unripe, but advancing society, who forgot for many a day the short, eloquent address then delivered by Judge Black, declaring the duty incumbent on the magistrate of administering justice according to the crime and the law, regardless of fear or favor. The just and incorruptible judge, he told them in substance, was the friend and protector of the helpless infant, the breeding woman, the honest laborer, the worthy citizen, and through these of the very Commonwealth itself; but the unjust and venal judge was the bitterest of foes to all these, a very wolf in sheep's clothing, unworthy alike of the honor of man or the mercy of God. At the conclusion of his address, as a most solemn and effective peroration, he pronounced sentence of death upon Mark Gibson according to the set formula.

When Mrs. Black met her husband at the entrance of their home that evening she looked anxiously and keenly into his eyes for one instant, then uttered a strange, low cry, and the tears began to rain down her cheeks. But this appearance of grief suggested an April shower rather than a November storm, for the sunshine of her smile belied her tears. There was, however, no ambiguity in the Judge's reception, for she flung her arms round his neck and kissed him fondly.

"You don't know how happy you have made me, Arthur. If you had yielded, I think I should have died of grief."

"Why, Clara, what can you mean?"

"You have been tempted—threatened—and have refused to be swayed from your duty."

The strong man turned pale. "You saw that letter, then?" he asked, in a shaken voice.

"I knew it before I saw the letter. Let them threaten; I am contented. If they shoot you from behind a tree, my hero will still live. If you had yielded, though you had lived to a hundred, my hero would have been dead forever!"

And although, even before the just sentence was executed, while riding alone toward the country courts in his circuit, the Judge was indeed "shot at from behind a tree," and not once only, but three several times,—as good fortune would have it without fatal result,—he never regretted the act that won from his devoted wife these words of praise. Glowing words were they, indeed, but not undeserved, for a hero he was. The bravest soldier is he who is afraid, but yet will not run; and the stoutest hero is not he who is never tempted, but he who is and refuses to yield. Such, indeed, are the great whose secret struggles we never know.

Louis Pendleton

NOTES

¶ We announce with pleasure the foundation of a "Society for the Suppression of Iconoclasts." The object of this society is " to provide for the extinction of that class of society, so prominent in the present day, whose chief business in life is the overthrow of the most cherished ideals of mankind." It is understood that the society has already in its employ a number of trusted agents, whose duty consists in the quiet removal from life's active scenes of those who come under the ban. One of the first to require the attention of this benevolent association was the man whose delinquencies, related in the Rochester *Post-Express*, are characteristic of the iconoclastic tribe. The *Post-Express* says : " One summer Sunday night, some years ago, a stranger paused at the door of a village church and listened to the congregation singing, ' By cool Siloam's shady rill.' He hung around until meeting was through, and stopping the minister when he came out said, ' Excuse me, sir, but I've been to Siloam, and I assure you there is no rill of any sort thereabout.' " Iconoclasm ceases to be a joke, however, when it aims at the overthrow of the beliefs that have been the inspiration of poets and painters for centuries, and that have played a part in the amelioration of mankind no less important than the utilitarian invention of science. One Prince de Valori has been poking about in the dust of old libraries and amassing facts to prove that Laura, Petrarch's Laura, was an elderly married woman with eleven children to her credit, and somewhat scandalous relation with the great poet to her discredit. Now, really, we do not care in the least whether the Petrarch and Laura of romance ever existed or not, but to have this miserable little prince, with his published revelation in the *Nouvelle Revue*, coming around and confronting us with Laura *en famille* is too much. It is decidedly bad taste in him ! We hereby call the attention of the society to his case.

¶ *The Lark* has essayed a new flight. There has come to us "Number 1 " of " Phyllida ; or, the Milkmaid. A bi-weekly review devoted to Literary Topics, and Reflections upon the Doings of the Town." From their first number we should judge that its mission is to be the glorification of California and all things Californian. Mr. Aiken complains bitterly that

" the ardent workers in Art, Literature, and Music in California have long endured either condescending and chary praise, or ignorant condemnation from many Eastern and foreign critics." If that be so, Mr. Aiken would much more wisely hold his peace concerning the fact. To continually remind everyone that you have always been called a boy, is not the best way to be considered a man. We are almost forced to conclude that Mr. Gelett Burgess and his associates are having a covert fling at their fellow *Californian*, and that the national hoax of the *Lark* is being localized in " Phillyda." It is a great man who does not take himself seriously, but is clever enough to make everyone else do so.

¶ There is a time to stop in the elaboration of theories, as well as in everything else. The man who always carries his opinions to their logical consequences, is likely to find that one of the " logical consequences " of such a course will be to find himself in very hot water. A crank is a man who insists upon making his theories keep on growing after they have reached maturity.

The Spectator, after all, is not entirely wrong when it cavils at Mr. Gladstone for calling book collecting a " vitalizing" process. If the book collector were always a book lover, the question would have another aspect. In fact, however, many collectors know nothing of their books beyond title page and binding. The man who pays high prices for rare editions, does little for the cause of learning beyond prolonging the existence of volumes that otherwise might quickly disappear from view.

The Spectator asks, not unjustly, why book collecting should vitalize anybody to a greater extent than collecting stamps, or shaving dishes, or buttons, or other things, which idle men with money and a " false kind of diligence " delight in.

Costly bindings may give to the rich man a satisfaction akin ·to that produced by costly furniture or bric-à-brac. Musty, if rare, old volumes may sometimes have a value aside from their cost, by speaking to him of the days in which they were first given to the world. But the genuine book-lover, I could easily prove, is almost indifferent to the seductions of fine bindings and limited editions. The books with which he surrounds himself are his friends. They help him in his work or they amuse him in his hours of leisure. Never could he lower himself to collect them as mere goods and chattels. Books may vitalize (this is Mr. Gladstone's barbarism), but book collecting in itself is never a vitalizing process.

THE failure to quite achieve, the success that stops just short of actual attainment, is the most melancholy verdict that has to be pronounced by the critic. There is an ever increasing body of writers whose epitaph must be " almost." Possessing facility, cleverness, and a degree of skill, yet is there " the one thing lacking." It may be that they have never arrived above a place in the ranks, but the possibility of the attainment that might have been theirs still stands before them, a blank wall of regret. It is the half successes that break hearts.

These somewhat somber reflections were caused by reading that wholly pleasant and readable little series of essays written by Joseph Edgar Chamberlain for the *Transcript*, under the " Listener " column, and reprinted by Copeland & Day in two volumes, with the titles, " The Listener in the Town," and " The Listener in the Country." (75 cents each.)

Mr. Chamberlain reminds one of Leigh Hunt in his ability to write cleverly and entertainingly of the fancies of the moment, but the essays lack imagination and power. Taken for what they were intended, that is, light and sketchy newspaper fragments, they are agreeable and amusing. Of the two volumes, the " Listener in the Country " is by far the better. There is a genuine love of Nature and sympathy with her moods shown in every line.

❡ Lee & Shepard have just published in an attractive volume the second edition of Oscar Fay Adams's " Story of Jane Austen's Life." The author, in his preface, announces that it is his intention to place Jane Austen before the world as the winsome, delightful woman that she was, and thus dispel the unattractive, not to say forbidding, mental picture which so many have formed of her. Mr. Adams visited many of the places once familiar to Jane Austen, and carefully noted his impression of the places described in her books. The book contains a very careful and thorough bibliography, covering everything that has been written concerning Miss Austen and her work. The crowning feature of the work is the eighteen full-page illustrations scattered through the volume, many of which were taken expressly for the author, and others of which were furnished him by members of the Austen family. All readers and admirers of "Sense and Sensibility" and "Pride and Prejudice" will welcome this new edition of Mr. Adams's book. ($2.00.)

¶ Book lovers and collectors will appreciate most heartily Curtis Guild's "Chat about Celebrities; or, the Story of a Book." Mr. Guild has been "extra illustrating" a copy of James T. Fields's "Yesterdays with Authors," until the original little book has swelled to four large volumes. With this book as a basis, Mr. Guild chats pleasantly of his experiences and observations of the last fifty years. Particularly amusing is that portion of the book devoted to Dickens, and in it are told many anecdotes that have never before been published. But it is of our own well-known Boston men, Longfellow, Holmes, Prescott, Bancroft, and Lowell, that Mr. Guild writes most intimately and lovingly. His experience as a dramatic critic thirty years ago made the prominent actors and actresses of that day personally known to him, and he has many entertaining things to say of them. The reader cannot help feeling a touch of sadness at the thought that many of those mentioned who were, as Mr. Guild says in his title, "celebrities," are now little more than names. The book is decidedly of more than ordinary interest. (Lee & Shepard, $1.50.)

¶ "Quo Vadis" is, without reservation, the noblest book of the last half of the nineteenth century. Henryk Sienkiewicz, the great Polish author, has given us his best work in this picture of the times of Nero. The book depicts the conflict of Christianity with the Roman Empire, and so exactly is the spirit caught, and so vividly is the story told, that we feel ourselves transported back through the centuries as at the touch of a magician. It is the misfortune that we have to contend with in the case of a popular book, that we must approach it with a sort of negative prejudice. We are likely to try to see behind the scenes, and to endeavor to analyze the means by which the effect is produced, and oftentimes the wires by which the puppets are moved are then made visible, when, to an unprejudiced reader, they would be unnoticed. "Quo Vadis" so sweeps the reader with the current of the story that he soon ceases to look for the showman behind the stage, and gives himself up to the breathless interest of the piece. The dramatic intensity and brilliancy of Sienkiewicz's style has often been commented upon. No one can adequately describe Sienkiewicz's work who has not, to some degree, his power of expression. The book is of those that all must read sooner or later. The student of history will welcome the book for its accurate picture of life in Rome during Nero's reign, and the lover of fiction will find in it the best of his favorite literature. (Little, Brown & Co., $2.00.)

The Red Letter

An Illustrated Monthly

Published by H. Walter Stephenson
Edited by Harry Draper Hunt
Under the art direction of E. B. Bird

The subscription rate is one dollar a year. Entered at the Boston Post Office as second-class mail matter. The trade supplied by the American News Company and its branches. Advertising rates on application.

The Red Letter Magazine,

Boston.

~···

¶ THIS issue completes Volume I. *The Poster* subscribers who were transferred to THE RED LETTER, having received six issues, will please notice that their subscriptions expire with this number. The editor will be glad to continue them on the list after receiving their subscriptions for another year. We might here state that the offer made sometime ago is still continued: those sending in four subscriptions will receive their own free.

¶ THE March issue will appear in a new dress: a permanent cover by Mr. Bertram Goodhue, whose work has won distinction in this country and abroad; and will contain illustrated articles, one on Orson Lowell, by P. McArthur, and one on F. H. Nankerville, by Percival Pollard. Miss Frances H. Doughty will contribute a clever story entitled " Ghosts Across the Water."

····~~~~

¶ THE series of " Impressions of Southern Spain," by Marcus Waterman, is continued through this issue, and Harry Gordon White sends " Carmena's Flitting."

FACTS AND IDEAS FOR ALL!

Advertising Experience.... Formerly

The Trade Press

CHICAGO....

A Monthly Magazine devoted to
Facts in Advertising....

Price, 10 cents a copy.
$1.00 a year.

THE·RED LETTER

AN·ILLVSTRATED MONTHLY

VOLVME·2·NVMBER·1
MARCH·MDCCCXCVII

Contents.

Drawn by
Orson Lowell

Permission of Scribner's

The Red Letter

An Illustrated Monthly.

"'T will while away an hour or so with picturings and print."—MARLOWE.

Keats

WITHIN the halls where from her saffron bed
Aurora cool awakes, I saw a bard;
Unmoved he stared, clutching, with hand stone hard,
A lyre, with festal marigolds all dead.

Philip Becker Goetz

Half-light Stories

CARMENA'S FLITTING.

CLEVE was playing *chamirittas* on the guitar, for he was averse to painting when nooks and corners in the dark end of the studio were given over to dusky uncertainty; and Carmena, as she rested on the corner divan, was smoking cigarettes as only Carmena could. Carmena was the model.

Carmena's hair was black, and her face an olive oval. Her eyes were of the darkest, deepest brown, when the long-lashed, drooping lids did not veil them from view, and her figure was lithe and slender, even unto slightness, with graceful, sweeping lines beneath the tightly drawn *crepe* shawl. She was a Lusitanian, not without a strain of gypsy blood.

Cleve liked the music just at dusk, and he liked to sit by Carmena, too. As for that worthy young person, she also liked the tinkle of the wire strings when the day's pose was ended, and she sat and smoked. So what more need be said?

All the fellows humored Carmena, because when she was pleased she laughed; and when she laughed she had dimples in her cheeks, that, with the lace *rebozo* and high shell comb, that had been her mother's and her grandmother's before they had found their present resting-place, had many times ere this been inspirations for some painter's canvas.

Besides, even now, if perchance some passing caprice willed, Carmena's feet could trip as lightly through the peasant-gypsy dances as on the day she bade farewell to her beloved *meza*, to wander, like the bird of passage that she was, in that world-wide country men call Bohemia, lingering here and there on a model throne, as a bird may pause in transit.

So Cleve, in secret hoping, played. But to-day another mood had worked a spell, and, though the *chamirittas* coaxed, they were in vain. The feet were coy, and answered not.

And when the shadows left the corners and crept along the floor until the ending day was driven out, even the dimples faded from sight, and only the dull red glow of the cigarette shone through the shreds of fragrant, curling smoke. So, in despair, Cleve played instead a sad and wailing melody that he had learned long years before; and as he played the slow, sweet chords he sang aloud in the old-time Lusitanian tongue a weird, heart-rending thing, with words as ancient as the hills and mountain-sides where yet it lingers with unlettered folk,—a last, deep sigh of Bobadilla and his Moorish followers. And as he crooned the song's first lulling chant the cigarette grew dim there in the dusky corner seat, and Carmena sighed.

For in her old life days the mountain goatherds sang it as they tended their flocks. Yes, and Luzian used to chant it, too,—her brother Luzian, who had gone away forever to the war. That eve before he went, when through the still moonlight the singing goatherd's voice had come from up the mountain side, they had chanted back to him! Then Luzian went away, and she had flown afar! And now those half-forgotten strains came from this Americano's lips,—this, her brother Luzian's farewell song. And that is why Carmena sighed.

Then, in its might, the chanting voice rose up. No tinkling music now, but vibrant with a solemn grandeur; slow at first, then quickening with a beating rhythm, like the tread of unnumbered hosts, until it faded like some dying ember, as the tenor voice and droning of the wire strings ebbed quite away; even as the goatherd's voice had died upon the evening air, —as Luzian's voice had died away; alas, forever, now. Ah! why should this Americano sing to her dead Luzian's song? And the rising moon that struggled through the city haze shone dimly through the great north-light and changed to dusk the blackness of the corner seat, where the raven head with its lace *rebozo* and high shell comb, the black crepe shawl

Drawn by
Florence P. England

and cigarette. were half revealed. a formless mass amid the pillows gathered there. and Carmena wept subdued. half-whispered sobs. like grief personified.

  .   .   .   .

Cleve bent gently over her. and strove to lift her up and brush her tears away. But Carmena needed no assistance. nor would she suffer him to touch her in her frenzied passion. With a gesture of her clinched white hand she pushed him from her. reaching the open floor with a mighty bound. And as she stood there in the light of the strengthening moon, with hair disheveled and half-trailing shawl. Cleve gazed in wonderment: no longer she of dimpled smiles and downcast eyes, but a new and strange Carmena. of glittering eyes and teeth. No more the grace of languor, but of suppleness and strength. Thus, all unknowing. had his music worked this spell. He who played in vain the *chamiritta* dance. should see the dancing Carmena now. With a quick movement she seized the instrument from his unresisting hands. In the uncanny light of the rising moon she sang and played, the like of which none ever heard before. nor will again : for words and music were alike unstudied creations of this new-born passion. flashed out like an ascending spark on some dark night.—a moment luminous, then gone forever.

" O Motherland of Olive. thou callest unto me.
  I. who afar off, weep with the cadence of thy voice.
Singest thou sweet. O Mother. with the voice of the Southland's wind.
    Words of longing for me. thy daughter, who dwelleth not in thy loving
    embrace."

And when the voice. low. deep. and trembling. ebbed into sobbing as she danced. he was amazed. for none before had heard the like come forth from Carmena's throat. Lips could never make that sound. No falsetto that. as, in the days gone by. she used to sing. but deep, rich alto. out from her very heart. And when the chords rang out again. the voice welled forth and he listened to her soul. Souls are never seen. but heard : and the words burned in the ear like coals :—

" Reach out thy hands. O my Vineland Mother.
Thy white-sailed hands that sail the great deep sea.
And in the hollow of their palms I will comfort me. and wipe my sorrow-
  ing tears away.
O thou Homeland. sunshine plays upon thy hillsides,
And in thy vales the fountain ever tinkles like a little bell."

And as she played and sang. her slender form waved to and fro in the dim moon's rays like some slender reed blown by the driving gale. now bending back, then quivering with the music's ecstasy; or recovering, when she seemed about to fall, she stood again before him, tall and straight as a willow wand.

Again the song broke forth, but more softly, now that her strength was nearly spent, and the fierceness of her mood was gone, and only gentleness remained.

" Thy children, Motherland, the brethren of my youth,
    Forever sing the songs of my ancestral folk,—
Songs of the sighing Moor, who never more will roam ;
And in the still moonlight the faun men and the wood sprites dance
Amid the river mist, when the night is hushed in solitude.
Cease thy calling, O thou Firstland Mother ;
Thy daughter heareth thee, and cometh to thy bosom."

And when the moon had risen from out the city haze and shone in all his splendor upon the dancing girl, the mood's fierce flame consumed itself, and gathering close the black crêpe shawl, this bird of passage sped away, as in the spring her feathered prototype flies ever onward to its native heath.

But from the darkness of the stairway landing the old-time salutation came, as we hear the birdnotes in the night,—perhaps a little sadly now,— " Viva Senhor, Adios."

Harry Gordon White

Rondeau

FAREWELL, dear Youth, our paths divide ;
    No longer may we side by side
        Tread hand in hand the pleasant way,
        For I must reach the world to-day,
    And enter on its surging tide.

Alas ! would that we might abide
Together while the twilight died,
    And stars beamed out to close the day.
        Farewell, dear Youth !

And yet, if worn and burden-tried
In some far future, it betide
    Once more my weary feet should stray
    Among the paths, oh ! come, I pray,
To meet me then ; but this denied,
        Farewell, dear Youth !

F. A. Nankivell

IT is a serious fact, and one too seldom noted, that whenever a man shows that his grip on the ladder of success is fairly secure, the number of persons pretending to have been instrumental in that success becomes ludicrously large. You may, if you go about and abroad sufficiently, meet all kinds of people who will tell you that they discovered the star in question. In the case of my good friend Frank A. Nankivell, for instance, the number of his "discoverers" assures me, were there no other reason, that he is on the high road to be considered successful. San Francisco teems with these persons, and the New York crop promises abundant harvest.

Waiving the matter of these explorers, however,—though it should be noted as quaint that their taste in art is usually of a sort to make one doubt the genuineness of their claims,—it remains a fact that Mr. Nankivell was certainly worth discovering. In the present force and originality of his black and white, as in his promise for the future, I consider Mr. Nankivell the strongest artist in America. That sounds like a large order, but I look to the future with easy confidence. There are artists to-day, whose names the general public pretends to know, who have not half the bold, dashing originality that informs Mr. Nankivell's line. At first sketch he frequently achieves results, by the grace of God, as it were, that most artists will never get if they stipple until they die.

Within a few months of his coming to New York, Mr. Nankivell was made a staff artist on *Puck*; a paper that has, artistically, a position in America similar to the one occupied in England by *Punch*, in that it by no means accepts sketches from Tom, Dick, and Harry, but relies altogether on a carefully chosen staff of artists. The Sunday edition of the *New York Journal* also shows much of Mr. Nankivell's work, though frequently, where using the color press, spoiling his drawings by poor printing.

In posters this artist has shown qualities that various observers find also in Dudley Hardy and Cheret. As against much of the work produced by those poster artists to whom the freakishness of the Beardsley and Bradley models were godsends, Nankivell's posters always show strength of drawing. The decorativeness follows as a natural result; it does not hide bad drawing. Two posters for the *Echo*, two for the *Journal's* "L" station display in New York, and finally a theatrical three-sheet for a music hall performer, Marie Halton, comprise his posters. The latter design, but just out, I consider the finest music hall poster this side of Jules Cheret. Collectors can safely star it as the gem of the American-born posters.

S

Drawn by
Frank A. Nankivell

It is from his arrival in America, in June, 1894, that Mr. Nankivell dates
as a prominent artist in black and white. An Australian, apprenticed
variously to an architect and to a civil engineer, Mr. Nankivell was always
an artist in his hopes and nature, and his hand evolved caricatures in very
early days. In 1892, deserting everything but art, Mr. Nankivell left Syd-
ney for Japan, where he spent the few years before he reached San Francisco. In that town he started *Chic*, a fortnightly that was too good to
live, and so died inside of a year. Its files contain some of the best of
Nankivell's caricatures in his earlier manner; he illustrated every number
throughout, and it is doubtful if, in the matter of sketches, there was ever
a better "one man" paper than *Chic*. The *Examiner* and the *Call*, of
San Francisco, also used much of the artist's work; the *Call*, at one time,
using a caricature of his almost daily in a column of hotel interviews, done
by R. H. Davis, one of the editors of *Chic*. In March, 1896, the move to
New York was made, and since then continued improvement in facility
and force, and the gradual evolution of an entirely individual style, have
brought Mr. Nankivell surely into prominence.

My own acquaintance with this artist's work dates from one day in
Chicago, when R. L. Ketchum, the Western story writer, came in from
San Francisco with a copy of *Chic*. It was evident at once that here were
sketches of the rapid, spontaneous sort that American periodicals had
hitherto been sadly innocent of. As against the work of Raven Hill in
the *Butterfly*, of Phil May in the *Sketch*, of Manuel, Eckhard, and others
in England, America was apparently able to show nothing but labored
efforts at "finished" work, at "detail," at everything save originality.
Since then I am happy to say that the friendship for the man's work
has developed into a personal friendship that time, I trust, will continue to
strengthen. Friendship, however, should have nothing to do with criticism.

It is only in the last few months that Mr. Nankivell's work has shown a
definite style of its own. There was always individuality, but the technique was at one time akin to Phil May's; at another, somewhat indefinite.
In the matter of adopting May's technique Mr. Nankivell is easily justified, since there is no better method to-day,—nor one more dangerous to
the incompetent. The fact that this artist's style is now so strictly his own,
shows that his way toward it was a safe one.

In caricature the readers of the RED LETTER have already seen a striking example of Mr. Nankivell's power. In color his posters are elegant—
though they go but a slight way to show his skill in oils, as some few of us
have seen it. And in black and white line,—well, keep your eyes open,
ladies and gentlemen, and remember what I was bold enough to aver early
in this article.

Percival Pollard

"Three Times—and Out"

"THE de—— I beg your pardon!"

"How dare you—how dare you swear at me?"

"Great Scott!" I ejaculated helplessly. "I—I beg your pardon—I apologize most humbly; but you know the fact of the matter is, I did not—ah—swear, and, besides, I thought—that is—I supposed—I—you see I—ah—didn't know it was you." My ill-timed attempt at levity enraged my *vis-a-vis* the more apparently.

"How perfectly absurd!" she stormed. "How could you know it was I? I don't know you! I never saw you."

"No, you don't," I admitted. "If you did, you would know that I don't swear,—at least not often, and never at a lady."

"Pray, what do you call swearing?" she retorted with sarcastic scorn.

"Shall I really tell you? I ——"

"Certainly not. The—the—! the devil' is quite bad enough."

A pair of sapphire eyes were all this time blazing up into my face, and the small person confronting me was quite oblivious of the mass of humanity surging around us.

"Yes; as he's painted he is rather black," I acquiesced; "but, honestly, as a matter of fact, I did not intend invoking his satanic majesty. I was about to say 'the deuce,' and you ought to do me the justice to remember that I changed my mind the moment I saw that I was—ah—confronting a lady."

"That only makes it worse—a thousand times worse!" she ran on fiercely. "It would have been exactly as inexcusable if I had been a—a shopgirl. Of course you did not know it was I! How should you? But a gentleman would not use such language before any lady."

"By Jo—that is, upon my word, madam, you are quick to draw conclusions." I mustered the dignity of the worm that turns. "I intended to imply that I believed—that is, I thought, you know,—I supposed you—ah—were a man!"

"A man!" Words entirely fail to convey the explosive indignation of the small person who had just crushed into me with the force of a New York pedestrian at holiday time. "A man!" she ejaculated. "Do I *look* like a man?"

"Far from it," I groaned despairingly. No man ever stamped his foot or flipped his head about in the fierce and altogether charming manner that a small woman assumes when she is angry. This, I take it, by the way, is why men—even self-controlled men—do, on occasions, swear. "Far from it; but, if you will permit me, dodging these infer—I beg pardon —these exasperating trolley cars gives one the smallest possible opportunity to see anything. I hadn't so much as a glimpse of you until you—that is we—I should say I —was so unfortunate as to—to run into you, you know." (There are times when the plain, unvarnished truth is not safe.) As a matter of fact, I was not hurrying at all. I stood between the two tracks on the 23d Street crossing, waiting for a west-bound car on the second track to clear the crossing. I was nearly knocked off my feet by what I naturally supposed to be a man. The figure emerged suddenly from behind the car, and was making a dash to cross the other track in front of a rapidly approaching Lexington cable. The collision took place on the crossing from Madison Avenue to 23d Street, just where the Lexington Avenue cars swing round onto Broadway. The coming car was under full current, ready to take the curve, and I do not doubt that the raging lady before me would have been ground under it if I had not furnished an unwelcome barrier to her progress. Why there is not a daily demolition of the populace at this point, it would puzzle a pessimist to explain. But this digression robs the scene I am attempting to depict of its ludicrous suddenness and violence. "That's just it," my lady retorted sharply to my attempted explanation. "You have no business to rush so; it isn't safe."

I gasped. This was a straw too much. "Madam," I said with irony that would, in my humble opinion, have been less brutally expressed by some mild and well-chosen explosive, "allow me to remind you that the accident was the result of your own haste and the unalterable laws of motion."

What an adept at maneuver, woman is!

"I don't in the least know what you are talking about," she flung out loftily, "but you've no right to keep me standing here in the middle of the street, after first nearly knocking me down, and then using such language as no gentleman would use to a lady, or indeed to anyone."

"Well, I swear!" I ejaculated helplessly, under my breath, I supposed.

"I dare say you will," retorted my lady, with fiery scorn.

What could I say? I lifted my hat with what grace I could muster, and this small feminine whirlwind graciously condescended not to be kept waiting any longer.

"That's what it is to have red hair," I reflected, as she swept deliciously over the crossing to the pavement. "By Jove! and she doesn't like to be sworn at! She was as pretty as a picture, and I like her spirit, though it was certainly misdirected. Hullo! What's this? Well, I am in luck! Here's her card-case, or pocketbook, or whatever women call those nondescript things they carry."

Sure enough, there were cards in the monkey-skin affair, and to my great satisfaction they bore an address,—

Miss Helen Leighton,
No. 40 Ashton Place,
Brooklyn.

"Infernal place to get to—Brooklyn," I ruminated, "but I'll get there."

I could see my lady scudding away beyond reach toward the Third Avenue L on 23d Street. Truth to say, I wouldn't have caught her if I could. It would be vastly more interesting to call on her next day, when her resentment had cooled. Give those auburn-haired people time enough, and they will make generous amends for every impulsive injustice they have dealt you. The red-haired disposition is not really bad, take it the year round; quite the contrary. Perhaps she would even be apologetic, though I found it difficult to picture her in this pose.

All the world knows what the imagination will create out of nothing. I pressed the electric button of "No. 40 Ashton Place, Brooklyn," the next afternoon, with the feeling that I was ringing up the curtain on one of those delightful nineteenth century dramas which end with such unfailing felicity for all concerned.

I purposely omit the record of my adventures in finding the place. The intricacies of travel in Brooklyn is a sore point between the two cities which the legislators purpose to transform into a sort of Siamese twin.

I was admitted by a—well, a cross between buttons, butler, office boy, and elder brother. He ushered me into the "parlor," and disappeared with my card.

Alas! the fearful uncertainty of American interiors! Anyone would have fitted Miss Leighton instinctively into an artistic, or, at least, a tasteful setting. I would not have believed she could permit so atrocious a room in any house she called home. After five minutes of it I was just concluding that I would sacrifice my pretty little episode rather than sit another moment on that moss-green upholstery gazing at the ultramarine carpet, generously besprinkled with huge copper-colored roses, when I heard the trailing of feminine garb down the stairs.

My drooping spirits revived. How would she meet me after her absurd abuse of yesterday? She would smile a radiant smile. I could see just how her face would light up. She would even burst into a gay little laugh, blush all over her piquant face, and with charming frankness and a throw-myself-on-your-mercy air.

Shades of Olympus! the creature that entered that door! I stood, staring, near the door to which I had advanced to meet her.

"You wished to see me?" the creature demanded with a manner that exacted prompt and definite justification of my visit.

Wished to see her! Never! " I—ah—yes: that is, no. I beg your pardon. I mean—there must be some mistake," I stammered. " I called to see Miss Leighton—Miss Helen Leighton."

" I am Miss Leighton," she replied stiffly.

I could only stare helplessly at the gaunt, awkward, aggressive, altogether formidable woman before me.

" Did you wish to see me on business?" The voice recalled me to the necessity of an explanation.

I mechanically took the cardcase from my pocket. Her face went through the process that would be called " lighting up " in a pretty girl.

" Is it yours?" I ejaculated rudely. Such a solution had not before occurred to me.

" Yes; I think I can satisfy you that it is my property," she answered in a glib, detestable, business-like tone. She enumerated the contents. I handed her the pocketbook and made my escape. I believe she expressed proper gratitude; I am not sure. I was pondering the disposition to be made of a dainty cambric handkerchief which I had transferred from the pocketbook to my breast pocket, and struggling to conceal my chagrin.

" What a fool!" I groaned as the front door closed behind me. " I run over a charming girl, or she runs over me,—but no matter about that now,—and find a cardcase. I infer, like an imbecile, that the girl and the card-case belong to each other. The worst of it is that I know no more about Miss Pepper-pot, and never shall, than I knew before she shot out from behind that beastly car."

Ah, those blessed accidents! those remarkable coincidences that we are always exciting ourselves about! I wouldn't exchange my heritage of luck for the divine right of kings, which seems, indeed, to have been a moderately uncomfortable inheritance.

Nearly three months after the beginning and apparent end of my little romance I was taking an early spin along the boulevard. Only two or three wheelmen were out. Scarcely anyone had discovered that the early New York spring was upon us. I was riding slowly, watching the lovely, dull lights of early morning on the Hudson. Just ahead of me a woman turned the corner of 86th Street, riding quite rapidly. It was the lady of the crossing. As I drove my wheel ahead to come up beside her, a yellow streak flashed across my path from the left, steered past the girl between her wheel and the curb, and with a scorcher's indifference to consequences scorched away into the distance. The poor girl was lying in a limp heap on the asphalt. There was no one in sight, barring the vanishing yellow streak, and a policeman serenely walking away from the scene, after the manner of his kind, in the vicinity of 78th Street.

I did what I could, and the blue eyes opened in an astonishingly short space of time.

"Oh, do go away!" said the girl, with unflattering emphasis.

"Impossible," I replied calmly, though I was exasperated. What right had this chit of a girl to hold me responsible for every mishap that befell her? It was bad enough that she never revealed herself to me except under violent conditions. To deal out nothing but upbraidings was not to be borne. Moreover, I intended to stop it here and now.

"How dare you go riding around the country like that?" she went on, as soon as she could find breath enough. "You ought to be arrested." She pulled herself into an upright position too suddenly; the blood dropped out of her face again, and she sank back helplessly onto my arm.

"There's a policeman down there," I said brutally; "when you feel strong enough we will ride after him, and you can prefer your charges."

"If you were a gentleman," she began hotly, and stopped to save herself from a burst of tears.

"You pretty clearly established the contrary, you know, once before, so we scarcely need discuss the question now," I said relentlessly.

"Oh! you are—it is detestable of you to—to speak of it," she exclaimed wildly. "You know quite well I've a right to be indignant now, and—and yet you—you sit there and—and justify yourself, and—and——"

"Oh, is *that* what I am doing?" I interrupted with renewed sarcasm. "I was under the impression that I was very submissive to your ladyship's reproaches."

"How dare you—how dare you imply that I am unjust?" She jumped to her feet, and the hot color found its way to her face in a great wave.

"As a matter of fact," I said, picking up her wheel, "I did not knock you over. That, however, is not of the slightest importance compared to the question whether or not you are the worse for your fall."

"I suppose the fault was mine," she said fiercely, ignoring my solicitation, "as it was before."

"Then you *do* remember me, do you?"

"Remember you! Do you suppose I can ever forget you?"

"Heaven forbid," I replied fervently.

She was giving little dabs to her face, and flicking the dust from her skirt with my handkerchief, which she had unconsciously taken from my hand. She was so sudden in her movements that it was difficult to keep up with her, but I did not intend that she should escape from me a second time without an explanation, and I kept a firm hold on her handle bars.

"Don't let me detain you," she remarked, with that ridiculous lift of her eyebrows affected by very small women when they want to be especially crushing.

"I don't know any more than you do," I began calmly, without yielding up her wheel to her, "why fate chooses to throw us together with such violence. I do know that you have twice shown me great injustice, and I shall not let you go away from me this time without an explanation."

Dignified silence from my lady.

"Do you see that spot up there on top of the rise?" I continued, pointing toward 125th Street.

She deigned to turn her lovely eyes, but vouchsafed no reply.

"*That* is the man who upset you," I persisted.

She lifted an incredulous face to mine.

"My sole offense," I went on inhumanly, "is that I picked you up from under your wheel and did what I could to resuscitate you."

"How perfectly dreadful!" she sobbed, burying her face in my handkerchief.

"For hea—that is—don't you know, don't cry." I can't stand a woman's tears. My heart hardened, however, as I realized what she had said. "By jove!" I continued recklessly, "I don't see how you can reasonably object to my picking you up out of the street. In my opinion it would have been decidedly *more* dreadful if I had left you there."

She had dropped onto the curb and was genuinely crying now; and as soon as I could dispose of the wheel, I sat down awkwardly beside her. It's instinctive to put your arm around a woman that cries, or take her hand, or pat her head, or do something; but I'd as soon think of caressing a meteor as this fiery young damsel, and besides I really was angry at her prudishness.

"You must be a very finicky young woman, indeed," I continued, urging my wrath on. "if you object to what I have done. I suppose I should have ridden for the scorcher or the policeman to introduce me to you before I picked you up."

"Oh, oh, *don't* be so stupid!" she gasped hysterically; "and I'm *not* finicky at all."

"Neither am I stupid," I growled resentfully.

"I m-meant how dud-dreadful to have th-thought you did-did it," she sobbed; "and to huh-have been so c-cross, and-and horrid. I knew all the t-time it was my fault more than y-yours on 23d Street; and I felt dud-dreadfully that I couldn't write and-and apologize; but, of course, I didn't know where you lived or-or anything. And then when I opened my eyes, and saw you, I was so angry to think you had d-done it again that I forgot all about it."

She had the better of her tears before she finished, and the absurdity of our present position moved us to a hilarity that would have been the scandal of the boulevard, except that the hour was too early for the aristocratic west-siders to witness it.

How I allowed that young woman to escape me without imparting her name, I don't know. She didn't vouchsafe it in return for my card, which

I promptly tendered her; and I trusted to our homeward spin to give me the opportunity for furthering our acquaintance. She chatted bravely as we rode back through 86th Street to her home near the park, with an air of talking against time, and I actually saw her disappear into the basement door of a handsome brown stone with her wheel, without daring to ask her name. The thought of my pocket handkerchief, which she had unsuspiciously put into her pocket, gave me a ray of hope, which was justified next morning.

The post brought me the handkerchief, together with a most gracious note from my fate, as I began to consider the little lady. After generous apologies for what she was pleased to style her absurd injustice, she said: "Harry, my brother, tells me you were a classmate of his at college, and is very indignant that you did not let us know you were in the city. You must come to see us as soon as possible. I assure you I will be very quiet while you are in the house, and we will try to avoid accident."

The letter was signed Alice Moore.

"Harry Moore! Well, he took mighty good pains to keep any of us from knowing he had a sister. He had brothers enough. There was Ralph, a senior when we entered, and a married brother, and John, a 'sub' when we left. By Jove! I suppose she was an infant. She isn't more than twenty or twenty-two now; and I'm—great Scott! am I thirty-five? She was rather below the importance of mentioning thirteen years ago. But plenty of happy —— " Well, I didn't exactly articulate my very irrelevant thoughts about disparity of age in its relation to marriage. "'As soon as possible.' That's to-night," I concluded; and with this happy reflection I sought the office of "Bell Bros., Limited."

My recent lesson in the evils of profanity exerted a restraining influence as I read a telegram demanding my immediate presence in St. Louis. I didn't swear—much. The trip concerned a contract that I had been trying for over a year to secure. There was no help for it; I must go. I had deferred writing Miss Moore until I should reach St. Louis. I secured the contract, and also some wandering germs of diphtheria. Two days after reaching St. Louis I was taken to the hospital. It was over a month before I was permitted to leave, and then only with a recommendation to rest, a sea voyage, etc., to restore my cardiac organ to its usual tone. My heart, indeed! I fancied I could give the learned man of pills points on the diagnosis of my case.

I went to New York, to 86th Street. The house was closed. The boarded-up door seemed like the impenetrable bar to my future. I studied the directory, where the Moores were as thick as blackberries in June—or Smiths. I found John and Henry with different offices and the same residence. I visited the offices: Henry was in St. Louis, on business; John was taking a two months' vacation. Why did I ever suppose that I could arrange a prosaic meeting with this will-o'-the-wisp,—this firefly? In disgust at my helplessness and weariness of existence, I determined to follow the doctor's prescription to go abroad.

I found her, of course. This was the way of it: Two weeks after I landed at Liverpool I found myself a tramp in Scotland. I steered clear of the cities, and, for the most part, of the railroads and conventional routes.

Just as the sun was getting low one evening I stumbled onto the prettiest little lake imaginable on the edge of a deep wood, where I had been sulking for a couple of hours. The sun poured a red glow, slanting over the smooth sheet. It was lovely. For the first time in weeks I was glad to be alive. There seemed to be no living thing there except myself; and such silence I have never—well, why not?—heard. I sprang up a great rocky slope that was attempting to hide the last bit of sun from me. There on the very edge of the rocky height was Alice—my Alice.

" O Jack, dear, isn't it lovely?" she called out, sending a chill to my heart.

"Now, who the devil is ' Jack, dear,'" I exclaimed, rushing to her and seizing both her hands. " Alice! where have you been? How came you here, and who is 'Jack'?"

Her pugnacious little chin squared itself. " How dare you—how dare you use such language to me?" she said, punctuating her wrath by a violent shake of my two hands.

" O, never mind that now," I rushed on, gladness making me insensible of everything but this new indication that this lovely girl was my destiny.

" But I *do* mind, and I won't have it," she replied, with a vigor that reminded me of former occasions. " If you are going to be always rushing at me in this ridiculous way, at least you shall not swear at me."

"O Alice, nonsense; you know I could not swear at you. It was just my surprise and my gladness." I had forgotten to let go of her hands. " Do tell me who Jack is at once—dear! "

" Who Jack is! The question is, who the devil are you, sir?" This shot came from a man who had apparently bounded up over the rock from the direction opposite to that by which I had entered this scene. I turned toward him. It was Jack Moore. I observed that my lady found no fault with *his* language. As for me, I would cheerfully have dropped Jack into the lake, if I had contemplated any opposition from him. As it was, I fell to berating him good-naturedly for concealing the fact that he had a sister all these years.

" A sister?" he exclaimed, with an interrogatory stare at Alice. " I haven't."

" What! " I exclaimed.

He and Alice looked at each other blankly.

"You used to be Harry Moore's brother," I said, testily; "and unless you've changed all that, I suppose you are the brother of Harry's sister."

"No," said Jack; "I'm not. I'm only connected with Harry's sister-in-law by marriage. I'm her husband."

"The devil!" said I.

E. M. Boult

Drawn by
Orson Lowell

Mr. Orson Lowell

HREE years ago Mr. Orson Lowell arrived in New York; since then he has made such rapid progress that he would be quite justified in writing a booklet on "How to Succeed." Of course he will never do anything so absurd, but it is not fair that the great secret should die with him; and that it may not, the writer has made him the subject of a special study. In consequence, he is able to announce that the way to succeed is to get "fun" out of life. And this statement immediately makes it necessary to define "fun" as the word is used by Mr. Lowell.

As nearly as can be learned, "fun," in his opinion, is "the privilege to do an unlimited amount of work to accomplish something one has in view." When an undertaking presents difficulties that call into play all the resources of his art, and causes struggles that would discourage a man of less energy, he gets unlimited "fun" out of it all, and that is exactly why he has succeeded so well. He enjoys his work, and for that reason the pictures he produces are thoroughly enjoyed by others. But before proceeding to a consideration of his work and methods, it may be well to record a few facts that will be of assistance to his future biographer.

Mr. Lowell was born just twenty-five years ago in Wyoming, Iowa. It was natural that his mind should be directed toward art, for his father was an artist of very considerable attainments, who watched with much interest, but without undue encouragement, the development of his son's talents. In the public schools Mr. Lowell went through the grind that all young Americans are fortunately forced to endure; but he enlivened it with much sketching and caricaturing, seldom allowing a day to pass in which he did not make an original picture, or copy one that happened to catch his fancy.

Considering the thoroughly "legitimate" character of his present work, it is amusing, as well as surprising, to learn that for many years his ambition was to be a cartoonist. The artists of the humorous press were all heroes to him, and the chief of his hopes was that he might some day make a picture worthy of acceptance by some red-faced comic paper.

When Mr. Lowell was eleven years of age the family moved to Chicago, where, besides having the privilege of attending better schools, he was soon able to study art seriously. In 1887 he entered the Art Institute, and became a pupil of Vanderpoel and Grover. Under them he acquired the technical skill and mastery of different mediums that afterwards enabled him to open a studio in New York, not as a novice, but as one who had served his apprenticeship, and was fitted to work beside the illustrators who had already found favor with the public.

When he removed to New York, in 1893, he had the good fortune to attract the attention of Mr. Jaccaci, who was at that time art manager of *McClure's Magazine*. Mr. Jaccaci was quick to recognize Mr. Lowell's ability, and to give him many opportunities of enjoying the kind of "fun" which, in these days of fads and flashy work, is peculiar to a lamentably small band of sincere workers. When Mr. Jaccaci assumed the management of the Art Department of *Scribner's Magazine*, he promptly availed himself of Mr. Lowell's artistic talents, with the result that the work of the young artist quickly received a wide and appreciative recognition.

In considering Mr. Lowell's work as an illustrator, the critic cannot help being struck by the decorative quality of his compositions. Full of character as they are, there is in them all that admirable balance of effects that makes a picture delightful without consideration of the story that is being told. Mr. Lowell's illustrations not only illuminate the meaning of the author whose work he is interpreting pictorially, but add to it a charm that is peculiarly individual, and springs from that artistic instinct which is innate and can never be acquired in the schools. Sometimes it seems as if there were a struggle in the mind of the artist as to whether the picture under consideration should be made a decoration or an illustration, but the result is almost invariably a design that carries the charm of the one and the interpretive value of the other.

Perhaps nothing in Mr. Lowell's work shows so much the ever-present artistic bent of his mind as the beauty with which he produces still life effects in his designs. The technical cleverness with which he expresses texture and detail of every kind, gives constant evidence of the assiduity with which he has studied. The analytical critic cannot help feeling that every object in his illustrations has been drawn many times, not perhaps for the work in hand, but rather when a few moments not otherwise occupied gave him the opportunity to increase his skill by depicting some trifle that attracted his attention.

Drawn by
    Orson Lowell

Another interesting thing about his artistic success, that is probably more creditable to him than anything else, is that with all his skill in portraying beauty he has never developed a "Lowell girl." He has pictured many beautiful women, but each has been a character study, and he has avoided the disaster of developing a type such as calls into existence hordes of amateurish imitators and stifles true art. Besides, he is able to do what few illustrators can do—draw an interesting man. His men have fiber and character, and are not merely racks on which to hang dress suits.

But though Mr. Lowell is best known as an illustrator, and is ambitious to succeed in that department of art rather than in painting, it must not be forgotten that he has had considerable success as a colorist. He has exhibited landscapes and figure studies at the exhibitions of the Society of American Artists, the New York Water Color Society, and the Water Color Club. Most of these have been sketches made in his summer itinerancies, and are full of sunshine and color. Many of them deal with subjects so full of varying hues, that one is almost staggered at his audacity in undertaking pictures requiring so much minute and discriminating attention. But in them all there is evidence of his thorough enjoyment of color as a medium of expression, and it is certain that as he proceeds he will learn the subtle art of eliminating all but essential that is indispensable to effective painting. At the present time he is preparing a series of illustrations in color to be reproduced by lithography in *New York Truth*, and his friends are looking forward with much interest to see what the result will be when he adds color to his graceful compositions.

Before concluding, a few more facts must be recorded for the benefit of the above-mentioned biographer. While working for the magazines, Mr. Lowell has illustrated many books for Scribner's; Little, Brown & Co., Boston; Harper Brothers; and he has just completed a series of illustrations for the two last volumes of Bret Harte's stories, that are to be issued shortly by Houghton, Mifflin & Co. He has also done occasional drawings for *Life*, *Truth*, *Vogue*, and other publications.

In conclusion there is little to say, save that the best thing about Mr. Lowell's work is that, with all its excellence, it promises so much for the future.

P. McArthur

Hidden

BETWEEN two narrow walls gold sunlight often shines:
And so a golden thought oft creeps between two lines.

Charles Hanson Towne

Ghosts Across the Water

NLY a tall, thin girl in a plain, dark serge dress; no one will be likely to give her a second glance as she steps into the Public Library with shawl and handbag on her arm. She sinks into the first vacant chair with a half-suppressed sigh of relief. Is she very tired? Her face can lay no claim to beauty, but it has a certain lovable quality and a pleasing mobility of expression· Her eyes at once seek the clock on the wall.

"Twenty minutes of five; is that all? How tiresome it was, that pacing up and down my room after everything was done and the express had taken my trunk! I felt like a caged lion wild to be set free. Yes, I knew it would be better to wait here the rest of the time; here, where I am only one of a crowd. Suppose one of those lodgers had come into my room and begun to prod me with questions? An hour and a quarter yet before the train starts! I won't go to the depot till the last minute; he might be seen standing round there, too; some one might recognize us. What a nuisance to have to think of people now when they are nothing to us; but soon we shall be far away from their prying eyes and meddlesome tongues."

A glow mounts this girl's pale cheeks as an image arises before her mind's eye; an impetuous movement betokens the restlessness of an imminent future waiting for her own hand to raise the curtain; only one more scene, this in the Library.

The chubby, roughly clad boy reading the *Youth's Companion* next to her looks up as she moves her chair. No one else seems to be observing this newcomer, though fifty or more quiet readers occupy the hall, and persons are continually walking in and out.

Only yesterday Helen Mayfield was part of a machine,—one of the type-writer girls of Bond & Co. Orphaned at the age of fourteen, she began to work for the firm for three dollars a week, owing the balance of her support to the hospitality of some remote kinsman, whom she relieved of the burden as soon as possible.

Now that she is earning ten dollars a week, and is able to live independently, in dingy lodgings, doubtless, as the world goes, she is tolerably fortunate; for she gets food, lodging, and clothing out of life, and possessed of a kind of wiry strength in her seeming fragility, breadwinning is not likely to kill her. It is true that she has not yet been able to save a dollar to depend on in case she should contract some fatal disease; but she would be well cared for in the charity ward of the City Hospital, those same distant relatives would have her decently buried, her fellow-workers would subscribe to a floral tribute to lay on her coffin, and attend the funeral in a body. Heaven would come at last, if she had been faithful to the end,—according to the frequent assurance of an eloquent minister at the South End.

Bond & Co. at ten dollars per week on earth, plus the promise of heaven as a sequel,—ought not this to satisfy any honest working girl?

But the heaven of the church seems very vague to this girl now, and the sky above her has never answered a single one of her questionings when she has gazed up to it with wistful eyes out of her lonely universe. Her only certainty is that something within her cries insatiably for a happiness different from any she has known: for a happiness here, before the time comes to put off this garment of flesh. Instincts, dreams, books, the birds, the wind, the flowers, the deep tones of the organ, the high, clear notes of the tenor in the church choir,—all have awakened this longing anew and ministered to its growth.

The beautiful and luxurious persistently denied this young woman should have little imagination: the cravings and tendencies that have fought so fiercely against her environment have not come down to her from her immediate ancestors: possibly it is a case of atavism. Finding time to read in the evenings, to look at pictures in the windows of Williams & Everett's on her way home from work, and attending the Lowell Institute free lectures occasionally, the deficiencies of her early education are not very apparent: there is an adaptability, a power of sympathy, that might even render her companionable to some well-informed person.

"Duffield: Peabody: Jones," the clerk at the desk calls out, with monotonous intervals between the names. The drop of the books, the tramp of a heavy boot, the creaking of a shoe, the flutter of leaves, the rustling of skirts,—Helen hears all these sounds, but they come to her ears as out of a dream world. Nothing in this Library is real to her except the clock,—the clock, her bounding pulses, her fevered heart.

"He longs to deliver me from the house of bondage. Haven't I wasted enough of my young days? What a delight it will be to typewrite his book for him—'Italian Vistas': the name sets me in a tremble. We'll have long walks through palaces in the moonlight: fountains will be playing: we'll go out in little boats to see gorgeous sunsets: those black-eyed children like the pictures in the Art Museum will sing to the guitar: he'll buy me fresh bunches of those big luscious grapes I never have tasted; best of all, nobody that we ever saw or heard of will be near to watch us." Closing her eyes for a moment, to make anticipation more like reality, her lips part slightly: those pink spots high up on her cheeks burn deeper. "There's a mysterious look in his eyes I don't understand: it draws me all out of myself till I don't know where I am. How handsome he is! But I'd love him just the same if he was marked with smallpox, I know I would! It must be Stephen now, or nobody; I couldn't care for such men as Miss Haynes, and Miss Pollock, and those other girls married, now that I've met him!"

A thrill of repulsion runs through her,—a potent anticlimax to the attractions of Stephen Lambert. Suddenly, irresistibly, her muscles clamor for action, thought having become oppressive.

The clock? Five minutes past five only, and it seems to her that she has been waiting an hour.

She rises impetuously and hurries by the grave, automatic policeman who stands in the archway between this hall and the reading room beyond; he might be a wax Tussaud policeman, the sham guardian of the Library. Everybody in the world has become a mere wax figure to Helen,—everybody except Stephen Lambert.

Some magazines and papers are lying on a desk in the inner room to the left of the policeman. She picks up one of them at random, an observer would say; but an observer is oftenest indiscriminating. Even in this moment of delirious expectancy her choice of a magazine to while away the intervening time is half consciously influenced by the valuable suggestions for remodeling dresses that she has received from other issues of this cheap print, called "The Ladies' Own."

She drops down on a bench and follows her old habit of turning to the colored fashion plates of impossible ladies.

Presently a soft smile creeps over her face, as if another lamp were lit from within; perhaps a term of joy is all this woman needs to make her beautiful.

"They'll be no more use to me now; I won't have to sew, and we'll stop in Paris," is what comes to her mind.

Her thoughts roving in the half-defined scenes of the promised land, her fingers continue to toy nervously with the leaves of the magazine. She glances at the printed characters; the title of a story attracts her; it is the simple directness of the style that succeeds finally in holding her attention.

The print is clear; the letters seem to fairly stand out from the page as she reads on to a certain critical point as follows:—

. .

"The woman said: 'For our dear Lord's sake, wait a moment! Do not shudder and gather up your dress; hear my story. I was walking along the common highway; there was one who walked close by my side. We saw many obstacles ahead, and we turned into a path that looked easier to follow. The people in the highway called out to us sternly. "The wrong road! Beware!" Some of them began to write on tablets, some put up signposts. He took my hand in his and said, "Do not heed them!" We wandered on till we came to a swiftly flowing river. A gilded pleasure boat floated to the bank, a winged figure was at the prow. We seized the oars. Music filled the air. A rosy haze enveloped the opposite shore, and through it we could see shadowy forms: their white arms seemed to beckon us to join them in the Kingdom of Happiness. We rowed across the river, we landed, and boat was carried away by the current. The fog lifted. All the sky grew cold and gray. The figures were all pale shadows: the reflection of a soul in torture was set in every face. " Who are you?" I cried in agony. " We are the ghosts of our dead joys. You will become like us. Why were you persuaded to cross that lying river?" Then I saw what was before me: I could not seem happy, and soon he left me. The sun went down. Through cruel straits I got back to this highway, but no traveler will notice me. I am alone in the Great Desert. I see only those ghosts across the water: I shall see them till I die!'"

Helen Mayfield shivers from head to foot as she finishes these terse sentences. A December frost has nipped her summer bloom: she wants to tear the book in her hand to fragments, but a perception of the Library and its obligations penetrates to her brain through the shock and restrains her. Starting up from the bench she walks to a window. Two readers glance at her: she obstructs their light. Her heart beats with such violence that she unconsciously presses one hand against it, the other still holds the magazine.

" Oh! why didn't I escape out of this city before I ever saw this?"

She can hear Stephen's voice pleading, echoing from yesterday,—

" You have only me. Come!"

" I am coming," her spirit answers; " I will go with you to the ends of the earth. Do you think I could let you sail away from me to-morrow to stay for years? God, let me die rather than give him up!"

The magazine feels heavy: she looks at it with a dumb terror. " I'll get rid of it,—forget it!"

She throws it hastily on the desk where she found it and walks away. An eager plunge through the heavy doors in the hall, and she is in the street.

The twilight is gathering. On the sidewalk she halts, as if to assure herself that all her belongings are safe, her gaze fixed in the direction of the Providence Depot, the building hidden by a turn of the street. Thought runs ahead :—

" He is there by this time. Good-by old Boston; I have loved you well: but now ——"

Suddenly her feet cling to the pavement. Why does she not go on?

She has a Titan to throttle: the Accustomed has caught her in its grip. Dull, sodden thing she has found it until this moment, when it springs upon her endued with the accumulated force of ages.

Two blocks beyond her, trains are being made up, engines are puffing premonitory blasts, and a well-built young man casts searching glances at every feminine figure among the travelers as he leaps onto the platform of a rear car.

"In the front car before this, as I told her," he decides, in failing to see the person he is looking for.

"All aboard!" cries the brakeman. The Known and the Unknown are fighting fiercely for that slender reed of a girl in front of the Public Library; she sways helplessly back and forth in the conflict. Up and down through the Common, men and women are passing to their homes for the night, the leafless trees clothed in icy garments above their heads. Helen looks over there with a wild, staring question,—

"And shall I never be among them again,—never as I am now?"

"Never!" echoes the Titan.

"Would they scorn and shun me if I came back to the Long Path, old and homesick?"

"Forever!" says the Titan.

The wind rises, and the great white boughs of the trees beyond the highway wave toward her, then away from her, like those ghostly arms across the lying river.

A clock strikes out clearly in the frosty air—one, two, three, four, five, six. Helen knows the hour without counting; she gives a bound forward as if to reach the depot in time, then falls back and grasps an iron railing to steady herself.

"Too late! He has gone. Oh! why was it so sweet?"

Desolation sweeps over her in a tidal wave. Two great tears melt the frozen dread in her eyes, and roll down her cheeks, her lips clenched with anguish.

Another moment and she draws herself up; she can remember everything,—the life of yesterday that she is to take hold of again. As she turns squarely round to encounter her world of toil, a meager figure in a shabby water-proof jostles her,—a middle-aged woman with a wilted face under an old-fashioned bonnet. Their eyes meet through the gloaming in an abstracted glance, each soul locked in with its own woe : they meet as strangers now,—strangers, it may be, forever. This woman is a writer, on her way into the Library, to look at her story in print. She goes at once to a desk in the inner room and picks up a magazine that is lying where Helen Mayfield dropped it. The author has never seen her story since the day she mailed the manuscript to a literary bureau six months ago, after having tried vainly several of the first-class periodicals. This morning she received a letter from the Bureau, informing her that her "admirable sketch" is in print in the current issue of "The Ladies' Own," and inclosing a check for five dollars in payment therefor.

"Oh! why did I get discouraged so soon?" is her self-accusing cry. "I put my soul into this story, and if I had only waited, some good chance for it would have come. I know it would; but I was so poor, so tired of hope deferred! I am getting old now; I shall never do any better work than this, and here it is buried in a fourth-rate fashion magazine!"

Her thin fingers turn over the leaves, and her feeling is the nearest she will ever know to that of a mother who mourns a dead child.

"I could stand giving it away for a mere song, much as I need money, if it would lead to anything, or if it would do anybody any good; but it is lost to fame, lost to the world. Who will ever read it now? Oh! why was I made to write, yet forbidden to succeed? Must I bury my talent in a napkin? Is there no room for it, for me, on the earth? My God, it is hard!"

Frances Albert Doughty.

The Arts and Crafts Exhibition

T is now about five years ago that the first Arts and Crafts Exhibition was held in England. The influences which led up to this were chiefly the awakened interest in applied art and handicraft, due to the teaching and work of such men as William Morris, Walter Crane, and others. The enormous production, by means of machinery, of things which enter into the interior furnishing of buildings, seemed gradually eliminating any art which might be in the workman, and was speedily turning the artisan into a mere human machine.

Morris says: "To give people pleasure in the things they must perforce use, that is one great office of decoration; to give people pleasure in the things they must perforce make, that is the other use of it."

This was the gospel of the whole movement, and so to-day, throughout all England, we find schools of handicraft doing work of honest motive and praiseworthy effort, and striving to weld the beautiful with the useful. It is significant that great influences in art have traveled from the East westward. We do not know whether the modern revival of handicraft in Old England is about to influence New England, beginning at Boston, or what other motives have suggested an Arts and Crafts Exhibition. As we look backward, it seems as if the energies of our workers and their intellectual activities have gone out too much in the channels of scientific invention and mechanical ingenuity, leaving our lives, even if more comfortable, cold and bare. Let us hope a new influence has come, which will infuse some warmth of art and poetry into the surroundings of everyday life.

The success of such exhibitions depends not on the men who initiate them, but on the enthusiasm and spirit of the workers who contribute. If we have no art handicraft to show worthy of the name, how can we have an exhibition? There is one aspect of this movement which is well to consider,—that relating to the artist and his work as affected by fashion. The commercial spirit says to the artist, " You must design thus and so, because the public want that." If designing silks or wall papers, he will be told, perhaps, that they must be French in style. All of which is most pernicious. It is like telling a poet he must write a certain kind of verse only. Now, in an exhibition like this about to be held, let full recognition be given to the works of artists that show the creations of a free man, untrammeled by any conditions whatsoever. Thus only will be developed a true individual art.

Again, special encouragement should be given to such works which, *both in design and execution*, are the work of one man. The man who handles the tools will be the better if he can conceive and design his work, and the designer will likewise benefit by handling the tools and mastering the technique of execution. This exhibition exalts hopes and expectations to us which, if realized, will do much good.

In active life we know the various artistic professions are fairly crowded, —take for instance Architecture and Pictorial Painting,—and the aspirants for success in these professions are not always wholly fitted for such work. Many have not risen to that standard of excellence which will insure them a livelihood at a period when competition is most bitter. Perhaps these very individuals, if they turned their talents into the work of decorative and applied art in connection with our handicrafts, might achieve a greater success and a comfortable living.

And this requires, in turn, on the part of the public,—the buyers of furniture and of everything that enters into their houses and buildings,— that they should give preference and encouragement to such furnishings, made by handicraftsmen, which show artistic qualities to the benefit of both; so that the things made may be, as Morris has it, "A joy to the maker and a joy to the user."

Robert Brown, Jr.

Impressions of Southern Spain

III

ALHAMBRA

S Granada is on the road to nowhere, one only goes there to see the Alhambra, and come back again. "You are going to Granada?" said an English commercial traveler whom I met at the station. "Ah, well, you will get there this afternoon. You can see the Alhambra and the Generaliffe in the morning, go over to the Cartuja after dinner, and take the night train back." You may well suppose that I put this astounding statement to the credit of English insensibility. What! The Alhambra in the fraction of a morning? That enchanted, golden palace where Irving lived, and where Gautier slept, and where De Amicis reveled in a dream of Oriental voluptuousness! What heresy,—what a base, commercial way of looking at this beautiful world!

Well, I have spent—not a half day, but many weeks there, and the more I see of Englishmen, the more convinced I am that they have a vast deal of practical good sense.

I don't suppose that those persons whose only idea of the Alhambra is formed from books and photographs, have any conception of what the real thing is like. I am going to try to tell the truth about it, since nobody has ever done so.

The Alhambra was built a good many centuries ago by the Moorish invaders of Spain. It was partly a pleasure house, and very much a fortification.

Whenever the Moors build any important structure, you will find fine masses enriched by fine detail in its proper place. Their good taste is unerring and inevitable. To undervalue their talent in these matters would be a piece of ridiculous conceit quite unworthy of an Anglo-Saxon. It is for this reason that I believe the Alhambra to have been what the Moors themselves considered it to be—one of the most beautiful palaces in the world.

But anyone at all familiar with Moorish construction must be struck by the fact that the interior of the palace was built, perhaps hurriedly, but certainly cheaply. It has the appearance of being erected more for a temporary residence than for a lasting monument. It looks as if its builders had no confidence in the perpetuity of their reign in Spain.

The external walls—the fortifications—were sufficiently well laid courses of brick and mud, alternating with courses of stone. This does not sound like an enduring mode of construction, but experience has shown that it outlasts solid stone work; and the Alhambra walls have stood pretty well the test of several earthquakes which have wrecked the more recent masonry of Charles the Fifth. Indeed, the old Roman wall of Algiers, something like two thousand years old, is built in much the same way, and has stood the same test. The Alhambra walls, which, built of red brick, red earth, and red stone, gave its name to the palace, remain to a great extent, and with their beautiful arched gateways seem to me by far the finest part of the present structure. But the interior of the palace appears to have been built with the greatest possible saving of time and expense. The stonework—what bits there are of it—is vastly inferior to that of any respectable Moorish private house; and the stucco, which was the principal ornament, however fine in design, was with them as it would be with us, an obvious economy,—a substitute for the carved stone which they themselves used in the mosque at Cordova.

To form any conception of the original palace one must trace back its history. I am not going to do this, which any guide book will do for me. I will only say that the Alhambra was built and enlarged, decorated and redecorated, and more or less restored by the Moors, then taken possession of by the Spanish kings, who had it repainted and restored by Italian decorators; then half demolished and deserted; and after being occupied by military garrisons, by monks who whitewashed it an inch thick, by gypsies who defaced it and befouled it, finally came into the hands of French troops, who tore down everything above the main floor,—that is to say, the greater part of the building,—and roofed in the rest to make comfortable barracks.

From that time the poor old ruin was allowed to moulder in peace until the Spanish government confided it to the hands of an enthusiastic and well-meaning amateur, who, Heaven forgive him, has gone about restoring it. Thus, after being alternately ravaged by French and Spanish conceit,—for the Spaniards would not hesitate to restore Solomon's Temple, nor the French to pull it down to build a boulevard,—the Alhambra is in much the same position as an old man in a wig,—it has neither the freshness of youth nor the dignity of old age.

You must understand that if the Moorish gold and color decoration ever existed, it entirely disappeared about four centuries ago, and the Italian restorations at least two centuries ago; and that the whole upper walls except one square tower, that is to say, the whole architectural design and effect of the building, were destroyed by the French invaders, for the alleged reason that they were unsafe. But as, at the same, they mined the whole palace,—with the purpose of blowing it up,—I am tempted to attribute their conduct to the jealous dislike which their nation has sometimes shown for things above their comprehension.

I have often tried to reconstruct vaguely in my own mind the effect of the original Alhambra, but the bare, staring, colorless reality is too freshly impressed upon me to allow me to do so with any great success.

I try to imagine the cool courts, shaded by great palms and many-hued awnings, and overhung by high walls pierced with delicate open galleries or jutting into fretted balconies, one above another: great *facades* like stone lacework, backed by masses of gold and glowing color, and all that endless variety of arrangement that none but the Moors have ever been able to invent. Everywhere shade and mystery, and the tinkling of fountains, and the scent of roses, and the sound of strange instruments, and the songs of birds.

But it is useless to try. The vision will not come. I can see nothing but the dreary, unshaded expanse of hot gravel, without a shrub or blade of grass; unbroken surfaces of new, low side wall, covered with meaningless, modernized stucco ornament,—for the restorer was too much a Spaniard not to improve on his original: plain, cheap-looking columns,—ten or a dozen feet high,—which were well enough when buried in dense shade, and topped by masses of rich architecture, but which are ridiculous in the dry glare of the sunlight, with nothing above them but a few feet of stuccoed ornament, and the whole—imagine it!—indiscriminately washed over with a fine, new, shining coat of what appears to be buff paint.

When I walked for the first time into the sickening reality of this restored Alhambra,—the fine old ruin of Irving's time converted into a decorator's workshop and a trap to catch *pesetas*,—I give you my word that, what with rage, what with disappointment, I had a great desire to cry. If it had not been for that beast of a custodian who was watching me, I really believe I should have done it.

I suppose I ought to speak more definitely of the so-called restorations of the Alhambra. I greatly dislike to do so. The amiable gentleman who has made them is still living, and does not dream that he is not doing the most commendable work. I do not feel inclined to blame him in the least. It is not his fault, since he has done the best that he could. It is merely the fault of the government that has employed an incompetent person. I believe, at his own request.

I dare say it is not generally known that the stuccowork of the Alhambra is precisely the same as that which is done to-day in Persia, in India, and to some extent in the Barbary States. If it was necessary to restore this ruin, which I doubt, workmen could have been found, probably no farther away than Tunis, who were accustomed to the manner of work and the daily use of the material. Competent Moorish architects could have superintended the work, and would have carried it out in its original spirit. The same national feeling which drove the native architects out of Algiers at the time of the French occupation, and forced them to take refuge in Tunis, would have made them proud to undertake a task which preserved the traditional glories of the Moorish empire in Spain, and the work would have been a work of art.

The restored portions of the Alhambra constitute about nine tenths of the wall surface in the various courts. There has been no attempt to use any color decoration except in one small, underground chamber, usually kept locked. The decoration of this room—in the baths—has no Moorish feeling whatever, being mostly done in broken colors and pale tints spread over large spaces. The original coloring of the Alhambra, as one may detect by careful investigation, was in a few full, positive colors, chiefly malachite, ultramarine, and dark vermilion, intimately mingled and united by a profuse use of gold. In this restoration, from want of funds— a very general want in Spain—bronze powder has been substituted for gold, and a very offensive pale lilac is the most prominent tint. The effect is not worth criticising.

The remainder of the stuccoed surface of the building has been painted with a universal tint about the color of an underdone loaf of bread. Anything more hideously new and dreary could not have been devised. When I add that the restored stucco is a mere repetition of three or four patterns, and has none of the rich, undulating character of the original, except in its outlines, being carefully reduced to an even surface, and all the edges sharpened with true Spanish formality, you may be able to understand why the modern Alhambra looks like a cardboard palace washed over with glue size.

The only distinctive thing about the Alhambra is the *faience* ornamentation, which forms the base of all the chambers. This, as is well known, instead of being of painted tiles, as is usual in Moorish buildings, consists of a mosaic in which intricate designs are made with bits of colored tile cut into geometrical shapes. In restoring this *faience*, instead of employing a similar material very easy to obtain in Spain, where this kind of manufacture is carried to great perfection, the decorator has resorted to the use of oil paint, colored wax, and bits of colored paper.

The want of money may be urged as an excuse for this childish playing at restoration. I am well aware that the annual allowance made by the government is so ridiculously small that the decorator has to eke out his support by the manufacture and sale to tourists of toy models of the Alhambra, which he colors according to his taste and fancy, sometimes in one way, sometimes in another. But the restoration was quite unnecessary, and should never have been undertaken. At most it should have been confined to cleaning off the accumulated whitewash and propping up the old walls and buildings. What business had this amateur decorator to make a new Alhambra with his paint pots and plaster of paris? Why convert this interesting old ruin into a cheap, span-new edifice, only fit for a *cafe concert?*

The Generaliffe, another Moorish palace within gunshot of the Alhambra, having the good fortune not to belong to the Spanish government,—being the private property of an old Italian family,—has escaped restoration, excepting a new roof here and there, and, although buried in whitewash, shows us what the Alhambra might have been if let alone. Its owners have confined themselves to keeping up its gardens and fountains; whereas the reformers of the Alhambra have rooted out all the gardens, with one exception, and the fountains are turned on, as the custodian informs you, only during the visit of distinguished strangers.

I will conclude my tirade against the Alhambra by a little abuse of the grove by which it is partly surrounded. On the hill of the Alhambra the ear of the stranger is astonished by an incessant blowing of noses, just as in the town below it is startled by a continual ringing of coin. The latter phenomenon is caused by the fact that although Spanish Munchausenades and complimentary excuses pass current everywhere by common consent, the coin of the realm has no such privilege, but must be rung many times by both parties to a bargain. The blowing of noses is due to the Duke of Wellington's beautiful elm grove, which is kept in a perpetual sloppy condition by the waste water of the Alhambra. The moment one passes from the street into this swamp through the massive old Spanish gateway, he is struck by a chill which is usually followed by an influenza.

But there is, unfortunately, something much worse to be dreaded here. Every stranger who spends more than a few days in this place is liable to be attacked by a peculiar kind of malarial fever, often very serious. I was myself so fortunate as to escape with the preliminary symptoms. The good-hearted old chambermaid, who seemed to know what was the matter, kindly volunteered a small pitcherful of a decoction of bark. By exhibiting the whole in one dose, and repeating the treatment the next morning, I managed to get on very well. I am, however, happy to inform the misguided tourist that there are several resident physicians who, I dare say, treat the complaint more scientifically, having much experience in it.

A great deal has been said of late about the bad effect of deforesting a country. Southern Spain, whose forests have entirely disappeared, is an exceptionally healthy country, both men and animals being in noticeably good condition. The cultivated olive, fig, and other fruit trees and the vegetables and vines seem to be amply able to keep the air pure, and are themselves extraordinarily productive. There is no lack of water for the purpose of irrigation, and I have long been of the opinion that an excess of moisture is one of the most active agents in producing disease and ill health.

The inundations of Murcia, so much quoted in this connection, were simply caused by the fact that the River Segura, which forms a wide basin in the middle of the town, is contracted into a very narrow gorge just below. A little inexpensive engineering would have saved the Murcianos from these disasters, and would now prevent their recurrence. Indeed, I am partly of the opinion that the river will itself in time break away a sufficient passage for the future, and thus save these modern antediluvians a world of unaccustomed trouble.

To come back to the Alhambra, one cannot well finish an account of it without saying something about the gypsies, who seem to be in their glory there, and are somehow mysteriously mixed up with the hotels and the guides.

From Fortuny's model, the king of the Gitanos, who is an excellent model, and always wants to sell his silver buttons at a singularly high rate, down to the small girls who perform quaint little gypsy songs and dances before you as you walk down the hill, ending with a sudden and unanimous demand for "*chovettas*," they are the most earnest and praiseworthy beggars in Granada.

I owe an apology to his majesty, which I here formally tender him, for having tacitly agreed to make the tour of the Albaycin—the gypsy quarter, and a nasty place—in his company and under his royal safeguard. I eluded him, and compromised the matter by handing him a small number of reals as I made my final adieus to the Alhambra. The mingled reproach and forgiveness of his silent smile are still vivid in my memory, accompanied by a faint sensation of remorse.

My remorse is, however, tempered by the fact that making this picturesque excursion is not an agreeable or entirely safe thing to do. His royal highness has a trick of getting you into a tight place somewhere and then setting on a mob of beggars of all ages and descriptions, who, if they do not pick your pockets, may at least colonize your person with vermin.

Spain is as full of this latter kind of pests as it was in the days of Sancho Panza. I was really driven out of Cartagena by them, and women may be seen everywhere sitting before their doors and tendering to each other and to their children those same touching and kindly offices that one always sees pass between monkeys in a cage.

There is something very odd about the Gitanos,—savage little animals, with glittering, wicked eyes, and an appearance of entire carelessness and irresponsibility. Strange as it may seem, very few of them can speak more than a dozen or two words of Spanish. I have no special dislike to them, if only they would not sing. Their singing is more Spanish than that of the Spaniards, and Spanish singing is a thing very difficult to describe. Suffice it to say that when a Grenadine desires to express a condition of perfect happiness and content of soul, he plays a wandering accompaniment on his guitar and bursts into a series of howls, moans, and groans, in which musical intervals are quite unnoticed.

There are, however, artists among the Gitanos, and in their strange songs one seems to hear the echo of some old world, long-forgotten system of melody such as one detects in the chants of the Mexican Indian, in the wail of old Celtic songs, and even in the plaintive and touching music of the Arabs. So they must have sung in the far East in the dim twilight of that old prehistoric world.

And so they must have danced; for the dancing of a Gitana is a thing wonderful and indescribable, and having no likeness to anything that exists. As travestied by ordinary performers, their dances are simply coarse and tiresome; but to see them rendered, as I have, by the *premiere danseuse* and jewel of the tribe, is a thing almost worth going to Granada for.

ALGIERS, January, 1883.

NOTES

¶ In that charming old, but ever new, volume of Leigh Hunt, "The Seer," under the heading "Bricklayers, and an Old Book," real and false art, "fads" and hobbies are thus deliciously touched upon: "The most elegant houses in the world, generally speaking, are built of clay. You have riches inside; costliness and beauty on the internal walls,—paintings, papers, fine draperies,—themselves compounded of the homeliest growths of the earth: but, pierce an inch or two outwards, and you come to the stuff of which the hovel is made. It is nothing but mind, at last, which throws elegance upon the richest as well as the poorest materials. Let a rich man give a hundred guineas for a daub, and people laugh at him and his daub together. The inside of his wall is no better than his out. But let him put Titian or Correggio upon it, and he puts mind there,—visible mind,—and, therefore, the most precious to all; his own mind, too, as well as the painters; for Love partakes of what it loves; and yet the painter's visible mind is not a bit different, except in degree, from the mind with which every lover of the graceful and the possible may adorn whatsoever it looks upon. The object will be perhaps rich in itself; but, if not, it will be rich, somehow or other, in association! And it cannot be too often repeated, as a truth in strictest logic, that every impression is real which is actually made upon us, whether by fact or fancy. No minds entirely divorce the two, or can divorce them, even if they evince the spiritual part of their faculties in doing nothing better than taking a fancy to a teacup or a hat."

¶ A painter of eminence was once resolved to finish a piece which should please the whole world. When, therefore, he had drawn a picture in which his utmost skill was exhausted, it was exposed in the public market-place, with directions at the bottom for every spectator to mark with a brush, which lay by, every limb and feature which seemed erroneous. The spectators came, and in general applauded; but each, willing to show his talent at criticism, marked whatever he thought proper. At evening, when the painter came, he was mortified to find the whole picture one universal blot; not a single stroke that was not stigmatized with marks of disapprobation. Not satisfied with this trial, the next day he was resolved to try them in a different manner, and, exposing his picture as before, desired that every spectator would mark those beauties he approved or admired. The people complied, and the artist, returning, found his picture replete with the marks of beauty : every stroke that had been yesterday condemned now received the character of approbation. "Well," cries the painter, "I now find that the best way to please one half of the world is not to mind what the other half says ; since what are faults in the eyes of these, shall be by those regarded as beauties."

● Just before Christmas last a London bookseller received an order from a lady for some Christmas stories as presents for her servants, leaving the selection to her bookseller. He sent up certain books published by the Religious Tract Society. The lady returned them on the ground that they were unsuitable for servants, because they had gilt edges !

● "The extraordinary difficulty of appraising Leighton's work at its right value, lies in the fact that it is so curious a mingling of true and sham art, whether you regard it from the point of view of the drama or of the classical spirit. His figures, in nearly every instance, not only act, but know that they are acting. Take, for example, the "Romeo and Juliet" : this is not, indeed, the death of Juliet as it was ; it is the very effective reproduction of the scene as it happened upon the stage. And you feel about all, or nearly all, the reposing or posing figures of other canvases that are acting the part, some well, some ill, but *acting* always."

● "There is a charm about half-fulfilled desire which nothing can quite equal : the gross touch of reality is not there to dispel illusion, and anticipation dances over all obstacles. Composers know the value of a pause in music, but it is curious that few people recognize its value in happiness : when the fruit is close to your hand, pause a moment before you touch it : when the doors of your cage are opened, wait a little before you fly away."

● "The beauty and joy of life is perhaps the greatest of all Art's themes. We are apt to think that the inspiration of joy. But this is only because joy is rarer emotion, and less easily understood. Almost every nature, however light, can sink, at least once, into the depths of sorrow, but only a few can ever rise to the heights of joy."

● The author of "Esther Waters," that wonderful, realistic story, writes the following letter to the *Saturday Review*. The literary amenities of authors occasionally are spicy, forsooth !

"To the Editor of the *Saturday Review :* Sir. — In this month's *Longmans* Mr. Andrew Lang comments somewhat strangely on my article entitled 'Since the Elizabethans,' published in *Cosmopolis* for October. It happened to me to spend a few days last summer in an English village. As I drove from the railway station to the lodging which had been hired for me, I noticed a pleasant river, which seemed to promise excellent fishing. I mentioned the river to my landlady. 'Oh, yes, sir,' she said, there is very good fishing here — many people come here for fishing.' 'What kind of people come here?' I asked, distractedly. 'Literary gentlemen come here very often, sir; we had Mr. Andrew Lang staying here.' 'Oh, really! Does he fish? Is he a good fisherman?' 'Yes, sir; he fishes beautifully.' 'Really! Does he catch much?' 'No, sir; he never catches anything; but he fishes beautifully.' Yours truly, George Moore."

¶ "Who shall decide when doctors disagree?"—when two such opposite "schools" as *The Chap-Book* and *The Literary World* (Boston) can say of Richard Le Gallienne's latest, "The Quest of the Golden Girl," the former, "The trouble with Mr. Le Gallienne is that he tries hard to be wicked, and only succeeds in being vulgar. He would have us think him no end a fellow at home, and we persist in looking on him as a rather foolish, weak-minded young man, with not even enough strength of character to be consistently immoral;" the latter, "For one who, gathering the best, may pass the evil unscathed, the book holds treasures"? Now the facts are with books, the stage, and in art, the *honi soit* principle will to the fore. "Nasty" (in the English sense) books, plays, pictures, and statues will be made, and there are those who will read, listen to, and look on the same. About all anyone can do is to raise his or her voice. A weak stomach digests poorly.

¶ ONE can see the road from the rim's edge :
        Always I look along the road,
    For down it something always comes
        Toward me ; something that doth smile,
            and something that doth weep.
    It is a woman, and a child.
        And the weeping woman faster goes
    Than doth the smiling child ;
        And both would give a drink to me,
    But the woman doth fetch the water up,
        And handeth me the pitcher full
    Quicker than doth the little child.
        The pitcher's rim is broken,
    Then both go hence, and I only think
        Of the woman that weeps ; but I forget,
    Always forget, the smiling child,
        Because it did not still my thirst ;
    And every day I go and watch
        The road, to see them coming.
    The touch of sorrow.

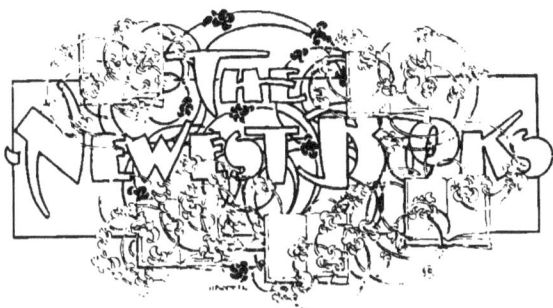

It is hard to see just why the author of "The End of the Beginning" saw fit to have it published anonymously, unless, perhaps, she (we take it for granted it *is* "she") felt that she had put too much of her soul and life into the book to bear that it should proclaim her identity to careless and disinterested readers. There is something peculiarly intimate and personal about the entire book; a something that compensates for the artificiality of epigrammatic conversation and somewhat strained situations. Armoret, the grandchild of a philosophizing old bookseller in a New England village, is the heroine, and about her development and tasting of the loves of life the story is built. The book might have been called "The Story of a Girl-hood." The other characters are Mr. Welby, a lovable old bookseller, whose "Philosophy of Life" remind one of the notable "Pilgrim's Scrip"; Robert Rodney, a *sansouciant* young artist; Henry Morland, an intro-spective man of culture and genius, whose disposal puts the author to some trouble; and Dr. Urquhart, the faithful young country doctor, whose wholesome goodness and naturalness at last win the girl from her rather morbid self-examinings and strivings for growth and the everlastingly talked of spiritual culture, to a good, healthy every-day life and love — and thus is concluded the whole matter in a most satisfactory manner.

The descriptions of season and scenery in the book are charming and full of sympathy. The curious selections given from Mr. Welby's "Philosophy of Life" are worthy of a wide circulation.

"Introspection has filled more insane asylums and made more unhappy homes than anything else that can be called a good."

"To have hated him was a religious education."

"We miss the unregions of the seen more than the regions of the unseen."

"'There is no sin to hearts that love,' says the poet. 'There is no love to hearts that sin.'"

"Are you doubtful? Wait. Are you sure? Then you can afford to wait."

¶ The peculiar trend of mind that has caused Prof. William James, of Harvard, to make a life-study of exceptional mental states, has given to his brother, Mr. Henry James, a power of psychological analysis that is scarcely equaled by any living novelist. Mr. James will take a single incident, a single situation, and upon that build a most elaborate structure of motives and moods, until the reader is quite lost in a maze of refinements. "The Spoils of Poynton" (Houghton, Mifflin & Co., $1.25) is in exact line with Mr. James's other novels. It is essentially a novel of civilization and complexities.

"The Spoils of Poynton" are the art treasures collected by Mrs. Gereth, and kept at the country seat, Poynton, left by her late husband's will to her son, Owen. Owen is a very weak, very helpless, impressionable young man, who is engaged to Mona Brigstock. Miss Brigstock's lack of appreciation for the artistic treasures about to pass into her possession determines Mrs. Gereth to prevent the marriage at any cost. Her young friend, Fleda Vetch, is thoroughly in sympathy with her devotion to the artistic and æsthetic; Mrs. Gereth accordingly determines that Owen shall marry this kindred soul. Fleda is already in love with Owen, and Owen is in that state of overflowing adoration for the opposite sex which requires merely an object for its satisfaction. Mrs. Gereth, as part of her plot, has removed almost all of the Poynton treasures to another home, thus stopping her son's marriage because Mona refuses to marry him unless Poynton is rehabilitated. In this deadlock Owen makes love to Fleda, and is accepted by her on condition that Mona relinquishes all right to him. Unfortunately Mrs. Gereth sends back the "spoils" prematurely, and Mona holds Owen to his promise. They are married and abroad when Poynton, art treasure and all, is burnt to the ground.

The force of the story is in the careful analysis of the mental condition of the character at different stages of the plot. Fleda Vetch, with her super-refined sensibilities and overwhelming love for the neutral and helpless Owen, is the central figure of the book, and hers is the point of view from which the story is told. As in all Mr. James's books the touch of the consummate stylist is seen in every sentence.

The Red Letter

An Illustrated Monthly

Published by H. Walter Stephenson
Edited by Harry Draper Hunt
Under the art direction of E. B. Bird

❡ The subscription rate is one dollar
a year. Entered at the Boston Post
Office as second-class mail matter.
The trade supplied by the American
News Company and its branches. Ad-
vertising rates on application.

The Red Letter Magazine,

Boston.

❡ SUBSCRIBERS to THE RED LETTER
can, by sending them to us, have their
first six numbers bound in cloth (and
returned to them), for fifty cents.

DODD'S
Advertising & Checking
AGENCY

THERE has never been a period when so much public interest was evinced in the advertising columns as there is at present. The enterprising advertiser who persistently pushes his commodity to public notice by means of ingenious devices of illustration, palatable truths and good judgment governed by thorough system and business principles, is as sure of prosperity as the certainty that day follows night. A continuous study for thirty years of the changing methods and requirements of the times has given us a good measure of success, attained only through the success of our clients. These thirty years of continuous dealing and careful service have given this agency a standing with advertisers equaled only by its influence with the publications.

You are uncertain what course to pursue to attain success? We invite correspondence — stating what methods you have used, amounts expended in the past, article to be introduced and points to be reached. We will then have our staff of artists, clever in their line and equal to any demands, prepare write-ups and designs.

If you are thinking of advertising in any newspaper, magazine or programme ANYWHERE, send to DODD'S Advertising & Checking AGENCY, 7 Water Street, Boston. St. Louis Branch, Globe-Democrat Building.

The Inland Printer

Leading Paper in the World in
the Printing Industry.

THE·RED LETTER

AN·ILLVSTRATED MONTHLY

TAVRVS

VOLVME·2·NVMBER·2
APRIL·MDCCCXCVII

Contents.

The Red
Letter

$1.00 A YEAR

✣ Profitable Advertising ✣

A Monthly. ✄ ✄ Fully Illustrated.
The Advertisers' Trade Journal.

Devoted to the interests of publishers and advertisers. ✄ Full of practical, profitable ideas. ✄ Tells what you want to know about advertising. ✄ Pays advertisers (write for rates). ✄ Is of great value to the subscriber.

KATE E. GRISWOLD,
Editor and Publisher,

Price, $1.00 per year.   No. 13 School Street, Boston, Mass. ✄
Send for sample copy, 10 cents.

THE.......

INLAND ✄
PRINTER

Leading Paper in the World
in the Printing Industry.

✄

Articles of General Interest
beautifully illustrated. With
large circulation. ✄ ✄ ✄ ✄

Only $2.00 per year; $1.00 for six
months; 20 cents a number. ✄ ✄
For sale by all Newsdealers.

THE INLAND PRINTER:

Nos. 212-214 Munroe Street,   No. 150 Nassau Street,
CHICAGO.   NEW YORK.

TO COLLECTORS

A few complete Sets of THE FLY LEAF, A PERI- ODICAL FOR CURIOUS PERSONS AND BOOK LOVERS, Edited by Walter Blackburn Harte, are offered for Sale at $1.00 per Set. ✼ ✼ ✼ ✼ ✼ ✼ ✼ ✼ ✼

Among the leading items of interest are: The Stir in Literature; The New Mysticism; The Jealous God; A Plague of Locusts; The Yellow Girl; The Vision of Youth; Icono- clasm; Adonis in Tatters; The New God; A Modest Proposal for the Rehabilitation of Letters in the Literary Show; The Stage and Its Culture; One Failure to Forget; Lucky Richard's Manual on How to Spend Money; Life and Death; New Bill for Prevention of Cruelty to Readers; The Apotheosis of the Harlot; Savages from Europe; Parilea's Dream; Conjugal Love.

These Sets are rare. The cargo of THE FLY LEAF was scuttled in the Irish Sea on April Fool's Day. Collectors will be glad to have a Complete File at this reasonable Price.

Address W. B. HARTE,

71 East 118th Street, New York.

Werther.
Pencil Study by Hallowell.

The Red Letter

An Illustrated Monthly.

"'*T'will while away an hour or so with picturings and print.*"—MARLOWE.

An Easter Blossom.

Oh, Easter flowers!
Say, did ye know through all the hours
Ye grew, thrilled through by sun and shade,
How fair and sweet ye would be made?

Oh, soul of mine!
Touched with a spark of life divine,
Knows't thou how fair thy robes shall be
When clothed with immortality?

Ah! dost thou still
Spur thyself on to do God's will,
To live with all thy utmost powers
His purpose out, as do the flowers?

Then trust to Him
Thy heavenly state, though faith be dim
And hope gaze out through mystery:
His Easter morn shall dawn for thee.

Isidor Day French.

A Knit Tommy.

BEFORE an old stone summerhouse, the front of which once faced the sea, but has now entirely crumbled away, walks a small boy in a white linen suit. He has in one hand a knit Tommy, and with the other is dragging over the uneven stones a little tin fire engine.

Behind the summerhouse, and showing through the openings that serve as windows, are tall, pink hollyhocks. Sitting on the stone bench inside, with her back to the flowers, is the Countess of Trenholm. She is wearing a white muslin frock and pink sash. Her sewing is idle in her lap, and her eyes are fixed on the blue Mediterranean, which dances and sparkles in the sunlight. The small boy comes inside and pulls at her frock. She takes him up, and holding him at arm's length says, "Did the sweetest boy want mother?"

"Baby tired," he says plainly, without any childish accent.

She holds him in her arms and sings to him gently.

He is soon sleeping.

Penelope smoothes the warm curls from his forehead.

He has the knit Tommy hugged closely to him.

The sound of the waves comes up from the beach below.

Suddenly Penelope starts.

Some one is whistling the "Fatherland." At last the whistle changes to song, and a man's voice rings out clear and fresh through the summer air. It is still the "Fatherland," and sung as only a German can sing it.

Penelope's arms tighten on the little burden she holds, and she draws her breath fast and hard.

A young German officer comes around the corner of the summerhouse. Penelope bows sweetly to him and holds out her hand.

He kisses it, and sits down beside her on the bench.

"Your son sleeps," he says.

"Yes." Penelope answers.

There is a long pause, in which she looks at the sea, and he looks at her.

"I have bad news," he says, at length. "We have our orders. We leave to-night."

"To-night, Paul," she says, looking at him quickly, and as quickly turning her eyes away.

"It had to come," he says slowly. "We're to go to the frontier. It will be sharp fighting."

"And you come back?"

"I can't tell when."

The baby wakes, and she puts him down on the ground.

"Before I go," Paul says slowly, and looking directly at her,—"in case I do not come back ——"

"Don't!" she cries sharply, as if the mere thought sent a pain through her heart.

"I want you to know in words," he continues, "what you must have known all through the months I have been here. I shouldn't tell you now if I were not going away, but if I do not come back it will be a comfort for me to know that you know of my love. I have loved you from the first day I saw you. Do you remember? You were in the fort with your husband."

" Yes," she says, and two tears run down her cheeks.

Kneeling beside her, he says softly, reverently, " Penelope, good-by."

Bending down, she kisses his forehead.

" Good-by," she says, " My Soldier and My Love."

She takes a heavy gold chain from her neck.

She winds it twice around his arm, and fastens it there.

" God bless you, and shield you from all danger," she says, raising her great, mournful eyes to his.

The baby runs to him and holds out the knit Tommy.

Paul takes the doll, and catching the child in his arms kisses him on each cheek.

" I will take your dolly with me," he says.

He leaves the summer house. Once he looks back. The sun is shining on the hollyhocks and on the golden hair of the child.

.   .   .   .

On a bright, warm day, when every bird is singing, and the perfume of the flowers is over everything, Penelope and her son are again sitting in the old summerhouse.

She is not looking at the blue water to-day, but away toward the distant North.

She sits so for some time, and then calls to her son, " Baby, father is coming."

The boy runs to meet the young man who is coming along the path with a joyous step.

He catches up the child and puts him on his shoulder. "Give mother her package," he says, as they enter the summerhouse.

The boy gives her a small box.

She opens it, and within she sees the knit Tommy.

He is stained red, and there is a hole through him.

On a scrap of paper, in faint letters, are the words, " My Love, good-by."

With a stifled sob she presses her lips to the blood-stained doll.

Her husband and child are playing before the summerhouse.

Annie E. Holden.

MacGahan War Correspondence Statue.

A Memory.

THERE is in France a village, which thirty years ago was the center of much artistic activity, where it was my fortune to pass several very happy years. In those years there came many delightful experiences, one of which may prove of interest to readers of the RED LETTER; for the comrade of whom I have to tell was a writer, eager to familiarize himself with every variety of life, that he might some day, in quiet hours, devote himself to pure literary work. Alas! the variety—North, South, East, and

West—he had, but the quiet life he longed for never came till he died a tragic death, and was buried at Pera, opposite Constantinople. I refer to Januarius A. MacGahan, than whom a braver or more lovable man I have never met.

He it was who first attracted attention to himself, as war correspondent, by letters written from Paris during the Franco-Prussian war,—graphic and truthful recitals of the lives of the Communists. His familiarity with the story of the siege made him an interesting guide ; and in company with a Boston friend we wandered about Paris when the blood was still red on the pavements, and the *petroleuses* were still being arrested in the streets and in their hiding places. His letter describing the shooting of Generals Clement Thomas and Le Comte, though one of two thousand or more words, was cabled to America, and from that compliment one may date his acknowledged success. We were together in 1875, in the month of May, riding over the Pyrenees as followers of Don Carlos. The romantic episodes of that Carlist war are never to be forgotten treasures in my memory. " Mac," as we called him, was loved everywhere by people of all social grades. Between the time we were together in Paris and our warlike experiences in the Basque provinces, he had been to Khiva, crossing the steppes in a wild chase, which he has so graphically described in his book, " Campaigning on the Oxus."

When we were together in Estella he received a telegram calling him back to Paris, whence Mr. James Gordon Bennett, of the *Herald*, wished to send him to the Arctic region on the Pandora, with an expedition then fitting out. Then, after his return, he was in Russia ; and finally, after assisting at many of the great battles between the Russians and the Turks, he died of the horrible black plague.

I must not omit in this short sketch to mention perhaps the most important of his achievements as correspondent. MacGahan was with Eugene Schuyler in that famous visit to Bulgaria, in 1876, and his letters to *The London Daily News*, read in the English Parliament, were the means of attracting England's attention to the atrocities committed in Bulgaria, and led to legislation which finally resulted in the freedom of that State.

Following the story of such an exciting life, the few lines that make up my peaceful tale may have little interest, yet I recall with pleasure the odd incident which led to our acquaintance, and offer this short story without apology.

One bright Sunday morning as I was busy with my breakfast, for at that time I was my own cook, a knock at my studio door, when answered, showed me two visitors ; one a Russian artist, with whom I was acquainted, and the other an entire stranger. This happened at Ecouen, some dozen miles away from Paris, to the North, a village where about twenty artists, bachelors and married men, were living. The stranger was presented to me by the Russian as a compatriot, a fellow-artist, who had come to the Inn the night before, and who, as he was but little familiar with French, had been brought to me as one of the old settlers. The Russian soon left us, probably wishing to use the fine day for sketching; and my new acquaintance—to whom I was drawn at first sight—excused me until my breakfast was cooked and eaten, and I was ready for a long promenade that I had planned for the day, in which he joined me most enthusiastically. I remember I had a volume of Tennyson's "Idyls of the King," which had been recently published, and this I slipped into my pocket, that we might refresh ourselves with its sweet singing as we lay by the wayside resting from our tramp. We crossed by wood and field, by highway and byway, to Montmorency, chatting, I remember, like magpies, of every variety of thing; nor did I notice until later that he ingeniously turned off the conversation from the subject of Art whenever he felt he would betray his unfamiliarity in a too apparent way. There was a *fete* at Montmorency, which he greatly relished; he had not been long on the Continent, and there was a fascinating freshness in his speech which delighted me. How it all comes back to me as I write of this first day's friendly outpourings and confidences on both sides! But the day finally ended, and we separated, he to his lodging at the inn and I to my bachelor's quarters at a peasant's house, *pere* Marin's, the wheelwright, where for two hundred francs—forty dollars—a year I had my bedroom, dining-room, studio, and a tiny kitchen as well. Those were jolly student days, and more than a happy twelvemonth did I spend in my attic home. We were tired, and doubtless slept well, but after the early coffee breakfast my new-found companion was on hand, and begged to accompany me to the spot out of doors I had chosen for that morning's sketching ground. He stayed and chatted for some time until he descried a funny leaning tower on a church a long way off, and decided he must go and explore that village.

That was the last I saw of him for several weeks, and I had quite made up my mind that I was never to see or hear from him again, that his appearance had been somewhat like that of a comet, unannounced and running off on some parabolic curve into space, when, at the end of a busy day's work, as I stood cleaning my palette, and at the same time looking out of the window, I descried my strange comrade of a day coming up the street. I knew him by his American walk long before I discovered that he had, by shaving, quite transformed his facial expression. I ran down to greet him, and as the sun set and the moon lighted us on our walk around the old wall of the Chateau of Montmorency, again we chatted away as though there had been no gap in our acquaintance. I remember how the confession of his deceit came out as we were sitting in the dim light looking off at the bright, twinkling lamps of Paris. I had been narrating the odd history of an old woman, Madame Lempereur, who lived at the wheel-wright's in a neat room on the floor below mine. It was a story of herself and her son, as she had told it to me; and as I talked, suddenly "Mac" turned, and looking me full in the face confessed that he was not a painter, but a writer, and that he wished some day to use my story; and then he begged would I forgive him, and let him come to live with me and do his share of my primitive housekeeping. He told me how, in his impulsive way, one Saturday night he had gone in Paris to the Northern Railway station, and had looked down the list for the name of a station that attracted him; how he had found one to his mind, Villiers-le-Bel; how he had purchased a ticket which was good until the following Monday; and how, when he reached the station, it proved to be out in the wide fields, with no town or village near it, but an omnibus waiting passengers; how he had climbed to the top of the "bus," and had refused to descend when it first reached the village of Villiers-le-Bel, but had gone on, until his heart failed when the vehicle began to climb a long hill, and seeing a light how he had applied for lodgings only to learn that it was an *estaminet*,* not an inn. Then he had followed directions, and plodded up the hill the way the "bus" had gone, and had at last reached the Hotel du Nord, at Ecouen. Here he was supposed to be an artist; had replied "No" once or twice to maid or man servant, but had decided if he were asked again he would say "Yes;" so possibly it was the host who asked him, and when he said "Yes," con-fidently presented him, as he was a foreigner, to the other foreigner who was at the inn,—my Russian friend, who brought him to me.

Thus was begun one of my sweetest friendships. We roomed together for three months or more in 1869, and then I went to Rome, whither his means did not permit him to accompany me. We corresponded frequently, but fate seemed not propitious to renewed acquaintance, as on my return from Rome to sail to America I passed him without knowing his where-abouts, on the Rhine, where he was studying German. But we met, as I have said, in Paris, and later spent several weeks together in Spain; then our ways parted.

Now there is talk in New York of erecting a statue to his memory. He is worthy of it, as such men as Archibald Forbes, Frank D. Millet, and a host of others can testify.

I hope these few lines of tribute to a dear friend may aid in interesting your readers to inform themselves concerning a bright and able man who was cut off in his prime before he could give in concrete form the result of his romantic experiences and mature judgments of his kind.

J. Wells Champney.

Estaminet is a drinking and smoking place rather than an inn.

The Thought and the Dream.

S he tossed in his sleep after a long and heavy slumber, the serene repose of the relaxed features blanched for a moment, as if they were seared by a fierce light, and then filled with a strange tide of woe and tears. Then all passed away in an instant like a shadow, and was succeeded by the vacancy of the profound sleep and death—the mortal mask of beatitude—when the heart and mind are at rest and peace. But, as dreamers know, this is often a mockery of oblivion, for there are the horrors of sleep as of waking, and perhaps death itself is not dreamless.

The early twilight of the gray dawn was just stealing through the curtained windows over the shadowy roofs, and falling upon his face. it lit the sorrow-lined mouth with softness and tenderness, that mirrored again the beauty and faith of early eager years—a picture one love-greedy woman's memory cherished.

Then the mouth was contorted by a strange stricture, as of one gasping for breath in some strangling horror: and the figure beside him started up, and watched his expression. There was a little gasp of anguish,—and again the reminiscence of the deep, careless sleep of childhood. She bent over him and smiled into his closed eyes.

It was his loved and loving wife. She bent her head noiselessly and cautiously over his face and brushed his lips tenderly, like a butterfly. Then she drew back and gazed into that unresponsive mask of sleep with eyes filled with that deeper tenderness that exists in woman's heart apart from the turbulence of passion.

She was always the first to awake, as he gave a good part of his nights to his labors. She awoke at the break of dawn, and sat silent and tremulous, afraid to stir, for fear of waking him, and loved him most in the relenting beauty of his sleep.

In the stress of life and care those lips could be severe and cynical: but in his slumber he became the child of nature again—the poet. the idealist. And as she looked her heart filled with the thought of the richness of his nature. the tenderness of his love in his most exalted hours and dreams. As he lay there, with all the harsh lines about his mouth and eyes smoothed out by the kindly magic of sleep, she had no scruple in whispering to herself in a gratified rapture of possession and tenderness: "Asleep he is angelic. Who says a man cannot be beautiful?"

And it was indeed true, for the finely chiseled face on the pillow, with the hush of sleep upon it, revealed all the poetry and spirit unperplexed of a rare nature.

It is this beauty which gives us a pang of sad solace in death ; it is the radiance of the spirit after life's many mocking masks of waking.

And so she sat and smiled, enraptured with loving and kissing her Beloved again and again.

But beneath this outward calm the sleeper's brain was busy with a troubled dream.

He dreamed he was suddenly enlightened to the point of absolute conviction of the faithlessness of his beloved Lucile, the wife of his first and great romantic passion, with whom marriage had been one dream of exalted love, in perfect confidence.

He knew the man who had lured her from him, surely by some magic, for they had loved in spirit as few men and women ever do. Her lover and betrayer was a trusted intimate. In a sudden entrance to his garden he had seen them in each others' arms in a leafy arbor, and start apart at his approach with swift guilt. Then he watched. The scene shifted in the quick play of dreams and life. She suddenly disappeared, and rumor or friends told him of her refuge,—a far away old sleepy town by the sea.

He traveled for many days and miles consumed with anger and sorrow. It was to some place in France or Spain they had fled. And finally he had a clue to them in some old town he could not recognize at first, but it loomed up in the gloom of midnight with maddening reminders of some fantastic town over which hung all the suffocating ribaldry and lust of a dissolute Church and State in an older century, that ruled all classes and conditions with a philosophy of cynical pleasure and greed. That was the romance of that old time, when all virtuous women were the prey of the gay cavalier and adventurer. But hearts were sad then, too, as he knew in his hour of dolor.

He and his had surely slipped back into the turmoil of the dark ages, and the love he knew was of the hungry senses, and not of the soul. All the world was sinning and pleasure making in grim and jovial earnest. Life was lived for the senses alone. Love was cheaply bought, and often paid for with a dagger thrust.

He was veritably in Touraine, and felt no surprise in his surroundings. He remembered perfectly to have visited, as a boy, the old university town in the train of a dissolute cardinal in a sacerdotal siege of the person of a famous and scandalous grand duchess.

Of course the unlit, narrow, rough-cobbled streets, with their impenetrable gloom of midnight, stained with blacker shadows of towers, and steeples, and high stone walls, were all familiar ; and there was nothing surprising

that he was skulking in the wake of a woman, wrapped in a dark cloak, hurrying alone through the perilous streets, in every dark corner, and turning, and doorway of which there might lurk some desperate and drunken ruffians.

He was undoubtedly in Touraine to settle an affair of love and honor. A cheated lover and husband, a cuckold, a jealous bravo, he was waiting to spit his rival, with a sudden dagger thrust, on the very threshold of his assignation. Of course he remembered every twist and turn of the dark and narrow ways of the old city, so famous for its amours and its crimes, its students of ribald life, and its famous clerics with their long retinues of harlots. He smiled at the recollection of the cardinal's adventures and amours; and now in this dark asylum of illicit loves and crimes he was skulking in the shadow of the woman he loved, and fearing to learn what he had come to learn. He was hazarding his life to avenge his honor.

He followed as close as he dared without attracting the woman's attention, with his hand on the hilt of a dagger in the fold of his waist.

Once or twice a crew of drunken students, reeling from wall to wall, tried to bar the woman's progress; but she turned silently aside and shot past them, and turned, as if following by instinct a well-known way, into the darkest and deepest intricacies of the town,—into the lower quarter, where crime lay festering behind every shutter, door, and wall.

The man followed close upon her heels, but in turning into a little alleyway he lost her. He felt cautiously along the wall, and found another opening, an impenetrably dark passageway, evidently roofed, for there was no sign of the sky above, and the air was fœtid and stifling.

He heard some one rapping softly against an iron panel at the far end of the passageway, and a woman's voice, his wife's, cried, "It is the hour; it is nigh midnight!" This was evidently a watchword—a token; for there came a voice back in greeting, a man's voice, ringing loud and reckless with joy and eagerness.

"God bless such a night," cried the man's voice; and at the same instant that it came full into the passage the watcher was suddenly stricken blind with a flood of light that streamed from an opened door.

It made the darkness where he stood so black he was unable to find the wall along which he had crept; and standing stunned he heard the woman's silks crushed and rustling in the man's fierce embrace, and he heard her cooing, choking, soft laugh of abandonment and pleasure.

And this was his wife, in old Touraine—the saint he had married!

"Ah," said the man's voice, "this is God's own night—made for love. A black night to hide poor love in security and oblivion; a very procuress of delight and sanctity, this old pitch-dark chaos of night.

"And love taught you the way in the dark. I will guard over you when you return in the twilight, for such beauty is in more peril in the dawn in Touraine, after a night of revel, than in this blessed curtain of secrecy."

"Love always finds a way," she answered. "But is there no peril?"

"Not until the dawn. Here we are as secret and secure as in a crypt. This is true love's other world in the most convenient corner of this world. Come, let us enter, and waste no moment of the precious hour of midnight. Love's grand climacteric is at this hour, and we shall wax sober with the dawn."

"Then I am with you, dearest life and love, sweet poison of my peace and all my future; I'm thine and Fate's till dawn. Till then I laugh at the cold, censorious world, and the irony of change. Oh that woman should change ——"

"A wise woman, knowing that, accepts her hour, takes Fate in good humor, and takes a starless sky as an omen of happy and blessed love. A sad world, shut out by the curtains of night and ecstasy."

"Ah!"—a long and piercing scream.

The woman had caught a pair of flame-lit eyes fixed on her at the other end of the passage.

In an instant she was swung across the threshold, and a door closed with a soft click in the surge of palpable darkness.

The watcher stumbled forward, feeling for the wall and the door; but in the hideous uncertainty of the darkness he scarcely dared to advance. "She must love him to come through this horror!" was his inner thought.

He groped about until he struck the wall, but he could not discover by touch any sign of a door or panel. In every direction, up and down the passage, he could only feel a stone wall, covered with damp and slime.

Then he became frenzied, and cried aloud in anguish and madness, but there was no answering cry or footstep, and he battered his fists against the wall in impotence until he struck something like an iron plate, and he fell forward into an opening of deeper darkness—and then a light broke.

He looked up. His wife bent over him and looked tenderly into his eyes, and kissed him with a kiss of delight and love.

"I have been thinking of my love for you for a whole hour," she said,—and folded him into her arms.

Walter Blackburne Harte.

The Hostelry.

ONE day—I cannot know
    If near or far it be—
It shall be mine to seek
    A narrow hostelry.

I shall put by my cares,
    I shall put by my fears,
And lay me down to sleep
    Through the unnumbered years.

I shall have done with love,
    With envy and with ire;
I shall have done with all
    The throbbings of desire.

How shall mine inn be told?
    Hands crossed upon the breast—
Such is the sign that marks
    The Hostelry of Rest.

Clinton Scollard.

Copying from the Original.

THE fierce noon sun shone straight down through the skylight into the main hall of the Corcoran Art Gallery upon the bent heads of the students at work there, absorbed, intent upon their copying. They glanced up at the glass overhead, and grumbled. The light was intense; it hurt their eyes. One girl, sitting almost underneath the skylight, was copying "The Odalisque." Dazzling reflections flashed from the brilliant draperies surrounding the glowing figure. It hung on the second row, so high up that she was forced to use an opera glass. Now and then she pressed her fingers against her eyes, to rest them from the glare. Nevertheless her copy, two thirds the size of the original, began to assume exquisite proportions.

Near her sat Ruth Millison, perched on a high stool, holding a great paint-laden palette over her left thumb and a brush in her right hand. This brush was poised in mid-air, while Ruth gazed frowningly at her copy of "Charlotte Corday." She looked like a child, propped so high that her feet rested on the last round of the stool, though the thoughtful expression of her profile, with its straight little nose and pouting lips, indicated her eighteen years. The sunshine touched some golden lights in her brown hair. It also threw her shadow slantingly beneath the stool, bringing her out in strong relief, like a picture,—and a very beautiful picture, too, thought Claude Larrimer, as he glanced at her over his shoulder, though he often wondered why she wasted her time on figures. He was painting "The Drove at the Ford," just two pictures beyond "Charlotte Corday." He cared nothing for faces or figures. The old world was too beautiful to burn daylight in painting mere people.

Ruth pressed her brush, thick with paint, distractedly to her lips. Claude leaned forward, at the peril of falling from his stool, and remonstrated with her. "If you eat paint like that, you'll die," said he, "and that's all there is to it. Don't you know that paint is poisonous?"

"I don't care," she answered somberly. "I might as well die; I can't paint."

"What's the matter now?" he asked, dismounting and going over to her, palette, brush, and all. "I thought you were doing beautifully with it. The handling is good."

"Yes; but how about the values? Don't say a word (as he frowned discouragingly); I know they are poor as they can be, and I can't help it. That's the worst of it. I am not in the mood; besides, I have made her eyes crossed."

Claude stepped back a pace, and looked at the copy through half-shut lids. It was true. In her supreme effort to attain the pathetic wistfulness of the Corday expression, she had slightly crossed the eyes.

"Well, straighten them out," said he; "that ought to be easy enough. Now, if it was a crooked road, I might help you: but eyes! I am not a portrait painter, thank goodness; I am not even a painter of fancy heads. You'll have to work it out yourself."

"I can't do it," she said disconsolately, her under lip quivering. "I've tried it for the last half hour."

"Put it away," advised Claude; "then tackle it again. Old Ulrich says one should never paint a minute after one is tired,—and he is authority, you know. Take his advice and mine, and quit."

"I can't," said Ruth, with a sigh; "I must work right along. I have only two days more; I am going home next week."

"'Only two days more,'" he echoed; "'going home next week!'"

"Yes; I was to stay six weeks, and the time will be up then."

"Have you really been painting here six weeks?" he asked, softly.

"Yes," she answered.

For a moment they did not speak. There was only the click of some visitors' heels on the polished floor, as they passed with their low-toned comments and criticisms from one picture to another, to break the silence.

"It seems only yesterday," he mused, "that I came here to paint, and found you perched before your easel, waiting for me."

She turned to him with wide, laughing eyes, for she had had no thought, in perching herself there, of waiting for him; but meeting his tender gaze she checked the saucy reply on her lips, blushed, and turned back to her copy. "I can't do this," she said, sighing again.

"Why did you copy that thing?" he asked; "it is so hackneyed. You see poor copies of it in nearly every parlor in Washington."

"But it is so beautiful," said she; "and then, you know, it isn't hackneyed at home."

"And where is your home?" he asked, gently.

"You know as well as I do," she cried. "I've told you a dozen times, Kentucky."

"O yes," said he. "I do remember now; but I never think of you as having a home on this common earth. I am always thinking of you as just having dropped down from Heaven."

"The next thing to it," said Ruth.—"'God's country;'" and she showed all her dimples and two rows of pearls in a ravishing smile.

He did not return the smile. His mood had changed. He moved away from her, and remounted his stool. Ruth also resumed her work, and they painted awhile in silence.

The visitors presently stood behind them, commenting audibly, and in no very complimentary terms, upon their copies. They were hardened to that. They painted on without listening: she, handling her colors rather more deftly now; and he, deep in the intricacies of purplish boughs laden with sun-flecked leaves.

Several of the students had quit work. They sat on the benches, surreptitiously eating their lunches out of little striped paper bags,—it was against the rules to lunch in the main galleries,—laughing and chattering in a subdued way, like magpies. Some had a pear or a bunch of white grapes; others, Maryland biscuit with thin slices of ham in between. They laughingly hid their little bags, and reached wildly for crumbs and grape hulls at the approach of the janitor.

At the other end of the hall the teacher who was employed to assist the students was criticising, in a loud voice, a young girl's copy of "The Helping Hand." His voice was so loud that the others might have heard if they had cared to listen. "Why in the world did you attempt it?" he stormed. "You will never be able to get that fine, misty, sea effect in the world,— never! It is too difficult for you. Drop it, and take up some simpler thing. You students have too much confidence in yourselves, entirely too much. You think you can copy anything in this gallery. Now, look at that! You ought to be copying from plaster casts right this minute, instead of plunging headlong into color. Look at the incorrectness of your drawing! Drop that, and take up some bit of landscape or a small head."

The girl seemed on the verge of tears, but when he left her she pressed the corner of her big painting apron to her eyes, and returned tremblingly to her work.

"I wouldn't mind him if I were you," whispered her neighbor, a girl who was copying a tiny landscape,—a flock of turkeys in a meadow fairly glittering with sunlight; "he doesn't know everything."

At those words of sympathy the apron went up to the eyes again, and the girl's shoulders shook with sobs.

"I wouldn't let him see me crying," said the other; "it will do him too much good. Hush now, hush now!"

Meanwhile, Claude worked furiously. He gave the impression that he was working off steam.

"It's lunch time, Claude," called out one of the girls, biting a biscuit half in two; but he never so much as turned his head.

Presently he spoke, without looking up. "I'm only a poor Virginian," he said, indicating a splotch or two of blue sky between the meshes of green leaves.

"Very poor?" asked Ruth, who, since she could not straighten Charlotte's eyes satisfactorily, left them for another day, and busied herself with the bars of the unfortunate girl's prison.

"Pretty poor," answered Claude; "the farm's all run down. You can't get help there in the country for love or money. The best negroes have all flocked to the cities, and the ones that are left ain't worth the powder to blow them up. The gov'ner lets the farm out on shares, and the poor whites that work it cheat the very life out of him."

"It don't look very encouraging," said Ruth, ungrammatically, laying a heavy shadow along the stone wall of the prison; "it certainly don't."

"I should think not," said Claude. "It's just about as discouraging as it possibly can be."

It appeared that he had suddenly sunk into the depths of despondency. He applied his brush with ferocious dabs to the splotches of sky, which were not sufficiently blue to suit his present mood.

Ruth glanced furtively at him from under her long lashes. His profile was intensely sad. The corners of his mouth drooped under his little blonde moustache. Was that all he was going to say? Why didn't he go on? She paused, mixing her colors with her brush a moment, waiting; then, "But you have your work," she said, brightly; "that counts for something, doesn't it?"

"Not much," he answered. Clearly, he was not to be lifted out of the depths. He remained there prostrate, with a grim sort of satisfaction in his own abject misery. "You see, the gov'ner hasn't any patience with my art work. 'It's all rubbish,' he says,—'plumb foolishness.' I might as well be mauling rails or pecking rock on a turnpike. You can catch a faint idea of what he thinks of Art by that. They put the jail birds to work pecking rock on turnpikes in Virginia."

Ruth nodded understandingly. "I know," she said; "so they do in Kentucky, too. I've seen them, poor fellows!"

"There's no telling whether I'll ever make a decent living with my art," he went on gloomily, feeling that, while he was in such dire need of sympathy, it was rather cruel of her to waste hers on jail birds. "Sometimes my pictures sell, and then, again, they don't. Oftenest they don't."

"Same here," said Ruth.

"Once in a while some idiot of a tourist, who knows about as much about Art as a kangaroo, will stroll through here and order a copy of some picture I happen to be at work on."

"It has happened to me, too, once or twice," remarked Ruth, with an humble show of pride, "and these pictures are worth something when we get through with them; for they are stamped with the Corcoran stamp. They won't let them go out of the Gallery unless they are good copies."

"But are they always good judges?" he asked, determined to see everything through blue glasses. "I've seen some awful ——"

"Shh,—don't talk treason! See those girls, how they are all stopping to listen."

"I paint landscapes from nature," he said, returning to the old theme, too intent upon his own troubles to care whether the girls listened or not, "and once in a great while they sell very well. I have now and then struck a buyer with more money than brains, who paid me fairly good prices, but the general outlook isn't brilliant; in fact, it's the very reverse," and his shoulders gave a downward droop of despair. "Sometimes I think the gov'ner was right, and I might as well be mauling rails."

"All artists think those things at times," said Ruth. "I do myself, though, of course, I am not much of an artist," she added, with an apologetic little laugh. Claude was too deeply absorbed to offer a polite disclaimer to this remark, and she went on: "All true artists are discouraged with their work. Their performance never quite comes up to their ideals. That is the reason of it, I think." She paused to note the effect of her reasoning, but, to her disappointment, he remained silent, vouchsafing not so much as a gesture of approval or admiration. "It is only upstarts who consider everything they do perfect," she concluded, with visibly waning enthusiasm.

"Now, if I had stayed on the farm," said he, still stubbornly pursuing his own train of thought, "I would have a good home to offer, if nothing else."

Ruth gave a little joyful start of surprise, and dropped her brush. She took a clean one from the brush-pot on the stand by her easel, and began to work vigorously at her iron bars without saying a word, though he had paused, as if for a reply. What reply could she make to a remark so irrelevant? There had been no question asked; there had been simply the statement of a fact.

Claude touched up some reflections in the ford through which the cattle were to pass—a most exquisite ford in the original, full of vari-colored lights and ripples, blue from the skies, green from the leaves, and yellow from the warmth of the sunlight; in the clearest depths there was even a little purple. "Now, you see," he resumed, with the deepest self-abasement, "I can't even paint these cows. I've got to get a friend of mine, a cattle painter, to put them in for me. I'm only a miserable landscape painter, who doesn't paint landscapes, even, very well."

"That's all right," said Ruth. "Every artist has his specialty. I know a painter who can't paint anything but cattle. He has to get somebody to put in the landscape around them, and that is worse. You can do without cattle in your landscape, but you can't very well do without landscape around your cattle," she concluded, with a rippling laugh. For some reason or other she was growing madly gay.

"There's Dick Brook, now," she began again, since he made no attempt to break the silence; "he paints negroes. You have seen his 'Parson's Visit,' in the next gallery, haven't you?"

He nodded assent.

"Fine, isn't it?" she asked. "And so each artist has his specialty, as I said before."

"But a landscape painter is the commonest of all," he reiterated, so sadly that a cloud passing over the skylight at that moment threw a shadow in the gallery seemingly in sympathy with his mood.

The girls eating their lunches looked up, to see if it rained.

"I've seen some lovely things you have done," said Ruth, in her sweet, low voice.

He worked feverishly, as if nerving himself to a difficult task. "And still, for all that," he said, his words following each other rapidly, and his brush, keeping pace with his heart-beats, flashing brilliant lights into the mirror-like ford, across which he was going to ask his friend to paint the cattle coming, "if a girl could run the risk of poverty for awhile, with the hope of something better in the future, with a fellow who, in six short weeks, has learned to love the brush she paints with, and the very shadow of the stool she sits on, why—why ——"

"What?" she asked, her face all alight with tenderness; for he by this time had sprung from his high stool, and stood close by her side, looking up into her face with beautiful, pleading eyes.

"Why," he said with a little catchy sob, "he would work his fingers to the bone for her; he would work for her until he died, and he would love her, love her, love her—as long as he drew the breath of life!"

"Hush," she said, with lowered lids; "the others are listening." But, beneath the big palette that hung over her left thumb he had found her little fingers; he clasped them close in his strong young hands.

She raised her lids and looked into his eyes; the compact was sealed; and the others, listening, heard only the click of the visitors' heels as they left the gallery,—for great love is silent, and heart-throbs make no sound.

Zoe Anderson Norris.

George H. Hallowell.

IF any one will take the trouble to look a little further than the picture exhibitions, which, after all, are only the surface of art in Boston, he will find several among the younger painters who show convincing evidence of artistic ability that is a guaranty of ultimate position. The man that has "arrived" is a known quantity, and in most cases the measure of his power is fixed. Hardly one in a hundred goes on from his first success to a higher level as John Sargent has done; usually the first fire burns itself out, or, at the best, never rises above its first flashes of achievement. With the men who as yet have not won their place we are at liberty to hope for something else, and keep on hoping until overtaken by disappointment.

Now and then those who find interest in searching out the younger men, digging into their piles of

sketches, analyzing their studies, making themselves familiar with their ambitions, motives, their
mental attitudes,—now and then such an one will
be rewarded by mines of considerable richness,
that promise great returns of precious ore when
once the plant is in good working order and the
project well capitalized.

Probably the majority of people who think about
this sort of thing are familiar with the Cadet
poster,—a sergeant of the First Corps,—and also
with the covers for the books issued for the Cadet
shows of "Excelsior, Jr." and "Simple Simon."
If the above-mentioned people know anything about
artistic matters, they will have recognized in these things a keen artistic
feeling, a remarkable decorative sense, a singular power on the part of
the designer over clean, competent line, together with quiet reserve to
a rather unusual degree. Very likely they will have said,
"This man has a future as a decorative designer." How
many of them know, however, that this ephemeral work is
only the froth of an artistic vitality of a nature and degree
sufficiently rare now-a-days to merit comment?

It is not until one gets below this decorative work—good
as it is—that one begins to find out something of the latent
possibilities of the man who made it. In it one sees, of
course, that the designer is a master of line and drawing, of
composition, of anatomy, but there is nothing in it to show
that he also has the rare and somewhat disdained qualities
of sane, vital imagination; that he is driven by an impulse—spiritual, emotional, whatever you see fit to call it—
of the same quality that made the "old masters"
masters, not amateurs.

To be convinced of this, one must know the
man, rummage through piles of sketches, study the
pencil and wash drawings of trees, and clouds, and
mountain slopes that would have made Turner grin
with delight; read through the blocked-in masses
of half-finished canvases the strong dramatic impulse, the amazing instinct for beauty of line, and
form, and color, and atmosphere; capture a note-
book crowded with the keenest observations of
nature; and then, after, when the pipe smoke is
thick enough, talk about it all. Follow this
course, and you will wonder if the immediate

future hasn't something rather remarkable in store for the artistic history of this country.

It is impossible to give to others, in the shape of sequent words and incidental drawings, the results of several years of personal knowledge, but even in the few things here reproduced, it is possible to see something of the competence in nearly all directions that is the most encouraging thing in George Hallowell's work. Examine the little pencil head of "Werther," and you will find not only a quality of line instinct with artistic power, but a spiritual element that is surprising. The fashionable art of the day is a Frankenstein,—deceptive as to outward appearance, but evil within, as are all things that are man-made and devoid of a soul.

"The Carter Stuck in the Mud," is an old sketch hustled off in three hours, but look at the power of it; the fine massing of light and shade, the strong, vigorous drawing, above all the element of the dramatic, which raises it at once above the level of illustration to the dignity of Art.

Next to his almost classical feeling for form and faultless line, this dramatic quality is, perhaps, the most salient note in Hallowell's work. There is a big study of his called only "The Destruction of the Forest." It is a modern scene in a lumber camp. Commonplace enough, and yet art has taken it and turned it into an awful tragedy : it is a horrible nightmare of brute force warring against the solemnity of nature. There is not a line of exaggeration in it, not a forced note, but the blind tragedy is there, implacable and full of terror.

This subject and its treatment are also indicative. There is nothing mediæval or affected in this work. It is healthy, manly, modern,—in a good sense. Even in the decorative religious work that Mr. Hallowell has just begun,—and that is quite evidently what lies nearest his heart,—there is no affectation, no posing, no aping of ancient models. Instead, a splendid sincerity, vitality : the influence of the old men is there, but not their dominance. We are slowly developing a great National school of monumental painters.

Several men are already accepted; their place is assured. There are others who possess equal ability, perhaps greater. Given the opportunity, they will stride to the front rank,—next to the great leader. Only the opportunity is wanting. Surely there must be those who will give it. The cost is comparatively small, the result incalculable.

R. A. Cram.

Impressions of Southern Spain.

IV.

MURCIA.

WISH I could put into words the impression I have of the city of Murcia. In color it would not be so difficult. Imagine a deep blue sky, so deep that the green fronds of the date palms are light against it, and their golden fruit glows like a flame, and below this the level, grey town sleeping in the hot sunlight, with here and there a quaint enameled dome, and, above all, the solitary spire of the old cathedral, a tawny, dust-colored spire, roofless houses, no color anywhere except in the little Moorish dome jeweled with dusty turquoise and lapis lazuli.

One feels in Murcia as if in a half doze with the soft perfumed air of an Indian summer blowing across one's face. It is the Lotus Eaters all over again : to breathe and feel your heart beat is a happiness.

May I whisper to you the golden secret of the charm of Murcia? Here it is : the tourist never comes here; English is not spoken. It is as unknown as the tongue that was talked at the founding of Babel.

One accumulates so many beautiful pictures in traveling—I mean in one's memory—from which one can draw the curtain at will forever; pictures that never fade or grow dull. Shall I show you one or two?

I can remember one of many summer nights on the blue water of the Gulf Stream. Under the awning on the deck are dusky forms grouped around, half seen, no light but the stars; just at my feet a young French sailor, half dressed, is singing love songs with a mellow, sweet voice that seems to caress the words.

Look again! See this sky, masked with masses of warm and formless vapor, through which the blue heaven peeps in one little vista, soon to be closed up. The clouds are so dense and low that you feel you could touch them with your walking stick, and yet the whole glows with a heavy richness like a Venetian picture. In front of you the great sails of an uncouth windmill slowly revolve, and whole forests of them are standing behind, and gradually fade into the misty horizon. Close beside you the green and weedy waters of a canal, stagnant between its still greener banks, reflect the yellow sky and the slow-moving sails of the mill.

Here comes a huge canal boat, barbarously daubed with color and drawn by a strange tandem. A woman in wooden shoes has harnessed herself to it, and a big dog is harnessed to the woman. A great, shapeless mass of black cotton and oilcloth stands in the stern, smoking a pipe, and steers the boat. At your elbow a little man, two feet high, with the lisp of innocence begs you for a cigar. You hand him a regalia, and he attaches himself to it and smokes with comfort and content.

A little farther on I see the narrow, blazing street of an Arab town. A sky of indigo, long rows of white, hot, one-storied huts, stained by the red earth which burns underfoot. Now and then a scrap of withered bamboo awning over a little door, where brown bundles of Arabs sit silent, sipping their tiny cups of thick coffee.

Down the street comes a group of earth-colored natives, children shouting, men and women laughing and chattering, and in the midst a mighty Bedawee leading a yellow lioness by a bit of string. Far off in the minute distance a long file of red-brown camels stalks across the plain.

I have hundreds of these living, unpaintable, indescribable pictures in my memory, bearing the dates of many years; but of all these, my private picture galleries, that of Murcia is, I think, the fullest.

Without moving from this writing table I can wander at will all over the town, and at every corner there is a picture. I see my long, narrow room, with its floor of alternate blue and white porcelain tiles, the ceiling so high overhead that one never notices it, and at the end of the room a great window, seven feet by ten, open to the floor.

I step out on the balcony in the early morning, sheltered by the wide awning which hangs over the iron rail. Away at the far end of the queer, old-fashioned street, from the mighty tower of the cathedral, just touched by the first sunlight, the open-mouthed bells swing out against the sky, pealing in harmonious confusion.

Below me, in the grey street, a peasant in a costume of three hundred years ago sweeps the dust of the pavement with a bamboo brush, into a palm-leaf basket. His donkey walks slowly before him, with his dust-laden paniers unaccountably balanced on his round back; for this little " burro " is round and fat,—everything and everybody in this wonderful city is round, and fat, and happy, and every face is broad and smiling.

Troops of goats begin to go by, with their great udders swollen with the morning's milk. Little housekeepers run on errands to and fro, with their shining black hair combed smoothly back in a pretty, womanly fashion, and coiled in a braid behind.

For a long time the sunshine has lain on the bamboo hencoops on the housetops, where the fowls march gravely about on the flat, terraced roofs, and around the chimneys, and along the eaves; and now thin lines of sunlight begin to steal into the street, between the great coarse awnings stretched from house to house.

Groups of peasants begin to ride by with loaded donkeys and carts, all going the same way; for the fair ground is at the farther end of the street, and this is the weekly market day. The women are gay with bright hand-kerchiefs and their blue-striped skirts. The men wear solemn black jackets and trousers and great flat felt hats, or little, pointed velvet caps. Every-thing is black; only the donkey is hung with scarlet tassels; and here and there you see one of those priceless old Epinardo blankets, with its deep-red ground and brilliant stripes—like a Roman scarf. The stout old man who carries it across his shoulders or over his saddle cloth, wove it fifty years ago with his own hands, and all these fifty years of sunlight have never dimmed its color.

Here comes a peasant of the poorest class, with his load of produce, dressed in a long, coarse, white shirt and short white stockings and sandals, and nothing else except a great flapping straw hat with a tall, pointed crown. And behind him, for contrast, walks a decent flower woman, with a red cotton apron over a red skirt, a red kerchief tied around her head and another over her shoulders, almost hiding her embroidered bodice. She is all in different shades of red, and in each hand is a big, conical bouquet, two feet high, blazing with scarlet and yellow and rose. For this is the land of flowers, and here, in October, you may buy for four or five cuartos a bunch of roses as large as your hat.

And here come tall, lumbering, wooden carts, each drawn by a yoke of stout little bulls, with collars of shining bells around their necks and red tassels hung wherever tassels will hang, and on their foreheads, where the ropes are twisted which hold the yoke, wonderful pads reaching high above the horns, and looking, for all the world, like old fashioned ruffled night-caps,—only these night caps are flaming with scarlet, and yellow, and blue, and green, laid on in a kind of savage embroidery.

Are you tired of all this stream of peasants? Then we will take our coffee and goat's milk and stroll down one of these side streets that lead, at the end, through the gates and out of the little city.

Everywhere we meet pretty, Moorish-looking women with little turned-up noses and Oriental eyes; stout, Moorish-looking men and jolly, Moorish-looking priests, with their black robes floating behind them; all so different from the clean-limbed, long-jawed Grenadines and their hungry, scowling Jesuits and painted, long-waisted señoras. All are busy and nobody hur-ries: they hurry so little that they are three hundred years behind the rest of the world.

Now we have come upon an open square, for the town is full of them. On one side is one of those quaint, brown churches crusted over with fine old mediæval saints with noble flowing drapery, but every figure, strange to say, with the very same twist in it,—for every statue in Spain seems to be contorted into the same undeviating line of beauty. All around are little booths and stands where the women sell cheap wares, and crocheted laces, and curious knitted things, stockings and babies' caps, full of knots and scroll patterns and zigzags; and in the middle a lazy crowd around two unshorn pilgrims,—real pilgrims with staff, and shell, and wallet, and coarse, patched garments,—so dirty,—who are preaching Heaven knows what, but I suspect there is money in it.

Or is it a charlatan, doing cheap tricks of sleight of hand and joking over his merchandise; or a group of Arab acrobats, with their fez caps and baggy pantaloons? Whichever you like, for whatever is incongruous and out of date drifts naturally into this anachronism of a city.

Now we come to the river banks. Down below there, to your left, is the narrow gorge where the great inundation destroyed so many houses. You may see the ruins of them still. But don't imagine to yourself any tremendous, sweeping, whirling rush of waters. Nothing ever rushes in Murcia: the river simply rose calmly and dissolved the houses, which were built of mud, and sticks, and little stones, as all Spain is built to this day.

Here to the right is the great public market place, reaching from the bridge through long lines of bamboo stalls, hung and shaded with mattings in every possible combination of picturesqueness, through heaps of yellow grain and glowing fruit, oranges and golden dates and bursting pomegranites, past old decayed convents, turned into pasadas, and tall, shapeless, crumbling walls—and so out of sight.

Never was there such a market as this: tanned, old, crazy booths in all shades of tawny browns, crowded with pleasant, busy, gayly dressed market women; all with that wonderful winning smile, the undying gift of the East; and all about bright fabrics and masses of sunny fruits, and overhead, the hot, dusty convent walls, and always, above all, that blue, blue sky, with the cathedral tower against it.

If I could only make you see it as I see it!

A little way farther on and we come to the very edge of the town, under the city walls. For this is a very little city: one can walk round it before breakfast. Do you hear those shrieks of distress? They are weighing a full-grown pig over there. They have taken three turns of a rope around his belly, and hung him to a steelyard. Two men hold up the steelyard by main force, and a third notes the weight. How delightfully simple everything is!

Wherever we turn we meet little cheerful, betasseled donkeys, and yoked bulls, with their red nightcaps; all hard-working, fat and good-humored like their masters. Everywhere we see dust-colored houses, with a look of decayed palaces and convents about them; with curious old carving and curious old Latin inscriptions over the doors. You feel yourself in an old, old world, reeking with the sunshine of past centuries. Only through the open doors, instead of ruffed dons, and stiff-skirted ladies, and solemn-faced priests, you get glimpses of picturesque inn yards, full of queer, hooded carts; of hand-weavers at their little looms; of girls busy with glistening silk; and countless, comfortable, white-capped old women, and children clothed only with innocence.

This man who speaks to us with such a frank smile is a maker of indigo-dyed fabrics. He is asking us to come into his house and see his processes. Here in two or three little rooms he spins his yarn, cotton, or wool; dyes them in the little vats, and weaves them in patterns of blue and white, on little hand-looms. He points out to us that his harnesses are worked by treadles; a recent improvement, he assures us, and a great saving of labor. How proud he is of his Old-World inventions. At his present rate of progress he will arrive at the steam engine in a very few centuries.

Farther on is a woman sitting in her doorway, winding silvery silk fibers on a great wooden spool, tending her baby with one hand and turning her wheel with the other. She, too, says "Come in," always with that wonderful Oriental smile. I can't tell you how this smile of the Eastern races affects me. It breaks out like the sun from a cloud. It is the same smile that one sees on the face of the Spanish Gitano, or the dusky Hindu, or the Arab of the desert. It is the same smile that has sat for thousands of years on the granite lips of Rameses, as he sits before the door of the great Nubian Temple.

Over there, in the doorway opposite, is a little girl of four years singing a gypsy song and dancing to the sound of her castanets, swaying her little half-clothed body and waving her round arms in perfect Gitana movement. In the street before her plays a naked baby, handsome as a young Hercules. In the sunshine beside the door sits the grandmother, and the young mother stands behind her chair and combs her long white hair. .

The castanets stop. We hear the sound of music, and four Spanish gentlemen march down the street, dressed in the old costume of the province, side by side, keeping step, each playing his guitar.

Would you like to know how they are dressed? They wear large, stiff, black felt hats, two feet across, with little pointed velvet crowns to them, and around the flat brim a velvet rim, turned up like the edge of a Japanese tray. They have embroidered white shirts without collar or neckerchief, black velvet waistcoats, open to the waist, and about the waist a black sash. They have short, black velvet jackets and tight-fitting black trousers.

There, I have shown you enough of my picture gallery. It is time to go home to dinner, and at the Patron's *fonda* you will get the best dinner that one can eat in Spain.

Late in the evening, as I smoke my cigarette, strolling up and down the Plateria, I hear slowly approaching military music, brazen and triumphant. There are lights of hundreds of candles, bayonets glisten through a smoky veil, rockets shoot into the darkness, and red and white fires flash on every side.

A long procession of gold-embroidered priests and white-robed boys defiles past me so slowly that they hardly seem to move. And here take off your hat like the others; it is the Vierje de Mercedes, the Madonna so famous for her miracles, making her progress through the city to visit the not less famous Madonna del Carmen.

There she is, in a forest of candles, a beautiful, painted, wooden statue, under a golden canopy, clothed in wonderful brocaded satin, and endless gold embroidery, and miraculous old lace. And the crowd shouts, the band plays, the rockets flash, and the women kneel and the men salute.

The hours go by; the lights are out, the streets are still. In the darkness I hear the musical chant of the night watchman as he cries the hour. There he is, just under my window :—

"Ave Maria Sanctissima, Media noce, Tiempo bel-lo."

And so "muy bono," as they say in Murcia.

ALGIERS, 1883.

NOTE EXPLANATORY.—Spanish coins : A *douro* is a dollar. A *peseta* is a franc, twenty cents. A *real*, or royal, is five cents. A *cuarto*, or quarter, was, I presume, originally a fourth of a real, but its value seems to vary. A *chavo*, or *chavetta*, and a *centimo*, or centime, are the smallest copper coins, and great numbers of them are in circulation. A *fonda* is a hotel, a *posada* is a cross between a caravansera and an inn.

In Murcia the Virgins of the different churches make periodical visits to each other, in the stately manner here described; the streets through which the procession is to pass, being decorated with flowers, draperies, and triumphal arches. What happens when they arrive at their destination I don't know, never having been present at the ceremony.

The *Plateria*, accent on the penultimate syllable, is the principal retail business street of Murcia. The name means the goldsmiths' or jewelers' row, *plata* being the word for silver.

Marcus Waterman.

David Gerry's Vision.

HE short afternoon light was gone, and David Gerry laid down his modeling tool with a sigh. Looking upon his almost completed work,—the portrait bust of a famous actress,—the young sculptor knew that he stood upon the threshold of success. The drooping lids intensified, by all the power of suggestion, the passion of the beautiful eyes; the full curves of the mouth whispered to what had lurked, unguessed at, in the heart of every man; the outspread fan, whose gauze and trifling sticks were wrought with a triumph of technical skill, drew the envious thought, by its affectation of concealment, to the lovely rounded breasts. Was his work, in truth, a success? Was there no more to render than physical perfection, and the tooling graved by a keen, bold intellect?

When David Gerry was a child his snow men were the wonder of the village. They were not the traditional figure, with columnar legs, a snow-ball nose, and clay pipe, but glistening statues, each with its own individuality. He cried when they melted, but when the snow fell again he built once more, confident that this time his work was for always. The statues all faced the West, and it was always the same face that David tried to render. When or how it had dawned upon him he did not know. Only the desire to give it form had been, from his cradle, the impelling impulse of his life. The longing to look straight and full upon it, if only for a fleeting instant, was never absent from his thoughts.

In those childish days the face had come to him in a far-off glimpse. Sometimes it was nearer, but veiled in a luminous mist. It shone upon him, nebulous, in a dream, from which he awoke crying, because at the very moment of seeing it in all its clearness it had vanished: It dawned upon him from out the music of the pines; it arose when he looked upon the stretch of ocean; it came in the light of setting suns, when in an agony of expectation and longing, he waited as though some inner force was about to break its bonds, and reveal life's infinite and remotest possibilities. But always as a suggestion; never face to face, as a reality.

He shuddered as he recalled that early life. He could hear his mother's high-pitched, querulous voice bidding him wipe his boots, or chiding him for having banged the door. He could see her small, erect figure, draped in a Paisley shawl with an elaborate border, and the wizened face in a coal-scuttle bonnet, over which towered hearse-like plumes. In his nostrils was the mingled odor of the cloves and peppermints that were to keep her from nodding in " meetin'-time," and the " camfire " with which her best clothes

were redolent. Mrs. Gerry had long ago been canonized in the village
rubric by reason of deafness, invalidism, and a familiar use of Scripture
texts wide of the mark. If, on Monday, Hannah's biscuit were "heavy as
lead," or "she should hev' a leetle more appetite for mutton broth if there
wuz only some one to speak kind to her; ol' folks needed to be coaxed to
eat," possibly the rheumatism attendant upon a draughty corner of the
meeting-house (Mrs. Gerry insisted upon attending divine service three
times a day) may have been accountable.

There was a set look about Hannah's mouth, as though her lips had
stiffened with repressed speech, oddly transformed, now and then, generally
at some grotesquely inappropriate moment, into the hideous travesty of a
smile,—the sport of a disease of the jaw bone contracted by her work in the
straw factory. David knew only by tradition that his sister had been young
and pretty in the days long ago, when she and Stephen Fletcher had sat
together in the village choir. Hannah's voice was strident, now, from constant speech with a deaf person, and her vocal *repertoire* was reduced to
two lines of a doleful meeting-house hymn, whose rendering accompanied
all her household labors :—

> " Fa-ar from mo-or-tal cares re-ee-treating,
> Sor-or-did ho-opes a-and va-ain dee-ee-sires."

The day came when Stephen told her that he had decided to break away
from the village life, and pleaded that she should be his wife; he would
gladly take upon himself the care of her mother and little Davy. But Mrs.
Gerry refused to tear herself away from her meeting-house and her pump.
If the great West had been an arid desert, or the pump had yielded the
waters of Zion, she could not have been more devotedly attached to it.

" The sun ariseth, they gather themselves together, and lay them down
in their dens," she added, solemnly.

" I will stay with you," declared the young man, when his sweetheart
acquainted him with her mother's decision.

But Hannah drew the thin little gold ring from her finger.

" It is your manhood that calls you," she said.

" By and by,"—— And the light of fealty was in Stephen's eyes.

But filial duty forbade Hannah's dwelling on a future where her mother
was not ; and vampire natures are long lived.

By and by Stephen's letters grew less frequent, and then ceased. He
had become the leading man in what was now a thriving western city.
He was spoken of as the next representative to Congress. One day a
neighbor came running in with a shawl over her head.

" I've left a batch o' pies in the oven, and the baby a screamin' with
colic," she gasped. " I thought as how you'd like to see this here that the

soap came done up in," and she thrust the fragment of an old newspaper into Hannah's hand. It contained the announcement of Stephen Fletcher's marriage.

After that day Hannah twisted what had become, in these latter years, a mere wisp of hair, into a hard little button at the back of her head. Stephen had liked to pass his hand over what had been heavy, lustrous braids, and for years after his departure Hannah tried to arrange her scanty, faded locks in the fashion that had pleased her lover. She took from her table the daguerreotype of a young man with sleek hair, and hands that, as they ostensibly toyed with an album, seemed groping for a hoe-handle. The inflamed New England conscience would not permit her to look upon the husband of another woman.

Every day she went to the straw factory that made the sole activity of the village. The immediate effects of the phosphorus employed in the bleaching process was to cause the hair to fall out and to injure the eye-sight; its ultimate result was to affect the lungs, usually with fatal termination. But the work in the bleaching room was better paid than in the other parts of the factory, and money was needed to buy her mother's medicines and keep little Davy comfortably clad. In the early morning and after work till late at night, she "red up" at home.

"I don' need much care. I ain't one of the kind that makes trouble for other folks," moaned Mrs. Gerry. "Hannah wuz allus rugged. She favors her father's folks," with a sigh that hinted of the mysterious and awful "trouble" dear to the internal organs of so many women. "I shall soon be gone,"—a chorus that had accompanied her every utterance since the memory of man. "'We may buy the poor for silver, and the needy for a pair of shoes!'"

In the evening, while her mother swayed back and forth before her in her favorite chair, Hannah read, at the top of her voice, the obituaries and quack medicine advertisements in Mrs. Gerry's religious weekly. When Davy was goaded past endurance by the nagging voice, he fled to the pine woods for never-failing solace. But Hannah did not mind. Hannah was never driven to the verge of madness by the querulous tones imploring that the stove door be opened "jest a grain," that five minutes before had been closed in response to the moan, "I'm a-freezin'; there ain't nobody to look after ol' folks nowadays," with an emphasis that could only hint of the volumes in the hands of the recording angel of her own youthful devotion to the aged. Hannah never betrayed impatience when asked to hand the fan within Mrs. Gerry's own reach, or to go to the attic to see if "the scuttle wasn't open," or to the cellar to still her mother's conviction that the pork barrel had sprung a-leak. If there was a rare moment in which she seated herself, it was only to rise at the bidding: "Can't you git me a grain o' sody? My supper ain't set jest right." And had she ever known a night when, sunk into wearied slumber, she was not aroused by the tones from the adjoining room, "Hannah, be you asleep? I ain't closed my eyes."

What did it matter? The galling chains of petty daily bondage could not chafe a nature like Hannah's. No agony of longing for a broad, free, rich life, of which dream glimpses had been hers; no hunger for the world of poetry, and music, and art preyed upon her soul. To Hannah no vision had ever come.

David worked in the designing room of the factory, where his facile fingers modeled the clay from which the plaster blocks were to be moulded into graceful modifications of, and unlooked-for improvements upon, the designs of the hats and bonnets that were the unvarying models of the other workmen. One day he threw down his " buffer." He was going to the city, to be a sculptor.

He found a little room —it was kitchen and bedroom as well as studio— four flights up, in a back street, overlooking a labyrinth of railroad tracks, but the light was good, and he was happy. The small art dealers bought his graceful and bizarre designs, and the money, little though it was, served to keep him in bread.

He thought when he came to the city, with its rich opportunities of art culture, its atmosphere of literary activity, that at last the vision would become clear. He haunted the Art Museum; in the calm beauty of Grecian sculpture he should find the object of his quest. He visited portrait galleries; to some master's eyes had been vouchsafed that which he sought. He was a never-failing attendant at the stately church where wealth and exclusiveness worshiped; embodied in some delicately attuned nature, vibrating to the most exalted emotions, he should see that of which he dreamt. Often as his purse permitted he stood in the theatre or concert hall, scanning the beauty and fashion of the city: his vision might be materialized in features perfected by the culture of generations.

Before the master pieces of ancient art he vaguely felt that the self-control that was their distinguishing characteristic belonged to his vision, but as an attribute, and not as its essence. Now and then, in the sweetness of a face that looked at him from some dim canvas, he seemed to catch sight of something that had belonged to the personality of the subject, but which the artist had failed to render. In church there was once and again a look upon a woman's face, as it was raised from prayer; a glimpse, at the theatre or concert, at the poet's impassioned words; or the notes of some great singer, as of a soul laid bare, that made him start eagerly forward. But the next moment either he lost sight of the face in the throng, or a veil had fallen over his own eyes. Sometimes, in the despair that the fruitless, goading quest brought upon him, he seemed to be ever further and further from its realization. In his sleep the luminous mist still came as of old; but when it dissolved and he was about to cry out with rapture, it was Hannah's grim, gaunt face that was revealed, with its hideous abortion of a smile, and he awoke with his pillow wet with childish tears.

He had never revisited his home, not even when his mother died; the scene of coarse village mourning would do his fine-strung sensibilities infinite harm. He shuddered at the thought of seeing again the picture Hannah had pasted on the kitchen wall,—a high-colored advertisement of somebody's miraculous soap; he could not even smile as he recalled his sister's collection of mortuary poetry, culled chiefly from her mother's paper, and thriftily preserved in an old receipt book. "Mrs. Ann Smiley's Gingerbread" pieced out a column of halting verse relating to the Rev. Nehemiah Bacheller's lamented "Departure for the Other Shore," and a doleful lyric on the "Passing Away of an Aged Couple," merged into a "Good Recipe for Soft Sope." Most of all, he shrank from Hannah herself; her stiff, ill-spelt letters lay unopened for days; and what was there in his own life of which he could write to her?

He drew the curtain from the western window. Absorbed in his work he had eaten nothing since daybreak, and was brought to the pitch of exaltation that comes with prolonged mental effort. In the light of the setting sun it seemed to him that the clay face assumed a distorted aspect; the hand, still represented by the sticks upon which the fingers were to be modeled, was that of a leper, hiding the loathsome secret within its breast from everyone but him. A fasting and feverish fantasy laid hold upon him that to him was about to be vouchsafed the hideous faculty of genius—to see the evil in every face.

He turned to anything that should distract the morbid current of his thoughts. On the table was a letter, whose familiar postmark had consigned it, unread, to the litter of rags and modeling tools. But the writing, he observed for the first time, was not Hannah's; half mechanically he tore open the envelope and read :—

"DEER DAVY,—I take my pen in hand considering it my duty to let you know concerning your sister Hanner. She's be'n ailing considerable since cold weather set in. One lung is most gone, and taint nowise likely she'll ever git round again. She aint be'n able to do no work this winter, not even at puttin' in linings in hats and bonnets at the factory, which is all she's be'n fit for, since she went blind a year ago come Christmas.

Yours respectfully,

MRS. MARTHA BIDDLE."

David read the letter again and yet again before its meaning, in dis-jointed rendering, reached his sense. Blind and ill! Out of work! Cold and hungry. In his highly wrought condition, thought succeeding thought were fused into a flash that well-nigh stunned him. What was this mes-sage that had come to him on the very eve of success?

A fierce resentment against everybody and everything seized him. For a moment he was capable of any mad excess of passion. He tore the fateful letter into fragments, and flung them from him. Shake off this fancied claim of the accident of birth! What right had the poor, stunted village nature to the sacrifice of a life so rich in promise? His talent was given him to use. Nay, what did it matter though thousands perished that genius might live?

He tried to think calmly. Why not send his sister the money for her support? He scarcely earned enough for his own sustenance. Though the world seldom fails to recognize genius, recognition is slow in coming, and slower yet in bringing financial reward. The only course that was open to him was to return to the designing room of the factory. Could he not go on with his work at home in spare hours and in the summer in-terim? The sordid atmosphere of the workroom, the stultifying village life, would stifle that which could attain its true growth only under its native conditions.

And the eyes and lips of clay whispered to his youthful blood of the pleasures that success would bring.

"Have I found my life only to lose it?" he cried in agony. "Who loses his life, though for another's sake, how shall he find it!"

Was it out of the radiance that there came the answer?

.   .

It was noon when David reached the station. Deacon Biddle, in his pung with the mangy buffalo robe, stared unrecognizing at anyone indulg-ing in the eccentricity of pedestrianism. As he walked along the village street Mrs. Breed's yellow cur snarled at him as of yore; he passed a group of factory girls with coarse voices and bold, conscious glances; the smell of the midday dinner issued from every white-painted, green-blinded house. There was a queer feeling in his throat, as of physical restriction, by the time he came in sight of the familiar pump. He pushed open the door and entered the tiny entry. The kitchen was empty and chill: the living room, too, had the penetrating dampness of an apartment that had long been fireless. He made his way, still like a man in a dream, up the narrow, crooked staircase, and unannounced entered the room above.

Several women were gathered about the four-posted feather bed; there was a stifling, sick-room atmosphere. At the sound of the opening door, Hannah had started from the pillows and stretched out her arms with unseeing, straining eyes.

"Davy!"

"Lor' knows how she's be'n alivin' this winter," said Mrs. Biddle, bustling to draw the coverlid about the sick woman's shoulders. "Sence she wuz took sick the neighbors hev' sot by her day and night," she added virtuously, while the other ghouls tiptoed near, with gloating eyes, to lose no gasp of the slow, stertorous breathing.

Hannah's head sank back upon the pillows; her fingers plucked at the "comfortable," whose hideous browns and purples wrung David's soul.

"Git used ter—the feelin'—farmboy. It—goes so—so; puttin' in linin's ain't chirky work. I—knew—you—would—wait, Steve. Yes, mother, I'm—comin'; the lamp's out.——Davy—mustn't—be—fretted ——"

'Far-ar fro-om mo-ortal ca-a-ares ——'"

There was a strange, hideous sound in Hannah's throat, followed by a few short breaths, at longer and longer intervals; they ceased.

There came that moment after death when, for a fleeting instant, the soul looks forth from what was, but now, its mortal guise,—and David Gerry looked upon the face of his vision.

"He idealizes his subjects," critics said of the great sculptor. But there were men and women who whispered,

"He sees the Divine in every face."

Edith Robinson.

Ebb Tide.

BEYOND the ghostly reaches of the sand
The sea ebbs out, lit by a 'boding moon,
And shadow gulls do scream and flit eftsoon,
While through the night the conch-shell's mystic rune
Sobs low about me where I dumbly stand.

The empty dunes shine with a mocking web
Of wraith-like mist; a sullen bittern flies
Lone and morose across the leaden skies.
Alone! alone! An inner echo cries,
The tide, and life, and love are at the ebb.

Elizabeth Alden Curtis.

The Appreciator.

I WAS descending the stoop of the Cleverton-Brassey residence, on West Fifty—— Street, and as I paused under the shelter of the awning, on the lowest of the broad stone steps, to settle the collar of my ulster about my ears and give a final twitch to my thick gloves, I felt a glow of inward satisfaction at having practically finished my day's work, and at the same time having gotten through easily that, to me, most disagreeable kind of newspaper work, a society assignment. The whole affair had been satisfactory, and devoid of unpleasant incident. Mrs. Cleverton-Brassey had sent an announcement of the impending function to the office early in the week, and that afternoon the City Editor had handed me the card with the remark :—

"Drop into this place this evening and see what is going on. You know Brassey is one of the partners in Hirshbaum, Ickelheimer & Schwab, the big department-store fellows who run the full-page ads. Sundays, so give them any notice in reason."

I had gone to my room, donned evening clothes, had a comfortable dinner, witnessed a good play at a theater where I was on friendly terms with the manager, and at about eleven o'clock presented myself at the Cleverton-Brassey mansion. I sent in my card to Mr. Brassey, was shown into his library, greeted cordially, and given an extensive report, which had been prepared in advance by Mrs. Cleverton-Brassey, of the evening's proceedings. I had refused Mr. Brassey's polite but perfunctory invitation to join his guests and to partake of refreshment, and I had accepted with thanks his large, fat cigar. In fact everything was as it should be ; I had nothing left to do but to write a few lines of introduction, tone down somewhat the exuberance of Mrs. Cleverton-Brassey's rhetoric, and send the article down to the *Reverberator* office by a messenger. Then I should be free to sup and go to bed. As I paused I heard the big mahogany door close again, and the next moment a pleasant voice at my elbow remarked :—

"I think I saw you inside ; delightful evening, was it not?"

"I was inside," I replied stiffly ; "but I can't say as to the evening. I went to see Mr. Brassey on business,—in fact, to report the affair ; I am a reporter on the *Reverberator*."

I always have a horror of being taken for a guest at these fashionable affairs, and I have discovered that there is no better way of shutting off the advances of a certain class of society people than to announce the fact boldly that I am a reporter. It is like hanging out a yellow quarantine flag.

" Precisely," replied the smiling stranger. " If I am not mistaken I have seen you at a number of places this winter, and, to speak frankly, I have become interested in your face, and should like to talk to you."

There was a subtle flattery in the man's manner which influenced me more than his words,—for none of us are impervious to flattery if delicately administered. I muttered some commonplace reply and turned to get a good look at my companion. We were under the big electric light on the corner of Sixth Avenue by this time, and had paused to allow a car to pass. Of course I had seen him before, at Mrs. Leo Hunter's and at the Brayton's. I fancied I remembered him at the Patriarch's and the Aborigines', but I had been a reporter only a year, and I was not sent to the more important functions myself; still I had seen him at scores of—not the very best—but all houses of the most irreproachable respectability; representatives of that semi-fashionable, semi-cultured set which aims to patronize Art with a capital A, and seeks to entertain lions. It is a step higher than the chromo-literary circle, which tries to copy it, and a step lower than real society. It is the circle where one meets " lions." In real society there are no lions, only men and women. I had seen him talking to Thumpowski, the great Russian pianist, at Mrs. Leo Hunter's last reception; he was among the first to press forward to compliment Rositina, the marvelous Spanish dancer, at the Brayton's; and this evening, as I glanced in at the drawing-room, he was foremost in paying homage at the shrine of Signor Bellowoni, the famous Italian basso. He was a pleasant-looking man, well groomed and well set up, regular features, hair slightly tinged with gray, and unobtrusively courteous manners, which marked a rather better grade of society than I had seen him in. His courtesy seemed born in him rather than acquired; an inheritance and a part of himself rather than a garment.

" So you have decided in my favor," he said with a queer smile, as I finished my scrutiny and started across the street.

" I only feared that you, a society man, and I, a humble reporter on a great daily newspaper, would have very little in common," I replied rather ungraciously. " I thought you took me for one of the guests,—one of your own set,—and I object to sailing under false colors," I added.

" God forbid," he exclaimed, still smiling. " No ; I knew your business, and, as I have said, was interested in you. I am a lonely man : in my line of business I have learned to depend largely upon my judgment of human nature, and I wanted to talk to you."

The explanation was so simply made that, though I had had a year's experience as a reporter, I could but be impressed by his evident sincerity, though I doubted his statement that he was a lonely man; it seemed preposterous, in view of the fact that I had seen him at nearly every social function I had attended in a professional capacity. We turned into a quiet chophouse, where I was accustomed to write out my notes when I had an up-town assignment, and, as we seated ourselves at one of the little tables, I said :—

" You will have to excuse me for a few minutes, as I have to fix this stuff and send it down to the office." He nodded amiably, lighted a cigar, and proceeded to amuse himself with the illustrated papers. My task was an easy one. Mrs. Cleverton-Brassey was accustomed to preparing reports of her entertainments for the press, and beyond inserting the names of two or three people who were friends of the City Editor, and cutting out a description of the gown of the wife of a man who wouldn't advertise in the *Reverberator*. I had nothing to do. I called a messenger boy, dispatched him with the copy, and turned to my companion with a sigh of relief.

" It is all a great bore, is it not?" he remarked sympathetically.

" It certainly is to one who does it from necessity," I replied.

" You don't fancy any one does it from pleasure, do you?" he queried, smiling. "Oh, no : there are the artists, the ' lions,' who are paid in some way or another, but generally in hard cash ; there are the business friends of the host, who go to oblige or curry favor with him ; there are the vast horde of climbers, who see in Mrs. Cleverton-Brassey's a step up on the social ladder ; there are the others who go because they want Mrs. Cleverton-Brassey at their receptions ; and there are you and I, who go on business."

" On business?" I echoed in surprise ; and the thought flashed through my mind, " A private detective, to see that the guests don't get away with the spoons."

" Yes," he replied ; " I am an appreciator."

I looked at him in puzzled silence : he laughed gently, and replied to my unspoken question.

" It is quite a new profession, and I think I may claim to be the inventor of it. Since the would-be fashionable people adopted the custom of inviting distinguished men and women to their receptions, the necessity of having some one who understands the prejudices, the fads, and the foibles of these social lions has developed. There must be some one who knows how to tickle their vanity ; in fact, some one who ' appreciates ' their genius. You remember the scene created by Herr von Grosenkopf, the German painter, at Mrs. Hardwicke-Browne's two seasons ago? He thinks himself a great classical figure painter : his silks, satins, and velvets are as true to nature as a loom could make them, but he does not like to be reminded of that. Mrs. Hardwicke-Browne complimented him upon his draperies until he flew into a rage, and swore for ten minutes in high German, winding up with ' Donnerwetter! Madame, 1 am not an upholsterer!' "

I laughed at the story, and my companion continued.

" There was dear old Mrs. Silas Lawson,—and whatever induced her to go lion hunting I could never understand,—who, after much effort, secured the attendance of Major Frost, the Arctic explorer, at one of her receptions, and straightway began to talk to him of the unwholesomeness of intoxicating liquors in cold climates, when it is a well-known fact that his last expedition in search of the Pole had to be abandoned because he broke all the scientific instruments for the sake of drinking the alcohol they contained; and Miss Sheridan, the daughter of old Sheridan, the contractor, who asked Jokofski, after he had played two or three of his most famous compositions, if he couldn't play some little thing of his own. Yes, society, so called, needed some one who could say just the right thing at the right time to the right person. I saw the demand, and filled it. I'm not a *claquer*, nor a professional distributor of flattery. I gently stroke the social lion on his most sensitive spots, and make him feel good and purr."

" And get paid for it." I said.

" Naturally we all get paid, and I am fortunate in receiving very liberal remuneration. It is not so easy as it looks, though. A lady contemplates giving a reception; she sends for me as she sends for her caterer : ' I shall want you on Thursday evening. Madame Squallini of Her Majesty's Opera, Signor Bifbing, the pianist, Swami Chunder Lal the, theosophist, and Hans Pflatz, the anarchist leader, will be there, and I want you to do your best.' Then I have to go to work and study up ; the musical people are comparatively easy ; the mention of two or three of their most successful appearances and a little flattery fixes them ; but Swami Chunder Lal requires a week's hard cramming of astral bodies, mahatmas, chelas, and all that sort of thing, and the anarchist wants revolutionary sentiments well drenched in gore, with a good dose of atheism thrown in. O, I can assure you it is not all play." And he smiled his peculiar, tolerant, quizical smile.

" Sorry, gentlemen, but it's closing time," interrupted the proprietor, apologetically. My companion insisted upon settling the modest check.

" Well, good-by ; we shall probably meet again," he said, as we parted on the corner. " I hope I have not bored you ; I have had a delightful evening."

As I walked down the street I was startled by a burst of Homeric laughter. I turned, and concluded that it came from a drunken man, who was seated on a stoop about half way up the block, so I paid no more attention to it.

The next day I was sent to report the departure of a European steamer. As I left the ship and was taking a last look at her from the dock, whom should I see but my friend of the previous evening, clad in ulster and travelling cap, leaning over the rail. Jim Spacer, of *The Earth*, was with me, and I grasped his elbow.

" Who is that?" I asked, hurriedly, pointing to the Appreciator.

" That? Why, that's Livingstone Stuyvesant, one of the best fellows about town, awfully rich, awfully eccentric, and one of the most notorious practical jokers in New York."

Just then he spied me, and another roar of laughter greeted my ears.

I said nothing, but I have often wondered if it was a case of mistaken identity, and that Jim really did not know who he was talking about; or if it had simply occurred to the eccentric young man, seeing my pocket full of neatly sharpened pencils, and all the other marks of my newness in my calling, that it would be fun to take a " rise " out of a green reporter.

Allan Forman.

Inland.

Encircled by the everlasting hills
    Lies restfulness, and summer days pass by
    Serenely neath the over-arching sky,
Touched by the season's spirit. Silence fills
Wide spaces whence tranquility distils ;
    And winds that ever bring the coolness nigh
    From uplands far away and yet more high
Lull to a deeper calmness tired wills.

Among the everlasting hills from age
To age these generations come and go
    Nobly with lifted eyes. O alien one !
Within thine ears there sounds the ebb and flow
Of distant surges,—thou must needs assuage
    Thy longing for the salt waves dashing in the sun !
                         O. H. S. D.

Notes.

¶ Any one who has read John Foster's life of Charles Dickens knows of the sorrows of childhood there depicted. "That I suffered," wrote Dickens, "in secret, and that I suffered exquisitely, no one ever knew but I. How much I suffered, it is, as I have said already, utterly beyond my power to tell. No man's imagination can overstep the reality. But I kept my own counsel, and I did my work." The many thousand, nay million, lives that do not become public property, could attest to the same or similar expressions, and many believe that but for these "sorrows" or trials the man and woman could not have done for the world what they have. Experience is, beyond question, the best, most thorough teacher, whether in sweetness or in sorrow. "My work was to cover the pots of paste blacking, and I did my work." Therein is the secret of Boz's success. Professor Sully, who has devoted himself for some years to a study of the psychological side of child life, says a contemporary, has risen up to explain that the "authorities" on the subject in recent stories and essays are, on the whole, incompetent observers. He does not like Mrs. Meynell's discourse: her "sonorous solemnity" fails to persuade him; and he is equally impervious to the allurements of Mr. Kenneth Grahame and Mr. Barrie. He says of the latter's "Sentimental Tommy" that it ought to be read as a pretty farce, and he goes on to express the hope that "one day Mr. Barrie may think it worth his while to con a child with something of the minute and patient study which he has devoted to its elders. It were surely better to create a living child than to produce what is, after all, rather too like a Scotch variant of the Immortal Tom Sawyer. One is encouraged in this hope of observing here and there in the story a skillful touching upon the eternally childlike." It is cheering to note that Professor Sully ignores Mr. Morrison's "Child of the Jago" entirely. That precious work is an atrocious libel upon child life, but it is being bolstered up at a great rate, just now, by English devotees of the brutally "virile" conception of life which the author happens to hold. Professor Sully concludes his suggestive paper with this remark: "What is wanted is a franker recognition of the truth that a child is a subject worthy in itself of the finest artistic portrayal, and that in the hands of a master it may be made admirable without being elongated into a prodigy, and highly entertaining without being broadened out into a huge joke."

¶ After the death of the Persian bard Hafiz, some of the religious among his countrymen protested strongly against allowing to him the right of sepulture, alleging, as their objection, the licentiousness of his poetry.

After much controversy it was agreed to leave the decision of the question to a mode of divination, not uncommon among the Persians, which consisted in opening the poet's book at random and taking the first verses that occurred. They happened to be these : —

> "Oh ! turn not coldly from the poet's bier,
> Nor check the sacred drops by Pity given ;
> For though to sin his body slumbereth here,
> His soul, absolved, already wings to Heaven."

These lines, says the legend, were looked upon as a Divine decree ; the religionists no longer enforced their objections, and the remains of the bard were left to take their quiet sleep by that "sweet bower of Mosellay" which he had so often celebrated in his verses.

¶ The influence of Sex ! Who shall say what it may not be? Mr. Alger, in his "Friendships of Women," prudently observes : "A man's best friend is a Wife of good sense and good heart, whom he loves and who loves him." To this Elizabeth Stuart Phelps-Ward, adds : "A woman's best friend is a Husband of intellect and of heart, whom she loves and who loves her. And I should like to add : A literary woman's best critic is her Husband ; and I cannot express in these few words the debt which I am proud to acknowledge to him who has never hindered my life's work by one hour of anything less than loyal delight in it, and who has never failed to urge me to my best, of which his ideal is higher than my own."

Of Dedications, two of the most beautiful instances I remember are Henry Mills Alden's in "A Study of Death," and Philip Gilbert Hamerton's in "The Intellectual Life." In the first-named book, even while the author wrote the study of the great invisible change that will come to all, the Helpmeet passed into Life. Thus runs the dedication :—

"My earliest written expression of intimate thought or cherished fancy was for your eyes only. It was my first approach to your maidenly heart, a mystical wooing, which neglected no resource, near or remote, for the enhancement of its charm, and so involved all other mystery in its own. In you childhood has been inviolate, never losing its power of leading me by an unspoken invocation to a green field ever kept fresh by a living fountain where the Shepherd tends His flock. Now, through a body racked with pain and sadly broken, still shines this unbroken childhood, teaching me Love's deepest mystery. It is fitting, then, that I should dedicate to you this book touching that mystery. It has been written in the shadow, but illumined by the brightness of an angel's face seen in the darkness, so that it has seemed easy and natural for me to find at the thorn's heart a secret and everlasting sweetness far surpassing that of the rose itself, which ceases in its own perfection. Whether that angel we have seen shall, for my need and comfort, and for your own longing, hold back his greatest gift, and leave you mine in the earthly ways we know and love, or shall hasten to make the heavenly surprises, the issue in either event will be a home coming : if *here*, yet already the deeper secret will have been, in part, disclosed ; and if *beyond*, that secret, fully known, will not betray the fondest hopes of loving hearts. Love never denied death, and death will not deny Love."

In the case of Mr. Hamerton, he has left this world and her to whom he wrote, a quarter of a century ago, these touching words :—

"We have shared together many hours of study, and you have been willing, at the cost of much patient labor, to cheer the difficult paths of intellectual toil by the unfailing sweetness of your beloved companionship. It seems to me that all those things which we have learned together are doubly my own, whilst those other studies which I have pursued in solitude have never yielded me more than a maimed and imperfect satisfaction. The dream of my life would be to associate you with all I do if that were possible ; but since the ideal can never be wholly realized, let me at least rejoice that we have been so little separated, and that the subtile influence of your finer taste and more delicate perception is ever, like some penetrating perfume, in the whole atmosphere around me."

> But yesterday I thought of Death as one
> Unkind, nay, cruel, insincere, and hard :
> Who came, and often ere we knew was gone,
> Taking our dear ones without regard
> To mental suffering. Death was to me
> A gaunt and grinning skeleton. I knew,
> Or thought I knew, Death was no friend ; but see
> My error. Death's is a woman's hand. True,
> At first we do not feel the tenderness
> That guides the hand to suage the rack and pain
> Our loved ones suffer from ; but none the less
> The woman-angel, Death, comes to sustain
> And help us bear our burdens with a grace
> That must, in time, bring heavenly calm and peace.

Book Notes.

¶ "Two pages of the most intense, vital interest to all lovers of music, and forty pages of commonplace narrative!" This constitutes an estimate of Wagner's "Pilgrimage to Beethoven," translated by Weyer, and bearing the imprint of The Open Court Company. This little book contains the story of a poor German musician who makes his way, with much difficulty, to Vienna to see the great composer. The journey and adventures are commonplace and uninteresting, but when Wagner puts into the mouth of the Master his own idea of the perfect opera, the book becomes a document of the greatest value to all students and amateurs. Beethoven says: "The instruments are, as it were, the representation of the primal media of the tones of creation and nature. That which they express can never be clearly defined or fixed; for they reproduce the very primal emotions themselves. . . . The genius of the human voice is of an entirely different character. The human voice is the representative of the human heart and its sequestered, individual feeling. . . . Bring these two elemental classes together, now, and combine them! To the unrestrained primal emotion of nature, soaring away into the infinite (representing them by the instruments), oppose the clear and determinate emotion of the human heart (representing it by the human voice)."

¶ "A Transatlantic Chatelaine," by Helen Choate Prince (Houghton, Mifflin & Co.), is the story of a rich young American widow who marries a titled Frenchman because she feels that it is her duty to do some good with her money, and because she believes that in building up the decayed fortunes of a noble family she will perform a true service for the world. Needless to say, her ideas of the nobility and fidelity to tradition of her husband are soon dispelled, and she finds that her life has been wrecked. At the time of her marriage she was really in love with a young Captain Reginer, but owing to misrepresentation she became alienated from him. After she has realized her husband's baseness she becomes convinced of Reginer's worth, and henceforth her life is a struggle between love and duty. The book is perfectly conventional, but the story is pleasantly told, and is sane and wholesome throughout.

¶ If all Indians were like "Lo-To-Kah" (The Continental Publishing Co., N. Y. $1.00), whose story is told by V. Z. Reed, we would all join the Indian Aid Association. Yet if Lo-To-Kah is idealized, an air of extreme truth is given to this account of his life and adventures. The story itself is divided into six episodes, each of which is a complete whole. Lo-

To-Kah is an aged Ute, who in youth had been a great man. He tells of his beautiful wife, Zeetah, whom he seized from the Navajos,—of Helen, the "golden woman," so wonderfully restored to her lover. Reading, we almost believe it all, for Mr. Reed is not only a master of good English, but a genuine story teller. We doubt only when we hear of Raymeya, the witch of Soledad. She is a kind of American "She" with a never-ending life, whose beginning antedates the Spanish conquest. It is her hopeless love for Lo-To-Kah which gives her so large a place in his story.

¶ "The Ape, The Idiot, and Other People," by W. C. Morrow (J. B. Lippincott Co., $1.25), is one more than a baker's dozen of clear-cut, short stories. Except the Ape and the Idiot, the "People" are connected with some one or another horrid tragedy. What boots so much tragedy, improbable, even though possible? One answer is that this almost Hawthornesque weirdness is exactly what the many like, especially as summer draws on, and time is so hard to kill. Mr. Morrow may be pardoned the horrors he shows us, for knowing how to tell a story clearly and without any waste of word. His is a crisp, incisive touch, and we are therefore almost ready to accept his monstrous Frankenstein,—more modern than Mary Shelley's,—his Permanent Stiletto, and all the others. Moreover, his stories are clean,—a virtue not always to be found in less bloody tales. "The Inmate of The Dungeon" and "The Hero of the Plague" have the ring of true pathos. Nearly all these stories, by the way, have their scene on the Pacific Coast.

¶ In "The Forge in the Forest" (Lamson, Wolffe and Co.), Mr. Chas. G. D. Roberts has given us a charming story of eighteenth century Acadia. It is certainly fitting that a poet, himself a son of Acadia, should paint us this picture of the past of a beautiful country. The central figures in this picture are Jean de Mer, a noted French ranger, and his son Marc; two beautiful English women, the widow Mizpah Hanford and her sister Prudence, the mad Grul, and La Garne, the Black Abbé, the last drawn strictly from life. In the dim background are De Ramezay, the French commander, the captain of a Boston vessel, and several Micmacs, some of whom are under the sinister influence of the Black Abbé. The latter is forever planning mischief to Jean de Mer, whom he hates. He instigates the abduction of Mizpah's child Philip, who, after many dangers, is restored to his mother. The loss of Philip draws Jean and Mizpah closely together, and the young Englishwoman at length admits her love for the stalwart Frenchman. Marc, too, finds his fate in Prudence, and love, as well as adventure, plays a considerable part in the story. Many of the adventures are thrilling, and Mr. Roberts' word painting of the Acadian scenery he knows so well is exquisite.

The Red Letter

An Illustrated Monthly

Published by H. Walter Stephenson
Edited by Harry Draper Hunt
Under the art direction of E. B. Bird

¶ The subscription rate is one dollar
a year. Entered at the Boston Post
Office as second-class mail matter.
The trade supplied by the American
News Company and its branches. Ad-
vertising rates on application.

The Red Letter Magazine,
Boston.
296 Boylston Street.

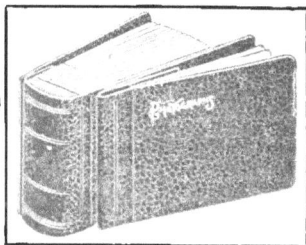